THE COMMUNIST PARTY IN MARYLAND, 1919–57

THE COMMUNIST PARTY IN MARYLAND, 1919-57

Vernon L. Pedersen

UNIVERSITY OF ILLINOIS PRESS

URBANA AND CHICAGO

Library of Congress Cataloging-in-Publication Data
Pedersen, Vernon L., 1955–
The Communist Party in Maryland, 1919–57 / Vernon L. Pedersen.
p.   cm.
Includes bibliographical references and index.
ISBN 0-252-02321-8 (cloth : alk. paper)
1. Communist Party of the United States of America (Md.)—History.
2. Communism—United States—Maryland—History.
3. United States. Congress. House. Committee on Un-American Activities.
I. Title.
JK2391.C5P38   2001
324.2752'075'0904—dc21   00-009609

C 5 4 3 2 1

To my grandmother,
who gave me my first history book,
and to my wife, Kate,
who convinced me I could write one of my own

Contents

Acknowledgments

This book would not have been possible without the support and encouragement of John Earl Haynes, who guided my early work, tolerated my often misplaced enthusiasm, and tried to discourage my frequent obsession with narrow topics. John allowed me to accompany him to Moscow in May of 1993, granting me the privilege of being one of the first three people to see the contents of Fond 515, the archives of the American Communist Party. John has often regretted that he never had the opportunity to teach history in an academic setting, but he has at least one very grateful student. I also extend deep thanks to Dasha Dimatrova Lotareva, my Moscow-based research associate. Dasha guided me through the intricacies of the Russian Center bureaucracy, translated guides, performed independent research, and saw to it that my photocopies and microfilm reached me. She also helped with apartment rental, translated restaurant menus, arranged tours of the city, and has been a very good friend as well as a professional colleague. I owe a great debt to Harvey Klehr of Emory University, who graciously allowed me to use a number of documents from his considerable collection and has been very generous in providing letters of reference.

Research on the history of Maryland communism took me to a number of libraries and archives, where I received unfailing courtesy and valuable assistance. I especially thank the staff of the Russian Center for the Preservation and Study of Documents of Recent History as well as Anne Turkos and the staff in the Maryland Room of the McKeldin Library at the University of Maryland. Their efficiency made my job much easier, and their interest in my work was very encouraging. I am grateful to the staff of the Special Collections Department in the Perkins Library at Duke University, the archival staff of the Hesburgh Library at Notre Dame University, the archivist of the Baltimore Archdiocese, and the staffs of the Maryland Room and the Microfilm Reading Room at the Enoch Pratt Library in Baltimore. Thanks are also due to the National Endowment for the Humanities, whose 1993 travel grant funded a large portion of the research for this book.

In 1989, I encountered Margaret Baldridge, then the executive secretary of the Communist Party of Maryland, at the New Era Bookshop, which began a five-year association with the members of the Maryland Party. I sat in on Party meetings, attended fund-raisers and social events, and served on the committee that ran the New Era Book Shop. Individual Party members invited me into their homes, and several veteran Party members allowed me to interview them. As a result of my exposure to inner-Party life, I have been able to create a much richer portrait of the Party's history than would otherwise have been possible. I thank George Meyers, Margaret Baldridge, Joe Henderson, Tim Wheeler, Howard Silverberg, Martha Richards, Ellen Painter, William Wood, Sirkka Lee Holm, and the other members of the Maryland Communist Party for their time and trust.

This study of Maryland communism began life as part of the Maryland Party's celebration of its seventieth anniversary. It then evolved into a dissertation, which shared the positive, sympathetic tone of the earlier work. In 1993, I visited the Russian Center archives for the first time and began reading the documentary history of the Maryland Communist Party. In 1994, I accepted a faculty position at the American University in Bulgaria, a job I continue to hold. The combination of careful study of the records of the Communist Party, USA, and the experience of living in a post-Communist country drastically altered my previous opinions of American communism. The current work, although incorporating some material from its earlier incarnations, is therefore radically different from my previous work and much more critical of the Maryland Party. It remains, I think, fair and evenhanded.

THE COMMUNIST PARTY IN MARYLAND, 1919–57

Introduction

Because Maryland combines seacoast and mountains with rolling farmland and rivers, its tourist bureau often calls it America in miniature. A similar comment could be made about the state's Communist Party, which is in many ways a microcosm of its parent organization, the Communist Party of the United States of America (CPUSA). At its height, its membership, composed of eastern European Jews, Finns, native-stock Americans, and a constantly shifting black population, paralleled that of the national organization. The Party's history in the state, from its founding in 1919, its height of influence during World War II, and its sharp decline during the McCarthy era, mirrors national patterns. Most important, members of the Maryland Party were engaged in all of the major activities, from political lobbying, civil rights work, and labor organizing to espionage, that characterized the Communist experience in the United States.

Despite its suitability as a case study, writings on the Communist Party of Maryland are very scarce and tend to focus on specific events and issues rather than a consideration of Party history as a whole. George Callcott included a chapter on the Party in his 1985 book, *Maryland and America, 1940 to 1980,* but it focused mainly on the passage of Maryland's infamous Ober law. Bruce Nelson, in *Workers on the Waterfront: Seamen, Longshoremen, and Unionism in the 1930s,* discussed the brief Communist takeover of seamen's relief and employment services in Fells Point, an incident known as the Baltimore Soviet. Linda Zeidman and Eric Hallengren covered the same ground in "Radicalism on the Waterfront" in *The Baltimore Book,* a collection of alternative essays on local history. Jo Ann Argersinger, in *Toward a New Deal in Baltimore: People and*

Government in the Great Depression, touched on Communist efforts to organize the unemployed in the early years of the Great Depression, but she devoted the bulk of her book to discussing New Deal agencies.

More detailed, but highly subjective accounts of Maryland communism are found in the memoirs of former Party members. Al Richmond, a longtime Communist, spent several years organizing in Baltimore and recounted his experiences in *A Long View from the Left: Memoirs of an American Revolutionary.* Communist seaman Charles Rubin's *Log of Rubin the Sailor* includes several chapters about Rubin's frequent visits to Baltimore and contains well-written portraits of prominent individuals. Whittaker Chambers's *Witness* captures the atmosphere of the Party's secret apparatus and describes the espionage network in the mid-Atlantic region. Although written from very different perspectives, all three books vividly describe people and places important to the history of the Maryland CPUSA and convey a sense of the excitement, idealism, frustration, and cynicism that characterized life in the Party.

Part of the reason that writings on Maryland communism are confined to portions of books on other topics is that the extremely irregular concentration of sources makes studying the CPUSA at the state level very difficult. Only two state studies exist; the most recent, Robin Kelley's *Hammer and Hoe: Alabama Communists during the Great Depression,* was published in 1990, while John Haynes's *Dubious Alliance: The Making of Minnesota's DFL Party,* was written in 1984. Both scholars deal with very brief periods of Party history, rely heavily on oral history and government records, and set their works in very atypical Party units. The Party in Minnesota existed in a unique political environment because Minnesota politics was dominated by the Farmer Labor Party, while the Alabama Communist Party was almost entirely black and rural, unlike the urban, ethnic makeup of the CPUSA in general. This study examines a very typical Party district, covers its history from its founding in 1919 to its near destruction in 1957, and draws on a broad range of previously unavailable primary sources.

The most important American collections are a series of unexpurgated FBI reports covering the Maryland Party from 1941 to 1945, the records of the Baltimore locals of the Industrial Union of Marine and Shipbuilding Workers of American (IUMSWA), and a microfilm collection of regional newspapers, all housed at the University of Maryland's McKeldin Library. Other valuable sources are the J. B. Matthews papers at Duke University and the John Francis Cronin papers at the University of Notre Dame. All of these collections pale in significance next to the resources available at the Russian Center for the Preservation and Study of Documents of Recent History (RTzKhIDNI). The Moscow-based archive holds the records of the Communist International

(Comintern), the Red International of Trade Unions (Profintern), and the central archives of the CPUSA itself.

The American Party records, recovered from remote storage in Siberia in 1993, are designated Fond 515 and consist of 4,400 separate folders representing the virtually complete files of the Central Committee of the American Communist Party from 1919 to 1944. Included in this treasure trove are minutes of Central Committee meetings, copies of communications with Moscow, and extensive files on the Party's local districts. References to Communist activities in Maryland are scattered throughout the collection but are concentrated in two areas. Most of the documents are in the records of District 3, which included Maryland, Delaware, the District of Columbia, and parts of Pennsylvania and Virginia. A smaller number are in the files of District 34, a Party section established in 1936 that contained only Maryland and the District of Columbia. Additional Maryland material, particularly post-1938 documents, can be found in the Comintern and Profintern files.

Before the opening of the Russian archives, scholarship on American communism was divided into two schools of thought. The first, or traditional school, established in the 1950s, saw the Party's connection to the Soviet Union as the most important aspect of its history. Its advocates, although conceding that opposition to the Party could be extreme, regarded the Party as a genuine threat to the United States. The second, or revisionist school, which grew out of "new left" historiography, dismissed the Soviet connection as ephemeral to the real issue: the correction of injustices in American society. Its supporters often credited the Party with having a beneficial effect on the United States and condemned the suppression of the Party during the McCarthy era as an exercise in paranoia and intolerance.

The opening of the Russian archives confirmed the traditionalists' long-held claims that the CPUSA was closely tied to the Soviet Union and that elements within the Party assisted in Soviet intelligence-gathering activity. These revelations produced reactions ranging from dismay to denial within the ranks of the revisionists. They ultimately settled on a "so what" response to the disclosures that continue to pour forth not only from the Russian archives but from the files of the CIA, FBI, and British intelligence services as well. The "so what" response acknowledges that a "small" number of Communists may have engaged in espionage and other clandestine and potentially subversive activities but that this is largely irrelevant because most Communists were unaware of the intelligence connection and joined the Party out of an idealism that remained untainted by the actions of a few. They argue that persistent focus on such an atypical aspect of Party history obscures the real nature of American communism and hides the Party's positive contributions to

American society. However, Party links to the Soviet Union extended far beyond intelligence gathering, and the positive contributions of the CPUSA are
ambiguous at best.

Several scholars, among them Fraser M. Ottanelli, in *The Communist Party of the United States from the Depression to World War II,* have put forth the
theory that the Communist Party, initially dominated by immigrants, underwent a gradual process of Americanization, leading to a completely national
outlook by World War II. The Maryland experience partly confirms this idea
but ultimately discredits it. At its birth in 1919, the Maryland Communist
Party drew its membership entirely from the immigrant community and organized itself on ethnic lines. Like many immigrant groups, the Party focused
its attention on events abroad, and Party members initially had trouble con-
sidering their revolutionary ideology as relevant to the United States.

By the late 1920s, the Party had become more American. Native-born,
"second-generation" immigrants dominated the organization, and membership had expanded to include some old-stock Americans as well. Most Party
clubs still organized themselves along ethnic lines, but several, reflecting the
assimilation of the immigrant groups, were established on a neighborhood or
occupational basis. In the late 1930s, the Communist Party began to celebrate
such purely "American" holidays as the Fourth of July, and Party clubs adopted
political designations. These changes reflected both a shift in Party policy and
a genuine lessening of the importance of ethnicity, illustrated by the fact that
some clubs voluntarily merged across ethnic lines. During World War II, the
Party followed the national pattern and subsumed ethnicity to the task of
victory over the Fascist powers. After the war, the Party did not revive any
strong sense of ethnic identity, although many individual Party members retained an interest in ethnic customs and folk culture.

On another level, however, Party members deliberately separated themselves from American society by immersing themselves in Soviet culture and
ideology to the point of saturation. In the 1920s and 1930s, literally hundreds
of Maryland Party members traveled to the USSR for extended stays. Top cadre received training and indoctrination at the Lenin School in Moscow, while
rank and filers labored on collective farms or helped build the Soviet industrial base. All but a handful returned fully convinced of the superiority of the
Soviet system. For those who could not travel to the USSR, the national Party
provided an unending supply of books, pamphlets, and films extolling the
virtues of the world's only socialist state.

After World War II and the beginning of the McCarthy era, Maryland
Communists identified even more strongly with the Soviet Union as a goal to
be attained, a justification for their sacrifices, and a source of physical com-

fort. Party members traveling to the Soviet Union and Eastern Europe received red-carpet treatment and often checked into resorts or hospitals for medical care. The glowing reports of Communists returning from trips to the Soviet block helped boost the moral of their less mobile comrades. As increasingly native-born residents of the United States, Communists responded like other Americans to the social forces that "Americanized" the descendants of the immigrant waves of the late nineteenth century and early twentieth. But at the same time, they intellectually alienated themselves through a conscious and systematic process of "Sovietization."

Revisionists make much of the Communist Party's advocacy of racial equality and integration long before the birth of the civil rights movement. Mark Naison, in *Communists in Harlem during the Depression,* records the training black activists received in Party organizations, and Robin Kelley, in *Hammer and Hoe: Black Radicalism and the Communist Party of Alabama,* offers a paean to the Party's work among black sharecroppers. Both writers suffer from a resolutely positive perspective of Party work among blacks, although Kelley is by far the worst offender. But the Communist Party was not the first or only organization to speak out against racism, and its record is not as unblemished as Naison and Kelley believe.

The Maryland Party did put tremendous effort into recruiting among blacks and transformed itself from an all-white organization in 1919 to one with a significant black membership, some estimates ranging as high as 50 percent by 1932. The Party regularly sponsored mixed-race dances, promoted several blacks to top party positions, and often ran blacks for local and state offices. A variety of front groups designed to appeal to blacks appeared over the years, and on two occasions Communist lawyers defended blacks accused of killing whites. The most important front group, the Total War Employment Committee (TWEC), operated during World War II and worked to grant blacks access to high-paying, formerly whites-only jobs in industry. A number of prominent black civil rights leaders in Maryland worked in Communist organizations, among them one of the state's most respected African Americans, Dr. John E. T. Camper, who was a loyal Party supporter for over thirty years. Besides Camper, the two most well-known black sympathizers were the civil rights activist Lillie Jackson and her daughter, Juanita Jackson Mitchell. Future Supreme Court justice Thurgood Marshall also had occasional contacts with the Party and once commented that the Party's legal efforts on behalf of blacks made it easier to raise money for the NAACP.

None of this effort ever gained the Party a secure place in the black community, however. Black Communist candidates never received more than a tiny fraction of the black vote, turnover among black Party members sometimes approached 90 percent a year, and the Party never gained a substantial following among the black residents of the Eastern Shore. Party failure to attract a stable black membership stemmed from a number of causes, but the single most important reason was that blacks refused to view class as more important than race. The majority of blacks who took an interest in the Communist Party did so only when it dealt with racial issues; only a tiny minority were attracted by its revolutionary program.

For that minority, life in the Party offered a mixed experience. Some enjoyed the opportunity to work with whites as equals, others dealt with residual racism and tokenism, and some took advantage of the Party's sensitivity toward "white chauvinism." One report to the Comintern despaired of the situation in Philadelphia, where an incompetent black organizer remained in his job because no one wanted to risk the charge of white chauvinism by criticizing him. Leonard Patterson, a black organizer in Baltimore, was continually promoted and eventually was sent to Moscow for training, despite a record of drinking and financial irresponsibility. Patterson rewarded the Party for its support by becoming a friendly witness for the House Committee on Un-American Activities in the 1950s. The Party deserves credit for being willing to challenge publicly one of America's most glaring injustices, but its contributions should not be overrated.

The collective experience of women in the Communist Party has received much less attention than that of blacks. Several studies of such individual leaders as Elizabeth Gurley Flynn, Anita Whitney, and Dorothy Healy exist, but there are no monographs addressing women as a whole. Harvey Klehr, one of the leading scholars of the traditional school, devoted a chapter to the role of women on the Party's Central Committee in his 1978 book, *Communist Cadre*. Klehr discovered that despite the Communist Party's commitment to gender equality, women in Party leadership positions advanced slower and remained at the top for much shorter periods than their male counterparts did. Although some subcommittees of the central body boasted large numbers of female members, Klehr concluded that women's advancement was handicapped by the stereotypes of mainstream society and the patriarchal traditions of the ethnic groups that supplied the bulk of Party membership.

Klehr's findings are borne out by the experiences of women in the Maryland Party. In 1919, only two women, Kate Ohsis and Bertha Zimmermann, occupied leadership positions, and both of them were married to prominent male Party leaders. During the period of militant sectarianism, several young women—such as Joan Hardy, who developed a reputation for tackling very large policemen—became prominent speakers and agitators. However, the most influential female Communists during the early and mid-thirties were Mary

Himoff and Clara Speer. Both women served briefly as head of the Washington, D.C., unit, and both gained their positions through their connections with male Communists. Himoff was the lover of Earl Reno, the head of the Maryland Party, while Speer, whose exact relationship cannot be determined, was extremely close to the Baltimore organizer Paul Cline. By the beginning of the Popular Front period, the only well-known female Communist was Dorothy Rose Blumberg, wife of the Maryland Party secretary Albert Blumberg.

A number of women attained prominence in the Maryland Party during World War II, a trend mirrored in mainstream society because millions of men were in the armed forces. Dorothy Rose Blumberg remained on the Maryland Central Committee, while Selma Wiess took over the Young Communist League from Hardy Scott. In the District of Columbia, Mary Stalcup rose from literature director to treasurer of the state Party, and Dorothy Strange and Elizabeth Searle wrote a pamphlet on postwar conditions that was distributed nationwide. These women aside, most female Communists did what women all over the country did during the war: filled vital but unheralded supporting roles. The fate of one high-ranking female Communist, Eva Chaney of Cumberland, Maryland, indicates that women were held to higher moral standards than their male comrades. In 1945, the District Committee stripped Chaney, whose Party membership was semisecret, of her Party offices because of her promiscuous lifestyle and past arrests on charges of disorderly conduct.

Revisionist writings about Communist labor activities are generally very positive, crediting Communist organizers with many of the early successes of the Congress of Industrial Organizations (CIO) and for much of the fighting spirit of the CIO's member unions. Roger Keeran, in *The Communist Party and the Auto Workers Union,* concludes that the Communist Party made substantial, "even crucial" contributions to the United Auto Workers in its formative years because of its dedication to the concept of industrial unionism and the willingness of its members to devote considerable time and energy to building unions and leading strikes. He dismisses charges that Communist loyalty to the international movement made it impossible for Party members to be legitimate trade unionists and counters that Communist were not only legitimate but often outstanding trade unionists. Keeran does concede that the demands of the Comintern sometimes led the Party to neglect the real interests of the workers, but he thinks that in the end the moral elan and intellectual strength the Communists drew from international ties outweighed the occasional problems.

Bruce Nelson, in *Workers on the Waterfront,* supports Keeran's thesis, praising the work of Communists in the maritime unions for their dedication and mildly rebuking them for the occasions when the Moscow line put them in opposition to the majority of organized seamen. Nelson describes the Baltimore Soviet as "an inspiring legend, a fighting program, and a crucible from which men went forward to leaven other struggles."[1] Later in his book, Nelson criticizes Harry Bridges, the leader of the International Longshoremen's Association and, unknown to Nelson, a secret Communist, for taking the Communist Party line against Roosevelt in 1940. However, Nelson quickly turns away from the issue of communism and, fixing on the union's refusal to back Bridges, praises the independence of the rank and file.

The situation in Maryland, where the Party enjoyed extensive influence on the waterfront and had footholds among textile, electrical, steel, and auto workers, presents a much more checkered record than the one outlined by Nelson and Keeran. Communists in organized labor in Maryland worked exceptionally hard to establish unions in their industries and keep them active. They often willingly took on such time-consuming jobs as committee members and union representatives. However, Party members channeled most of this hard work through semisecret Communist factions and pursued Party agendas tenaciously. Communist union members did not hesitate to abuse the rules of parliamentary procedure to dominate union meetings and ferociously attacked any opponents as Red-baiters, company stooges, or fascists. Local 43 of the Industrial Union of Marine and Shipbuilding Workers of America at the Fairfield Yards was in a state of permanent upheaval as the Communist faction and its opponents brutally fought for dominance. The Communists frequently denounced the unsavory tactics of their opponents but, when they lost power in 1945, promptly adopted the methods they had once deplored as disruptive and undemocratic.

Communist union members in Maryland put great effort into making their unions instruments of political action, the specifics of which changed dramatically depending on the foreign policy needs of the Soviet Union. Members of the National Maritime Union and the Baltimore shipbuilding unions loudly opposed Roosevelt's support of Britain in 1940 and threatened industrial slow-downs and sabotage to prevent supplies from reaching the beleaguered island. The day after the German invasion of the Soviet Union, these same people were demanding American intervention and supporting any production speed-up necessary to aid the nations opposing Hitler. Communist union organizers in Maryland did attempt to create better conditions for workers, but their primary objective was transforming unions into political tools to promote the Party line and support the Soviet Union.

A previously shadowy area, now illuminated by the opening of the Moscow archives, is the day-to-day life of Communist organizers and functionar-

ies. The letters and documents in the Russian Center reveal a world characterized by high turnover and difficult working conditions. In the 1920s and the
early 1930s, the national Party shifted organizers in and out of Maryland in a
seemingly endless chain. The first organizer, Louis Hendin, arrived in the city
from New York in the summer of 1919 and returned there less than a year later, following the upheavals of the Palmer raids. In 1925, the city had three
different organizers in the space of a few months. Initially, the city's organizers came from within the Baltimore Party. However, after the expulsion of the
Lovestonites, outside organizers were assigned to the city in dizzying succession, rarely remaining longer than a year. The turnover ruined the local Party, reducing it to less than fifty members by 1935. Intense work by Joseph Gaal
and Earl Reno restored the movement, and the Party branch was returned to
local control in 1937 under Albert Blumberg, a Baltimore native.

Party organizers consistently stretched their resources to the breaking
point, working long hours in difficult circumstances and sometimes in ill-
health. One Party organizer in Baltimore begged for relief because his throat
and voice were giving out from delivering three and four speeches day. Another functionary, attached to the Philadelphia district, requested additional
financial support because he was about to be evicted from his apartment and
could not afford to buy food. Reno, one of the most effective organizers who
passed through Maryland, put great effort into arranging for a Communist-
dominated delegation to attend the state American Federation of Labor convention. Much to his distress, the head of the delegation appeared at his office
hours after he was supposed to have departed saying the money given him for
expenses was insufficient. The last-minute defection put Reno's work back a
year and convinced him to head the next delegation himself.

Correspondence between Maryland Party leaders and the national offices
reveals an intriguing mixture of idealism, dedication, and violent factionalism. One of the first letters from District 3 in the Russian archives complains
of the activities of the "opposition." Norman Tallentire, a Philadelphia-based
organizer who frequently visited Maryland, sent lengthy handwritten letters
to New York denouncing his rival Alex Bail and bemoaning the opportunities
squandered by misguided policies. Paul Cline and Clara Speer fought a year-
long battle with the Jewish clubs in Baltimore and the District of Columbia.
George Meyers and Irving Kandel conducted a bruising fight for leadership of
the Party at the height of anti-Communist attacks.

At the same time, Party members could display tremendous idealism and
self-sacrifice. Mary Himoff, Earl Reno's tireless companion, wrote an impas-
sioned letter to national officials protesting the strain Reno was under and
requesting a busman's holiday in New York for both of them to hear Earl Brow-

der debate Norman Thomas. Years later, after Reno had broken with the Party and had been dragooned into testifying before the House Committee on Un-American Activities, he still spoke with pride about his accomplishments in Baltimore. Dorothy Rose Blumberg joined the Party out of loyalty to her husband but became one of its most eloquent defenders and went to prison for her beliefs. It is impossible not to like such people as Reno, Himoff, Blumberg, and the many other dedicated individuals who shaped the Party in Maryland. This work gives them the respect that is their due, but it also records that the cause to which they devoted their lives ultimately proved to be false.

Communists served the Party with great dedication, a dedication anti-Communists matched effort for effort. Anticommunism is usually skimmed over in revisionist histories or treated briefly as the actions of racists, reactionaries, or, in the more Marxist studies, victims of false consciousness. But most anti-Communists were just as principled as their radical opponents and fought the Party out of patriotic, ideological, or religious motives. In Maryland, the Catholic church spearheaded the anticommunism movement, and most of the Party's prominent opponents—such as John Francis Cronin, a labor priest; William J. Muth, a city council member; and Frank Ober, the author of Maryland's Ober law—were Catholics.

Catholic opposition to communism varied greatly over time, mirroring the ebbing and flowing of anticommunism in society in general. Anticommunism in Maryland was primarily reactive in nature, responding to specific events aboard or to openly Communist-led activities in the state. The broader Maryland public initially thought little about communism or considered the Party's antics an amusing aspect of Baltimore city life. Widespread acceptance of anticommunism came only during the first decades of the cold war and was a function of the perception of the Soviet Union as a threat to national security rather than a reflection of actual Party strength in Maryland.

No aspect of the Soviet threat aroused the public imagination more than accusations that Communist Party members spied for the Soviet Union. Clandestine work in Baltimore began in the early 1920s with the arrival of Prokope Suvorov. Suvorov came to the United States not to pry out military secrets but to keep an eye on Russian emigrant groups. In 1933, J. Peters, the head of underground activity in the United States, began construction of a secret apparatus in Baltimore. Because of its proximity to Washington, Peters considered the Baltimore organization to be one of the most important in the country and intended it as a conduit for secure communications and transfers of funds. While constructing Baltimore's secret apparatus, Peters recruited David Vernon Zimmerman, a Maryland Communist known by his Party name of David Carpenter, into the underground. Once Peters decided to turn the work of the secret apparatus toward espionage, Carpenter became closely involved and recruited the confessed State Department spy Henry Julian Wadleigh. Much to Carpenter's distress, Peters later merged his network into the one run by Whittaker Chambers.

The espionage networks remained carefully concealed, and there is no evidence that anyone in the Maryland Party, with the possible exception of Albert Blumberg, was aware of their existence. The revisionists are correct in pointing out that only a very few Communists engaged in spying, but they are wrong when they try to limit the significance of these activities. It is irrelevant how many individuals were involved in espionage since it was the atmosphere of willing support for the activities of the Soviet Union, shared by all Party members, not just underground operatives, that made the work possible. Nor can spying be seen as an isolated activity performed out of a sense of socialist duty. Instead, it was the extreme end of a continuum of covert practices that included virtually all Party members.

Only J. Peters knew the full details of David Carpenter's activities, but many individuals knew about Leonard Patterson and Stanley Bloomberg. The two men specialized in recruiting and infiltrating secret members of the Young Communist League into the Maryland National Guard, where they carried out propaganda work designed to demoralize their units. During the Popular Front period and World War II, almost all Party members practiced clandestine techniques because of the need to maintain secret Party cliques in labor unions and front groups. During the McCarthy era, at least a half-dozen Marylanders disappeared into the underground, and self-concealment became a matter of survival. When Margaret Baldridge took over as executive secretary of the Maryland Party in the early 1980s, she was amazed at the elaborate security measures that remained in place.

The combination of subversion and the Party's habit of self-concealment created an atmosphere of deception that tainted all of the Party's endeavors and in the end brought down the terrors of the McCarthy era on its members. Before that tragic denouement, however, Communists in Maryland and the nation enjoyed two heady periods of success. During the Popular Front period, the Maryland Party advocated antifascism, world peace, and centralized economic planning. Each goal made up part of the overall Party program, served the needs of both ideology and Soviet foreign policy, and appealed to many non-Communists. Thousands of Marylanders were convinced by the Great Depression that laissez-faire capitalism was inherently flawed, while thousands more feared the rise of aggressive Fascist regimes in Europe and Asia.

Serious domestic opposition to the Party developed by the late 1930s, plunging it into the trials of the "little Red scare." But the U.S. entry into World War

II on the side of the Soviet Union forestalled a concentrated assault on the Communists and allowed the Party to reach its height of influence. Communist success during World War II also rested on a wide range of goals. Among the most important were its resolute "win the war" stance, its demands for full employment, its support for government price controls, and its vision of a postwar world of cooperation and international peace. As a tremendous added bonus, support for the Soviet Union could be cast as patriotism. The seeming convergence of the Soviet and American visions of economic and social reform during the Popular Front period and the marriage of Soviet and American foreign policy during the war brought hundreds of members into the Maryland Party and swelled the ranks of its supporters into the tens of thousands.

Party advocacy of progressive goals and its success during these two periods account for much of its popularity in academic circles today. What is often forgotten is that the heart of Party activity was never a single issue or even a collection of issues. Selma Wiess put it best in regard to the American Youth for Democracy (AYD), a wartime front group. "It's up to us," she told a coworker, "to get persons interested enough in the program of the AYD to join . . . once in it's up to us to educate them around to communism."[2] Communism, as the history of the Soviet Union has painfully illustrated, was about not social justice but intolerance, authoritarianism, and the terrors of a police state.

1

Bolsheviks in Baltimore

Communism came to Maryland in the summer of 1919, along with twenty-four-year-old, Ukrainian-born Louis Hendin. Although he later claimed he had come to Baltimore only to practice dentistry, Hendin devoted most of his time to establishing and guiding the city's embryonic Communist Party. Hendin traveled to Baltimore from New York because two years earlier a combination of war, diplomatic miscalculation, personal weakness, and opportunism allowed the Bolsheviks to become masters of the Russian Empire. Thousands of people all over the world, dazzled by the promise of the Russian Revolution, sought to bring the benefits of the Bolshevik experiment to their own countries. During 1918, radicals in Hungary, Greece, and Germany organized Communist parties and launched short-lived revolutions. In the United States, Eugene V. Debs, leader of the Socialist Party, proudly declared, "From the crown of my head to the soles of my feet I am a Bolshevik and proud of it."[1]

Convinced that the revolution would spread and certain of the need for Bolshevik guidance of the emerging Communist movement, Vladimir Lenin created the Third Communist International (Comintern). In January of 1919, the Comintern issued an invitation for all like-minded organizations to send delegates to Moscow for its founding convention. Socialist parties worldwide split between those eager to emulate Lenin and the Bolsheviks and those convinced of the wisdom of less violent reformism. In the United States, Debs reconsidered his earlier support for the Communists and remained at the head of the traditional gradualist group.

A fiery collection of would-be revolutionaries emerged as Debs's opponents, but the coalition proved unstable and promptly divided into warring factions. John Reed, famous as an eyewitness to the Russian Revolution, led a small group of native-born radicals who favored a gradualist approach to revolution and the capture of the Socialist Party to provide a mass base for American communism. Reed's opponents, led by Louis Fraina, an Italian-born radical journalist from Boston, came overwhelmingly from the Socialist Party's immigrant-based, foreign-language federations. Fraina's supporters sought the immediate adoption of Bolshevik tactics in the United States and shunned any goals less drastic than the rapid destruction of the capitalist order. Reed planned to try to take over the Socialist Party convention to be held in Chicago on 30 August 1919. Fraina's group called for a separate Communist Party convention, also to be held in Chicago, on 1 September.[2]

In Maryland, the Socialist Party did not split so much as it flaked. Out of a membership of several thousand, barely two hundred individuals declared their allegiance to the radicals and joined Louis Hendin in organizing a prospective Party branch. Hendin's most enthusiastic followers came from the Latvian federation, whose head, Julius Ohsis, arranged for the entire membership to be transferred into Hendin's new party. Hendin and the Latvians, along with members of the Russian, Ukrainian, and Polish federations, established a skeleton Party apparatus, drew up a draft constitution, and elected the Latvian branch member David Zimmermann as their delegate to the 1 September convention.

Zimmermann returned to Baltimore on 17 September and two days later called to order the first official meeting of the Baltimore branch of the Communist Party of America (CPA). Fourteen people, representing the four founding language groups, listened intently as Zimmermann discussed the birth of the CPA, reported the election of Charles Ruthenberg as the national Party's chairman, and announced the acceptance of the Baltimore organization as a provisional Party branch. After Zimmermann's talk, the assembled Communists approved the draft constitution, fixed the level of dues, arranged for regular meetings, and elected officers. Hendin became the Party's new executive secretary, Zimmermann assumed the office of Party organizer, and Jacob Timoney, the Russian branch representative, became Party treasurer.[3]

As Party organizer, Zimmermann distributed literature, arranged meetings, and tried to recruit new members and extend the Party's influence over compatible organizations. The group most sympathetic to the Communist Party during the first few months of its life was the Union of Russian Workers, an organization that mixed socialism with strong doses of Russian populism and anarchism. Maurice Berezin, like Hendin a dentist by profession, headed the Baltimore chapter of the Union of Russian Workers. He espoused an interesting doctrine, which he called "anarcho-communism," combining socialist reformism and a populist concern for the individual with the centralism and discipline of the Communist Party. He and many of his followers were attracted by the Communists' activism, and a few individuals even held membership in both organizations.[4]

The Party enjoyed a similar relationship with the Industrial Workers of the World (IWW), or Wobblies. Founded in 1905 by the Socialist Party, the Western Federation of Miners, and several smaller radical groups, the IWW, America's most radical labor union, had prospered among the unorganized agricultural workers of the western United States. It also had achieved a respectable following among eastern textile workers, Gulf Coast longshoremen, lumbermen in the South and Northwest, and miners from Nevada's gold fields to Minnesota's iron range.

Convinced that World War I was nothing more than a rich man's struggle in which poor men did the dying, the IWW resolutely opposed U.S. entry into the war and publicly threatened to sabotage war industries. The Wilson administration branded the Wobblies disloyal elements and struck out at the union, arresting its members, raiding its offices, and confiscating its publications. The government crackdown destroyed the IWW as an effective organization and drove its membership further to the left. The Wobblies' national leader, William "Big Bill" Haywood, jumped bail on charges of subversion and defected to the Soviet Union. Many other Wobblies followed him, if not all the way to the Soviet Union at least into the Communist Party. The Maryland Party organizer David Zimmermann and his wife, Bertha, had both worked for the IWW in Chicago, while T. S. Wetter, secretary of the Baltimore IWW, offered assistance and cooperated extensively with the Communists.[5]

Beyond the Union of Russian Workers, the IWW, and the remaining foreign-language branches of the Socialist Party, the chances for recruiting dropped to nothing. However, a number of groups offered potentially sympathetic audiences if the Party could overcome its isolation in the immigrant community and reach out to them. The Socialist Party had several thousand English-speaking adherents in Baltimore, and many of them, like the members of the Union of Russian Workers, were attracted to the Communist commitment to action rather than talk. The Committee of Forty-eight, a radical organization modeled on Theodore Roosevelt's old Bull Moose Party, advocated public ownership of utilities, natural resources, transportation, and a program of gender and racial equality. Its local leader, Mercer G. Johnston, viewed the economic portions of the Communist Party agenda sympathetically and offered his support on several occasions.[6]

Baltimore also had many progressives in the Republican Party. Led by

Charles Joseph Bonaparte, a great-nephew of Napoléon Bonaparte, they pushed through a series of reforms in the areas of sanitation, housing regulation, and medical care for the city's poor. Bonaparte and a large number of like-minded Republicans deserted the party in 1912 to support former president Theodore Roosevelt's Bull Moose Party. Although frustrated by the nation's postwar turn away from reformism, Baltimore's progressives would remain aloof from the Communists until the political shifts of the 1930s.[7]

Baltimore's 80,000 black residents presented a more immediate audience. Most of the city's African Americans lived in a handful of the oldest, most crowded west Baltimore neighborhoods and were restricted to low-wage, low-skill jobs. However, Baltimore also boasted a well-organized black elite of professionals and businesspeople who strongly supported the progressive wing of the Republican Party and worked hard to improve the social and economic conditions of their fellow blacks. Since 1904, the black elite had fought a series of losing battles against the spread of Jim Crow laws. The loss of former liberties embittered them, and the shabby treatment of black soldiers during and after World War I did nothing to improve their attitude. Communists in Moscow and New York City believed that blacks represented a tremendous opportunity for Party growth, and in time the Maryland Party would reach out to them with its message of mandated racial equality.[8]

If Baltimore's ethnic enclaves, radicals, progressives, and blacks represented potential Communist sympathizers, the city's Catholics represented very real opponents. The church in Maryland traced its roots to the founding of the colony in 1634 as a refuge for Catholics facing persecution in their native England. Despite the state's creation as a Catholic enclave, Catholics never made up a majority of Maryland's population. They were, however, a substantial, self-conscious, and well-organized minority, which, in Baltimore alone, numbered well over 100,000 by 1919. They were thoroughly integrated into society, and though divided by wealth and ethnicity, Maryland's Catholics presented the image of a distinct, cohesive society because of the establishment of Catholic schools and the centrality of the church to the social lives of its communicants. Catholics viewed the militant atheism and secularism of the Communist Party as anathema to their basic beliefs and would become the Party's most dangerous and effective opponents.[9]

In 1919, Maryland boasted a population of nearly 1.5 million, spread over a striking variety of regions. The Sho', as the eastern peninsula was called by its residents, and the southern counties between the Potomac River and the Chesapeake Bay seemed, to the superficial glance, to exist suspended in time, unaffected by the changes that had carried the rest of the state into the twentieth century. A slow pace of life and a strong sense of kinship, unchanged from the antebellum period, dominated the life of the small towns and farms dotting the region. Traces of an even more distant past and patterns of life persisted among the watermen of Chesapeake Bay. Not only did the watermen wrest a living from the estuary in the same way they had in colonial times, but also traces of accents from Elizabethan England could still be heard among the residents of Smith Island and the remoter fishing communities.[10]

Despite appearances, the advance of time had affected eastern and southern Maryland. Farms shrank steadily in size from the end of the Civil War onward, reducing the wealth of their owners and filling these owners with a general sense of pessimism and persecution. The feeling of pressure from an alien, threatening, and immoral outside world inclined the residents of the Sho' toward conservatism, not radicalism. All of the Eastern Shore counties except Worcester—home to Ocean City, a seaside resort—had passed local acts of prohibition by 1908. The Eastern Shore also housed the second largest population of blacks in the state. As a group, blacks had suffered more than whites from the economic decline of agriculture. Every year more of them were pushed off their small farms and into low-wage jobs in the canning and food-processing factories that grew up around the towns of Salisbury and Cambridge. As a consequence, a growing stream of blacks abandoned the countryside for residence in Baltimore. The discontented portion that remained would be a constant, if ultimately frustrating, temptation to Communist organizers.[11]

To the north and west of Baltimore lay a wheat-growing region near the farming communities of Westminster and Frederick, which had been populated by Germans from Pennsylvania over the course of the eighteenth century. The farmers of northern Maryland upheld the values of the Protestant work ethic and clung to the familiarity and safety offered by small-town America. Evenly divided between Democrats and Republicans, the stolid, pragmatic residents of the piedmont region had little interest in radical politics. In 1912, when the Socialist Party reached the height of its electoral influence, capturing 6 percent of the presidential vote, it barely registered in Maryland's four central counties.[12]

Farther west in the panhandle region, which snakes between the Potomac River and the Pennsylvania border, Debs and the Socialists fared much better. As the twentieth century progressed, the fiercely independent, clan-oriented residents of Appalachia watched their distinctive way of life erode and found themselves forced off their subsistence farms and into the mills and mines around Cumberland and Hagerstown. The wrenching transformation, plus the struggle against poverty, radicalized many mountain residents. Extensive public works projects in the years before World War I improved the schools and paved the roads, ending the region's decades of isolation and demonstrating to many others the benefits of government activism. Eventually, the mountains of western Maryland would provide the Communist Party with its largest concentration of adherents outside of Baltimore.[13]

The Communist Party in Maryland confronted a situation remarkably like the one faced by the Party nationally: isolated in urban areas, burdened with a membership heavily weighted toward non-English speakers, but galvanized by its sense of destiny and armed with a compelling ideology. Since the Party was extremely small, it should have been able to go about attempting to exploit its advantages and struggling with its disadvantages in the comfort of total obscurity. Yet barely six months after the Party's founding, Maryland's Communists were subjected to intense public scrutiny and crushing government opposition.

The U.S. government's interest in obscure radical groups stemmed from the conjunction of a number of factors and was strongly colored by the hysteria and paranoia generated by America's entry into World War I. Quite suddenly, previously tolerated groups—such as resident aliens, pacifists, socialists, and a wide range of anarchist and labor organizations—were perceived as dangerously subversive. During 1917 and 1918, Congress passed several bills, known collectively as the Espionage Acts, which made it a crime to oppose the war, criticize the government, or advocate the overthrow of the United States by force and violence. To keep track of potential threats to national security, particularly German nationals, the government turned to a little-known branch of the Justice Department, the Bureau of Investigation.

Before World War I, the Bureau of Investigation's most exciting task had been a stepped-up effort, under Attorney General Thomas W. Gregory, to enforce the provisions of the Mann Act, which prohibited the transport of women across state lines for nefarious purposes. After 1917, however, the bureau gained three hundred new agents and a much more dynamic mission. Over the next two years, the invigorated bureau helped crush the IWW at the national level, rounded up numerous immigrants seen as either antiwar or pro-German, and arrested dozens of prominent socialists and anarchists, such as Eugene Debs and Emma Goldman.[14]

The fear of internal enemies working in collusion with adversaries abroad did not end with the fall of the kaiser. Instead, the focus shifted from German militarism to Russian communism. President Woodrow Wilson and the majority of Americans welcomed the fall of the tzar in March of 1917 as the long overdue end of a despotic regime. Opinion divided sharply, however, on the November seizure of power by the Bolsheviks. Socialists, anarchists, and Wobblies in the United States hailed the October Revolution as the beginning of Marx's dream of a classless society. But many more people viewed the Bolsheviks as international gangsters irrevocably opposed to cherished American values. The founding of the Comintern and its promulgation of an anticapitalist world revolution confirmed the government's worst fears and elevated Communists over German sympathizers as the gravest threat to American security.

Although the leaders of the Maryland Communist Party must have been aware of the rapidly rising level of official hostility, they displayed little evidence of it in the months after the Party's founding. Hendin wrote to the Communist Party chief Charles Ruthenberg to obtain a charter for the Baltimore Party. The Russian branch established a school dedicated to Communist studies and English lessons, and the Ukrainian Communists hosted a well-attended ball. David Zimmermann successfully enticed members of the Jewish and Lithuanian branches of the Socialist Party into the Communist camp. One of the Jewish branches, however, endured a sharp debate and a close vote that split the members; thirteen people remained with the Socialist Party, while fourteen joined the Communists. The extremely haphazard organization of left-wing groups in the city made it hard for Zimmermann to even find the Lithuanian branch, but by December eighteen of the twenty-two Lithuanians had enrolled in the Communist Party.[15]

While the Communists raided the ranks of the Socialist Party, the Socialists made numerous overtures to the deserters. None of the newly affiliated revolutionaries chose to return, however, prompting punitive tactics. The defecting members of the Jewish branch were threatened with legal action unless they returned the branch finances. In contrast, the Lithuanian branch simply divided its treasury equally between the Communist and Socialist factions.[16]

Another group eager to recruit CPA members was the Party's twin, the Communist Labor Party (CLP). Since its founding a day before the CPA, the Communist Labor Party had bombarded the CPA membership with calls for unification. Discussion of the CLP's overtures occupied a number of early Party meetings in Baltimore, and Hendin's second letter to Ruthenberg asked for advice on the issue of unity. Ruthenberg replied, and Hendin concurred, that unity could come only if the CLP members and branches joined the Communist Party of America on its terms.[17]

Eager to counter his rivals and to extend the Party's reach outside of Baltimore's ethnic enclaves, Hendin decided to organize a mass meeting conducted in English. He obtained Louis Fraina, currently the international secretary of the CPA, as a speaker and arranged for use of the B'rith Shalom Hall at 1012 East Baltimore Street. The meeting, held at two o'clock in the afternoon of 9 November 1919, drew a crowd of "five hundred men and twelve women." The chairman began the event with a brief speech stating that the purpose of meeting was to organize the Communist Party and to spread propaganda to the American working class. He then asked for donations to cover printing costs for two pamphlets entitled "Break the Blockade of Russia" and "Your Shop." A Communist from Philadelphia briefly addressed the crowd in Yiddish, and then Louis Fraina rose to speak.[18]

Fraina gave a fiery speech dedicated to the second anniversary of the Federated Soviet Socialist Republic of Russia. He castigated capitalists for taking the lion's share of the profits produced by the working class and predicted that all world governments would be socialist in nature within twenty-five years. Fraina sat down to thunderous applause while Party members passed the hat again, this time for the defense of recently arrested members of the Union of Russian Workers.

Hendin must have been pleased by the success of his plan to introduce the Communist Party of Baltimore to the wider community. Supporters donated over $250, several members of the audience signed Party cards, and two intensely interested individuals even took notes. Unfortunately, they were both agents in the employ of William M. Doyas, special agent in charge of the Baltimore office of the Bureau of Investigation. J. Edgar Hoover, the youthful director of the bureau, took a personal interest in both Communist parties. Agents under his control had infiltrated the two Chicago conventions and now had the twin parties under national surveillance in preparation for legal action against them. Special Agent Doyas, however, had been unable to discover any trace of Communist activity in Baltimore. Instead, he had concentrated his attention on the Union of Russian Workers, arresting Berezin and five of his followers on 7 November as part of a national raid against the group.[19]

The 9 November mass meeting alerted Doyas to the fact that the Communist Party existed in Baltimore, and he worked quickly to gather more information. Two of the imprisoned members of the Union of Russian Workers, Alexander Wolkov and Peter Soroka, also held membership in the Communist Party. Under questioning, both men named Louis Hendin as the primary Communist leader in Baltimore. More important, a search of Wolkov's belongings turned up a membership book listing the names and addresses of the members of the CPA's first Russian branch. Doyas used the book as the basis for drawing up a list of arrest-warrant requests and sent an agent to interview Hendin. Hendin proved to be very cooperative, telling Doyas's agent, Henry Stein, that the Communist Party differed from the Socialist Party in its advocacy of an industrial form of government, disclosing that the CPA financial officer in Baltimore was Jacob Timoney, and mentioning that the Party met regularly at 339 North Caroline Street.[20]

While waiting to move against the Communists, Doyas interrogated his small nest of imprisoned anarchists to determine if they had violated the Espionage Act by advocating the overthrow of the United States by force and violence. Doyas found they all had and turned them over to the immigration authorities, at that time housed in the Labor Department, for deportation. This technique—bureaucratic investigation followed by executive deportation—had been developed by J. Edgar Hoover to avoid a series of trials and their attendant difficulties of expense, publicity, and unpredictable juries. Eliminating treasonous individuals by bureaucratic procedure did have one drawback, however: it could be applied only to resident aliens. American citizens, whether native-born or naturalized, enjoyed the constitutional guarantee of a trial.

In Hoover's eyes, the trade-off cost little, since he estimated that at least 90 percent of the dangerous radicals in the United States were resident aliens. Unfortunately, the remaining 10 percent included such prominent Communists as the propagandist Robert Minor; John Reed, one of the Communist Labor Party's founders; and Charles Ruthenberg, the executive secretary of the CPA. In Baltimore, Special Agent Doyas discovered, much to his disappointment, that Louis Hendin had received his citizenship papers on 26 September 1919, slipping through the Justice Department's net by less than a month.[21]

Hendin's good fortune did not extend to the majority of Baltimore's Communists who were targeted for arrest by the Justice Department in the Baltimore rendition of the Palmer raids. Attorney General A. Mitchell Palmer, partly motivated by the bombing of his home in the summer of 1919, conceived of the raids that bore his name as a massive nationwide effort to destroy American communism in its infancy. Winston Churchill had sought the same ends internationally when he urged armed intervention in Russia to "strangle the Bolshevik baby in its cradle." The comparatively small-scale November raids against the Union of Russian Workers warmed up bureau agents and prepared them for the much more ambitious January undertaking.[22]

Doyas made his arrangements for the 2 January 1920 raids very carefully. He appointed four men to act with him as special agents, acquired the services of several stenographers and interpreters, secured the assistance of three police inspectors, and just hours before the raids recruited twelve plainclothes officers for additional manpower. Through a civilian source, he obtained the use of fourteen automobiles to deploy his men about the city. The Justice Department, to ensure simultaneous raids across the entire county, determined the exact time for each local effort. Doyas, instructed to launch his sweep at 9 P.M., felt the timing was very bad. At nine, most members of the working class were not at home but out at the moving-picture parlors dotting their neighborhoods. Six P.M., he later wrote to his superiors, would have been much better because the suspects could have been snared at dinner.[23]

Doyas and his operatives first descended on the residence of William Kade, whom they suspected of being the main organizer of the Baltimore branch of the Communist Labor Party. Although they seized several boxes of literature, they could find no membership books or any other kind of evidence indicating an active CLP in the city. Doyas's luck improved considerably when his men, led by Special Agent True D. Taylor, searched the home of Louis Hendin on East Baltimore Street. Although, as a U.S. citizen, Hendin could not be arrested, his home could be searched for "subversive material." Taylor confiscated several thousand CPA pamphlets, more membership lists for the first Russian branch of the Communist Party, and, most important, Hendin's carefully kept minutes of the CPA Central Committee meetings.[24]

The rest of Doyas's men concentrated on taking individual Party members into custody, using their automobiles to spread out through Baltimore's neighborhoods. One team surprised Thomas Truss, a prominent member of the Polish community in Baltimore, and his family at a late dinner. The Polish-speaking officer in charge of the arresting detail politely allowed Truss to finish eating before taking him into custody. Karl Karklin, a recent arrival in Baltimore, answered a knock at the door of his boardinghouse room, only to be arrested by waiting officers. The presence of the government agents electrified each neighborhood they visited. Doyas was convinced that word of the raid spread so rapidly that many of the radicals who had not gone out for the evening escaped from their homes and boardinghouses moments ahead of his men. Doyas was likely correct since only twenty-three of the seventy-three radicals for which he held arrest warrants could be found.[25]

Although low in quantity, Doyas's collection of Bolsheviks rated high in quality. Among those arrested were the Party organizer David Zimmermann and his wife, Bertha; the Latvian branch head Julius Ohsis and his wife, Kate; and Jacob Timoney, the Party treasurer. Most of the remaining detainees were rank-and-file members of the first Russian branch of the Party. Doyas spent part of the day after the raids talking to reporters, who published a dramatic and flattering account of the Baltimore arrests on their front pages, and then devoted himself to interrogating his prisoners. Because of a series of individual arrests following the main raid, the number of people to be questioned had reached thirty-four. To ensure that the suspected radicals were processed smoothly, bureau headquarters sent Doyas five pages of detailed interrogation guidelines, personally drawn up by J. Edgar Hoover.[26]

Hoover's outline began with a series of simple questions regarding the citizenship, background, and profession of the detainee. The interrogation then shifted to questions about the subject's membership in the Communist Party to establish that the person being questioned supported the principles of the CPA as outlined in its constitution. Then, to keep the subject off balance, questioning veered into identifying other Party members and meeting places. Finally, the interrogator would ask how the subject felt about the principles of the Communist International and whether the individual felt that destruction of property and assassination were legitimate political tools. Used correctly, the guidelines would force the accused individuals to condemn themselves as dangerous radicals by confessing to the major points of Hoover's legal briefs against the two Communist parties. Ideally, a rapid deportation would follow. However, as Doyas quickly discovered, the situation in Baltimore was far from ideal.[27]

Doyas began his interrogations with Julius Ohsis, whom Doyas considered the most active Communist in the city and whose long record of left-wing work fit the profile of a dangerous revolutionary. Although Ohsis readily admitted to being a Communist, he could not state positively what that meant, was unclear on the Party's relationship with the Comintern, and was uncertain about the number of other Party branches in Baltimore. Ohsis's wife, Katie, proved even less helpful. She declared that her only Party activities had been to sell calendars to raise funds, and she claimed to have no firm idea of the principles of the Communist Party because she had simply transferred her membership when the Latvian federation joined the new organization.[28]

Vasily Trimlove, a twenty-four-year-old Russian carpenter, admitted he was a member of the Communist Party but refused to concede he was a Communist. When asked to explain the discrepancy, Trimlove responded that he had joined the Party out of curiosity and hoped to learn what it was about over time. Since he confessed his embarrassment at being unable to speak English very well, part of Trimlove's interest may have been the language classes offered by the Russian branch. Trimlove did admit to attending a number of Party meetings, prompting Doyas to declare that the meetings must have focused on the need to overthrow the U.S. government. Trimlove denied the accusation, replying that the meetings were all about the new Soviet regime in Russia and never touched on the United States at all.[29]

Bertha Zimmermann gave answers remarkably similar to Trimlove's. When Doyas asserted, "You must know, if you read and understood it [the CPA constitution], that the Communist party of which you are a member preaches and teaches the overthrow of the government of this country," Zimmermann retorted sharply that the constitution said nothing of the sort. Doyas tried another approach and inquired if she believed in revolution. Zimmermann responded that of course she did, adding, "You don't know what contention there was in Russia. The people had to have a revolution there." When asked about a December meeting at which journalist Morris Olgin spoke, Zimmermann denied that anyone present criticized the U.S. government. Instead, she told Doyas, the talk focused on the evils of capitalism, how to improve the lot of workers, and the urgent need to lift the blockade prohibiting travel from the United States to Soviet Russia.[30]

When asked about her own activities as a member of the Communist Party, Zimmermann was less forthcoming. Although admitting that she made motions about bazaars and other fund-raising or social events, she neglected to mention her seat on the Baltimore Central Committee or her work, along with that of her husband, in distributing the Party's journal, the *Communist,* in Baltimore.[31]

Bertha's husband, David, denied that the Communist Party had anything to do with anarchism or its tactics of random violence. The main purpose of the Latvian branch of the Party, he insisted, was the education of the Latvian people in the United States. Zimmermann added that he wanted to remain permanently in the United States and preferred democratic government. Doyas questioned Zimmermann closely about the Comintern's general principles and its criticism of the Paris peace settlement. Zimmermann refused to commit himself, saying that both documents were difficult to understand and that he could not agree with everything they said without reservation.[32]

Toward the end of several interviews, Doyas expressed intense frustration with his subjects and demanded to know why they insisted on denying the facts. Some of Agent Doyas's anger was justified. In all likelihood, Julius Ohsis did know how many Party branches existed in the city, and David Zimmermann, as a delegate to the Party's founding convention, could probably discuss the meaning of the Comintern constitution at great length. However, much of what the novice Communists had to say has the ring of truth. Doyas was looking for a tightly organized ring of professional revolutionaries conspiring directly against the U.S. government. Instead, he found a newly formed organization that was little more than a loose collection of individuals caught up in the narrow concerns of their ethnic groups, well-informed about events in their former homelands, and remarkably oblivious to the issues gripping their adopted society.

Bertha Zimmermann is a perfect example of the difficult situation Doyas faced. Although she had lived in the United States for over ten years and spoke very good English, Zimmermann spent most of her time with fellow Latvians and thought of revolution almost entirely in terms of the Russian Empire. Zimmermann's work with the IWW branded her in Doyas's eyes as an opponent of the government. However, the Wobblies' war resistance had been an atypical excursion into politics; normally, members of the group even refused to vote. Zimmermann's IWW work predisposed her to envision an American revolution taking place on ten thousand shop floors, not at the gates of the White House.

Although Bertha Zimmermann did not fit Doyas's perception of an anti-American subversive, at least she was an ideologically motivated radical. Several of the other people arrested in the Palmer raids were little more than ethnic nationalists. John Kufel, a Russian Pole who had been a postal clerk in Turkmenistan before being jailed on false charges of subversion, is a perfect example. Upon his release from prison, Kufel joined the Russian Social Democratic Party out of spite and emigrated to the United States in 1909. Kufel found work as a tailor, eventually opened his own small shop on Baltimore's Fleet Street, and joined a variety of Polish patriotic organizations as well as the Union of Russian Workers. He set up housekeeping with Elena Lichtorowicz, a professional singer, who maintained connections with a number of radical organizations, including the first Russian branch of the Communist Party.[33]

John Kufel; Elena Lichtorowicz, who now called herself Helen Kufel; and their young daughter were all arrested and interrogated closely. Under questioning, John Kufel expressed no ill will toward the United States, claimed that he remained a socialist "to keep in step with the times," and stated that his fondest wish was to return to Russia now that the tzar had been overthrown. Helen Kufel proved even more unsuitable in the role of a cold-blooded revolutionary. She told her interrogators that she found membership in a variety of organizations a useful way to get singing engagements and confessed that she habitually distributed her husband's business cards at Party meetings.[34]

Thomas Truss, the man arrested at his dinner table, also personified the fluid, ethnic nature of Baltimore radicalism. Since Truss exercised considerable influence in the Polish community, it was only natural that Communist organizers, seeking to expand the Polish branch of the Party, should ask him for help. Truss, sympathetic to radical organizations because of their frequent work on behalf of immigrants, helped arrange two meetings and, as a sign of support, accepted a CPA membership card and donated fifty cents to the group. On the basis of a sketchy version of these events, Doyas ordered Truss's arrest in the January raids.[35]

Once out of jail, Truss secured the services of a well-respected Baltimore law firm, Niles, Wolf, Morrow and Barton, and sued the Bureau of Investigation for intimidation and false arrest. J. Edgar Hoover summoned Doyas to Washington to personally explain the situation. Doyas assured Hoover that the Truss arrest was fully justified and denounced the Reverend Charles Fox, who had stood up for Truss, as a dangerous German sympathizer. Hoover accepted his subordinate's report and ordered him to investigate the law firm for signs of radicalism. The investigation revealed that Embry Niles, the lawyer handling the Truss case, had been educated at the University of Maryland and at Oxford, favored Herbert Hoover's internationalist policies, and leaned toward socialism. Doyas evaluated him as "so well educated and so sincere [that] he might be considered a dangerous man." Niles proved very dangerous to the bureau's case; he persuaded officials at the Department of Labor to drop all the charges against Truss.[36]

Despite an increasing amount of evidence that most of his prisoners were nothing more than left-wingers and nationalists, William Doyas continued to search for a conspiracy against the U.S. government. Such single-minded persistence has caused some to condemn the bureau agents and their bosses, J. Edgar Hoover and A. Mitchell Palmer, as glory-seekers and fanatics, but these assessments are much too harsh. Hoover and Doyas were caught up in the powerful emotions that swept the country during the first "Red scare," poorly informed about the circumstances of immigrant life, and preoccupied with the situation in Soviet Russia. The Bolshevik government made no secret of its antipathy toward the capitalist nations of the West and maintained an international network of revolutionaries and espionage agents through the Comintern and the Cheka, precursor to the KGB.

In February of 1920, Doyas received a military intelligence report on the Comintern agent Anton Kotterhof. Kotterhof had crossed into the newly independent nation of Latvia in October of 1919 but was unable to secure transportation from Riga. Latvian police arrested the stranded agent, who was traveling under the alias of Pedrov, and relieved him of sixty diamonds and a letter to the American Communists from Nikolai Bukharin, the head of the Comintern. Subsequently released, Kotterhof made his way to Port of Spain, Trinidad. Now using the name Heifetz, he was believed to be a member of the crew of the USS *Owego,* en route to Baltimore.[37]

The letter taken from Kotterhof in Riga confirmed Doyas's worst fears about the international conspiracy he believed existed in Maryland. The communication gave detailed instructions about the recruitment of various left-wing groups into the Communist Party and encouraged the formation of paramilitary units from the ranks of veterans and sailors to counter "white-guard" organizations. Bukharin laid down the outlines of a general American program that included replacing the Senate and House of Representatives with Soviets and seizing control of industrial production.[38]

Bukharin doubtless intended his letter to be taken seriously, but it reads today like a parody of revolutionary fervor. The author blithely assumed that conditions in the United States matched those in Russia and that the tactics propelling the Bolsheviks to power could be applied across thousands of miles and a yawning cultural chasm. As an illustration of the degree of self-delusion and outrageous optimism that gripped the Bolsheviks in the early years of their rule, the letter is priceless. But to Doyas and his superiors, it chillingly spelled out in the dangers of communism and fully justified their actions. One of Doyas's special agents met the USS *Owego* when it docked, and several members of the crew were interrogated at bureau headquarters, but the illusive Kotterhof was not among them.[39]

Doyas's dark suspicions were further reinforced when the Baltimore CPA, following Comintern orders, began to go underground. Barely two weeks after the Palmer raids, Thomas Mirnoff went to see Hendin to have his teeth cleaned. Hendin informed Mirnoff that from now on only select individuals would be recruited and that all meetings would be small and secret. Unfortunately for Hendin, the circle of trusted individuals was not small and secret enough. Mirnoff left Hendin's office and promptly reported his conversation to K. C. Parrish, one of Special Agent Doyas's informants.[40]

Hendin's conspiratorial lapse is understandable because he was dividing his attention between running a dental practice, creating a clandestine organization, and attempting to get the arrested Communists out of jail. Initially, this last task seemed impossible because bail had been set at the astronomical figure of ten thousand dollars per prisoner. However, the bureau's tactics of avoiding a criminal case by relying on Labor Department procedures worked in the Party's favor. Betram Stump, the immigration agent who had jurisdiction over all the prisoners, soon found himself bombarded by requests from lawyers and family members to reduce bail.[41]

The number of pleas mounted so quickly that Stump not only reduced bail to one thousand dollars per person but also allowed it to be paid in Liberty Bonds. By 12 February, over forty-eight thousand dollars in bonds had been posted, and most of the arrested Communists had been set free. Michael Waszkiewiech obtained his freedom without even posting bail. Waszkiewiech had asked to be released on his own recognizance because he was the sole support of a wife and five children. After an investigation, Stump complied with Waszkiewiech's request, and eventually all charges against him were dropped.[42]

Funds to buy bonds for the reduced bails were raised by friends and family and channeled through the Workers Red Cross, an international organization created by the Comintern. A similar organization, the Worker's Defense Union (WDU), established during World War I by the IWW, also existed in Baltimore. Hendin approached the leaders of the WDU and suggested that they combine operations and extend their joint assistance to members of the Union of Russian Workers as well as jailed Wobblies and Communists. The arrangement worked out very well for the Communists and contributed to the drift of former members of the Union of Russian Workers and the IWW into the Party.[43]

On 8 May 1920, the Workers Red Cross, renamed the Workers Relief Society, held an end-of-the-season ball to raise funds for the remaining political prisoners. The name change resulted from the reluctance of the police to grant meeting permits to the Workers Red Cross because they felt the name verged on copyright infringement. The ball, attended by two informants, as well as assorted radicals, provides a glimpse of the uneven transformation of Baltimore's fledgling Communists into underground revolutionaries. The two informants reported back to Doyas that members of the Party now recognized each other by numbers rather than names and spoke in an elliptical fashion. Jacob Timoney, the former Party treasurer, addressed the crowd at the ball, saying, "It is hard to say anything these days—we give you enough meaning in our declaration," and then he spent the remainder of the meeting speaking in Russian to two strangers.[44]

Timoney's behavior matched that of a clandestine revolutionary very well, but closer examination of the informants' report indicates that the Party was still far from the cold-blooded terrorist organization that Doyas imagined. Other party-goers included Helen Kufel and John Kufel. Helen appeared to be looking for singing engagements, but John may have decided, as he did in Russia, that as long as he was going to be accused of being a Communist, he might as well be one. T. S. Wetter, the head of the IWW in Baltimore, came to the party as a gesture of continuing support, as did Natali Vovechek, a member of the Holy Trinity Independent Russian Orthodox Church. Vovechek attended the meeting at the invitation of Timoney and with the blessing of the church's pastor, Ivan Toltanoga, who leaned toward the left. She made a short speech inviting the assembled radicals to attend a dance sponsored by the church later in the summer. One informant learned that the Communists had considered using the church as a meeting hall but that Hendin was firmly opposed, believing that too close association with a religious body would tarnish the Party's reputation.

Refusing to allow the Party to become linked with the Holy Trinity Russian Independent Orthodox Church was Hendin's last significant act as head of the Baltimore CPA. In late May, a police officer in Fells Point approached Doyas and informed him that Hendin had left Baltimore. The officer had gone by Hendin's residence, which was also his place of business, and discovered the employees of a dental supply house removing the doctor's furnishings. The officer stopped to supervise and took the opportunity to search Hendin's remaining possessions, finding a series of letters from Communist Party headquarters in Chicago, which he gave to Doyas. Unbeknownst to Doyas, Hendin had returned to New York, where he remained active in the Communist

Party. In 1934, Party records show him serving on the New York City Executive Committee.[45]

As Doyas lost track of the Communist Party as an organization, those individuals he had arrested in the January raids began to slip through his fingers as well. This time the source of his troubles lay in Washington. As early as February 1920, some government officials began to express the fear that the Palmer raids were more damaging to American liberties than the radicalism the raids sought to suppress. One person determined to see that all the accused aliens received the full benefit of due process was Assistant Secretary of Labor Louis Post. Post reviewed Hoover's legal briefs against the two Communist parties, determined that no case existed against the Communist Labor Party, and dismissed charges against all its members. He then reviewed the charges against members of the Communist Party of America on an individual basis and threw the great majority out. In the end, only a handful of the people arrested in the Palmer raids were actually deported.[46]

By the summer of 1920, it had become increasingly clear to Agent Doyas that his attempt to destroy Bolshevism in his jurisdiction had failed. As the Communist Party slipped further and further underground, Doyas was reduced to chasing increasingly insubstantial ghosts. In June, he attempted, unsuccessfully, to track down rumors of the existence of Hungarian and Finnish branches of the Communist Party. In August, one of his informants summoned him urgently to Sparrows Point, where Doyas was forced to listen to rumors of fantastic Bolshevik schemes to flood the United States with propaganda smuggled in from Mexico. In September, Doyas painstakingly tracked a package containing twenty-five copies of *The Communist* to a house on North Chester Street, but all he discovered was that the magazines were to be passed on to David and Bertha Zimmermann. Since the Immigration Department had already ordered their deportation, there was nothing concrete to be done.[47]

2

The Lovestonite Expulsion

The retreat underground protected the fledgling Communist Party from the Bureau of Investigation but did nothing to relieve a growing atmosphere of factionalism that divided its members and drastically reduced its numbers. At the same time, the successive crises transformed the Party from the collection of amateurs discovered by William Doyas into a well-disciplined organization with a cadre of leaders acutely sensitive to instructions from the center. The first major upheaval came immediately after the founding of the twin parties, when both the CPA and the CLP sent delegations to Moscow to plead their case before the Comintern. Each party requested recognition as the genuine representative of the American working class, but the Comintern dismissed both sets of arguments and ordered the two groups to merge. When initial attempts at unification failed, the Comintern sent a delegation to New York that succeeded in bringing about a somewhat reluctant marriage in May of 1921.

Soon after unification, William Z. Foster's Chicago-based labor organization, the Trade Union Educational League (TUEL), and a group of socialists known as the Workers (Arbiters) Circles joined the Communist Party. No sooner had the Party absorbed these two small groups than it plunged into acrimonious debate over Comintern orders to establish an open, "legal" organization to complement the "illegal" underground Party. After a false start in July, a New York City convention established the open Workers Party in December of 1921.

Baltimore newspapers covered the convention, but, in contrast to the serious treatment they gave the Palmer raids, they seemed to consider the convention little more than a joke. One article gleefully recounted the near riot that erupted when James P. Cannon, the presiding officer, asked the delegates for more action and less talk and noted that Benjamin Gitlow, the Workers Party candidate for mayor of New York, had been nominated for the office by his mother. The same tone informed an article that quoted the American Federation of Labor's head, Samuel Gompers. After reading Workers Party press releases on the vigor of the organization, Gompers stated that he had "no exaggerated notion" of Communist influence and challenged them to try and take over his organization. He dismissed the Party's claims of growing radical strength as nothing more than the "vaporings of muddle-headed men and short-haired women."[1]

Whether comic or serious, press coverage throughout the early 1920s gave the impression that the local Communist Party had vanished in the Palmer raids. The misconception arose naturally from the secrecy maintained by the small surviving group and the disappearance of many of the founding members. Prominent by their absence after 1921 were Bertha and David Zimmermann, Kate and Julius Ohsis, Louis Hendin, and Jacob Timoney. The Zimmermanns had probably been deported, Hendin had returned to New York, and the others may have shared these fates or, perhaps, simply adopted a quieter life.

After unification, the Party organized itself into sixteen national districts. The districts varied in size from District 2, which covered the state of New York, to District 11, also known as the Agricultural District, which took in everything from Texas to Montana. Baltimore became a somewhat neglected branch of District 3, headquartered in Philadelphia. District 3 included eastern Pennsylvania, all of Delaware and Maryland, plus the District of Columbia and the cities of Norfolk and Richmond, Virginia. The district leadership did not intentionally disregard the needs of the Baltimore Party but found themselves hampered by the sheer size of the district, poor human resources, chronic factional fighting, and endless financial problems.

In 1922, the district organizer, who used the Party name of H. Cooper, criticized his colleagues for lacking the skills to fill out a simple transfer card. In the same letter, he accused another leading Party member of stirring up the opposition. The financial problems grew so severe that Cooper suggested he be allowed to retain a portion of the district dues to cover shortfalls in his salary. "Comrade Jones," a Party troubleshooter on temporary duty in District 3, complained to the New York headquarters that, because of his unpaid wages, he was three weeks behind in his rent and was having trouble feeding himself.[2]

Officials at Party headquarters sympathized with Cooper over the incessant challenges from the opposition but were much less accommodating when it came to the other difficulties. Headquarters responded to the continual complaints over funds with the reminder that it was the duty of the districts to finance the center, not the other way around. Commenting on a poorly attended demonstration, the New York office expressed disbelief that only half a dozen comrades had turned out and recommended that attendance be made compulsory in the future.[3]

The Communist Party suffered from high turnover and was frequently forced to shuffle its administration. Cooper resigned as the District 3 organizer in November of 1922 after being exposed as an active Communist. His successor, Abram Jakira, ran the district for the next four years but squandered much of his time in factional fighting. He was replaced in 1926 by Alex Bail. Bail, who had strong backing from Party chief Jay Lovestone, also indulged in Party infighting and left Philadelphia in 1927 after turning the district over to Herbert Benjamin. The Baltimore subdistrict endured similar instability in its leading cadre; in the spring of 1925, it had three city secretaries in less than two months.[4]

The earliest known head of the Baltimore Party, after Hendin and Timoney, was Irving Solinsky, occasionally referred to in Party correspondence as Solins. Solinsky, who first appears as the Baltimore secretary in 1924, had a brief tenure characterized by frequent conflicts with Party headquarters and few accomplishments. Part of the problem was Solinsky's own fault because he often tripped himself up with poor planning. But he also received little assistance from the Party's language branches, which continued to suffer from the same ambiguous mix of politics and ethnicity that had so confused Special Agent Doyas.[5]

While reliably radical, the ninety-member Finnish branch spent as much time on cultural affairs as on politics and was engaged in a struggle with the non-Communist Finns for control of Finn Hall. The fifty-member Czech branch had split between a left-wing faction, which followed the Party line, and a right-wing faction, which Solinsky feared would "soon turn the branch into some social affair." Solinsky despaired of any action from Abram Jakira, the district organizer, and requested that the national-level Czech organization send someone to Baltimore to sort out the problem. In contrast to the socially minded but at least lively Finn and Czech branches, the small Hungarian branch had sunk into apathy. Despite the best efforts of Solinsky and his successors, it disbanded in the summer of 1925. The Party's English branch, made up of native-born Americans, enjoyed higher morale but also disbanded in 1925, when several members left town.[6]

The Jewish branch remained well organized but suffered from an independent streak. Raphael Abramovich, a Menshevik opponent of the Bolshevik regime in Russia, planned to visit Baltimore in early 1925 as a part of a nationwide speaking tour. In some cities, Communists had violently broken up Abramovich's speeches but the leadership in District 3 contented itself with ordering Party members in the city to boycott the meeting. Despite the ban, several Jewish Communists attended the speech and quietly sat through Abramovich's denunciation of the Soviet Union, which earned them considerable ridicule in the pages of the *Jewish Daily Forward.* The district leadership wrote to Solinsky demanding to know why, if the Jewish comrades were willing to break Party discipline by attending the meeting, they were not willing to either disrupt the proceedings or at least challenge the defamation of the Soviet Union.[7]

Solinsky resigned at the end of March 1925 and was replaced by Thomas N. Owerking, a former Baltimore industrial organizer, who quit barely a month later and emigrated to the Soviet Union. The position of secretary then fell to Nicholas Ciattei, generally known as Chatty, an Americanized version of his name. Two reports, one written in July of 1925 and the second in February of 1926, provide the first clear picture of the Baltimore Communist Party since the Palmer raids and illustrate the challenges Chatty faced. The first, by A. Litvakoff, a district-level organizer, observed that industrial work in Baltimore was "completely demoralized and neglected" and recommended that "a capable comrade be sent to Baltimore for at least six months" to aid in a thorough reorganization. Litvakoff singled out the Philadelphia-based industrial organizer and future Central Committee member Harry Wickes for particular criticism, noting that after making a special trip to Baltimore, Wickes did nothing more substantial than organize a "Hands Off China" meeting.[8]

In February of 1926, a team of four district officials, led by Alex Bail and Norman Tallentire, "swooped down" on Baltimore to reorganize the branches and clubs. Their visit came in the wake of the dissolving of the "illegal," or underground, party and the changing of the Party's name from the Workers Party to the Workers (Communist) Party. The team found 124 registered Party members in Baltimore, with 23 more to be reregistered in the near future. Bail thought that most of the city's branches were functioning adequately and singled out the Finnish Club for particular praise.[9]

However, as Litvakoff before him, Bail thought that Party influence in the workplace left much to be desired. Only three shop organizations, called nuclei by the scientifically minded Communists, existed in Baltimore. The largest of the three, with fifty members, was made up of Communists employed in the tin plate department at Bethlehem Steel's sprawling Sparrows Point mill. The other two nuclei, one in a clothing manufactory and the other at the Crown Cork and Bottling Company, had only three members each. Although Bail wished the Party had a larger presence among the work force, there was little he could do to improve the situation. He instead contented himself with reorganizing the existing nuclei and establishing four street units to replace the soon-to-be-phased-out language branches. Since the new street units followed neighborhood and hence ethnic lines, the language branches disappeared in name only. Later renamed clubs, the street units were spoken of as Jewish, Finnish, or Italian "branches" until World War II.

Bail praised the dedication of the Baltimore Party's youthful leadership but was troubled by the situation in the Russian branch. He had discovered that with the approval of the national Russian-language organization, the Russian Communists regularly attended and supported the Independent Russian Orthodox Church in Baltimore. The branch leader, Prokope Suvorov, taught Russian-language classes for children at the church, while another Communist helped the congregation stage plays. The rest of the branch members sold literature at the church and generally, in Bail's words, made "themselves quite at home." Bail felt that something was definitely wrong, although he found it mildly reassuring that a large portrait of Lenin hung in the church. He asked his superiors to let him know what kind of a united front this represented and to contact the Russian bureau for advice.

Tantalizing clues about Suvorov have survived. Suvorov, who lived on Nicholson Street, first appears in the records of District 3 in July of 1924 as the secretary of the Russian branch. The next mention of him is in 1925 in a confidential letter from Party headquarters in New York to Jakira denying Suvorov permission to go to the Soviet Union. Suvorov wanted to return home because his mother was in ill health; however, the Soviet government denied the request on the grounds that Suvorov could not immigrate as an individual but had to be a member of an organized commune. Suvorov was not trying to immigrate but was attempting only to return to the country in which he still held citizenship. Nor was it hard to become attached to a commune; the files of District 3 are filled with correspondence regarding Communists traveling back and forth from the Soviet Union. In 1926, so many Communists from District 3 applied for permission to go to the Soviet Union that Norman Tallentire, the official who processed the requests, ran out of printed forms and had to write headquarters for a new supply.[10]

Suvorov never returned to Russia. He died of uncertain causes in Baltimore on 6 May 1926 at the age of twenty-eight. Less than four months later, a letter from Suvorov's mother addressed "America, Baltimore—to the Communist Party" arrived from New York. At some point in its delivery, someone had written across the top, "please forward this to the Party where he [her son] worked." In the letter, Suvorov's mother pleaded for assistance from the Baltimore Party because everyone in her home town thought her son had defected and she was unable to get state aid for herself and her three surviving children. The letter describes Suvorov as a "soldier," states that he was a member of the Communist Party of the Soviet Union, and makes it plain that he left Russia secretly under instructions to aid the American Communist Party. Suvorov's mother never explained exactly what she wanted from the Americans. She may have hoped for money, but more likely she wanted them to confirm that Suvorov was a loyal Communist who died while preforming his international duty. What reply the Americans made, if any, is unknown.[11]

The letter from Suvorov's mother could not have left the Soviet Union without the permission of either the OGPU (the Unified State Political Directorate, later the KGB) or the Communist Party, which strongly suggests that Suvorov was, as his mother claimed, a Soviet agent. Such a role explains his attachment to the Independent Russian Orthodox Church since the Soviet government made a point of keeping a careful watch on even sympathetic emigrant organizations. The government's refusal to let him return to Russia also makes sense in this context. In all likelihood, either Suvorov had not completed his main task or a suitable replacement had not been found. It is odd that Suvorov's mother should have been forced to such unorthodox methods to relieve her situation when a word from the right authority should have sufficed. However, this would hardly be the first example of someone falling through the cracks of the unwieldy and fragmented Soviet bureaucracy. The entire Suvorov affair has an air of confusion about it, not at all out of place in the general disarray of international communism during the 1920s.

Disarray lay at the heart of the Baltimore Party's major grievance against the central Party apparatus. Frequently speakers, painstakingly scheduled for rallies and celebrations, would cancel at the last minute, leaving the Baltimore organizers holding the bag. Besides the embarrassment at being unable to produce the promised celebrity, the local Party members found their recruiting efforts severely hampered. Sympathizers and interested individuals often accused the Party of advertising well-known speakers as a bait-and-switch tactic just to boost meeting attendance. Bail, a generally conservative Party worker, urged that the situation be corrected to allow work in Baltimore to progress. Tallentire, who was not known for moderation, phrased his recommendations in somewhat stronger language, branding the practice of canceling speakers as "reprehensible" and insisting that it must "absolutely" be stopped.[12]

Tallentire's exaggerated language and inability to get along with Bail eventually resulted in his transfer to Minneapolis, but his rhetoric seemed justified in this case. Throughout the mid-1920s, the Baltimore Party leadership labored under severe financial and organizational handicaps and could ill afford the losses associated with the cancellations. Ellen Zetron, the young secretary of the Baltimore Central Committee, carefully set up speaking engagements for such Party luminaries as Jay Lovestone, Benjamin Gitlow, and Rose Pastor Stokes, only to have them canceled or changed after they had been advertised. The Stokes cancellation, which took place half an hour before the meeting was to begin, so vexed Zetron that she demanded Stokes not only reschedule her engagement but issue a public letter of apology to her disappointed audience.[13]

Not all speakers canceled, of course. On 27 December 1926, Mercer G. Johnston, the former chair of the Committee of Forty-eight, served as master of ceremonies for Benjamin Gitlow, the Communist Party's second in command. Gitlow bombarded a large audience at the Hippodrome Theater with denouncements of capitalism's crimes, which included the American invasion of Nicaragua and the lavish Christmas gifts, some in the half-million dollar range, exchanged by New York socialites. Gitlow spent the question-and-answer period following his prepared remarks defending the Soviet Union from charges that it had "nationalized women" and stifled all opposition to the government. Ironically Gitlow, who spoke openly as a Communist, had been quoted in the Baltimore press, on the occasion of the founding of the Workers Party, as saying "the Communist Party is dead."[14]

Besides organizing meetings, the Party took concrete, if faltering, steps to extend its influence in progressive labor and political circles. In 1923, the Comintern had instructed the Workers Party to ally itself with, and eventually take over, a mass-based, progressive party. The New York leadership initially selected the Conference for Progressive Political Action (CPPA), whose leader, Wisconsin's Senator Robert La Follett, stood an outside chance of winning the 1924 presidential race. Opening contacts between the Party and the CPPA appeared promising, but the Comintern abruptly reversed its position, forcing Party delegates to the CPPA convention to loudly criticize La Follett. The alliance failed, and La Follett became a stanch anti-Communist.[15]

In 1925, the Comintern changed its mind again and instructed the Party to seek an alliance with the Farmer-Labor Party and to work within the American Federation of Labor (AFL). Since no branch of the Farmer-Labor Party existed in Maryland, Chatty chose to work with the Maryland People's Party (MPP), a small progressive organization with ties to the AFL. Chatty proposed either running a joint campaign with the People's Party or organizing an independent Workers Party campaign. Chatty preferred the second option because he thought that the MPP was a petite-bourgeois group that could not be easily brought into line with Communist goals. Alex Bail disagreed with Chatty, telling him that the Baltimore Party had "neither the experience or the comrades to make even a half hearted attempt" at a state electoral campaign. Instead, Bail instructed Chatty and David Howatt, a prominent local

Party member, to undertake a campaign for control of the MPP that would convert it into a genuine expression of working-class sentiment.[16]

Bail hoped that a closer alliance with the MPP would also reinforce the small, but real progress the Baltimore Party had begun to make in the AFL. Most of the progress was because of Howatt, who had gained a responsible position in the Baltimore Telegraphers Union. But a small group of Party members and sympathizers in the Baltimore Carpenters Union showed real promise and even led a revolt against that union's conservative leadership. The Communists' brief insurgency came in the wake of the expulsion of the Carpenters local from the Baltimore Federation of Labor (BFL). After the expulsion, the small Communist group printed a leaflet calling for a union meeting to protest the leadership's actions and to petition for readmittance to the BFL. The meeting began well, but the Communists and their sympathizers quickly lost control of the situation, allowing speakers loyal to the union leadership to dominate the gathering.[17]

Shortly afterward, a private detective and a union official questioned the printer who had run off the Communist leaflets in an attempt to learn the names of the men who ordered the flyers. The setback threw the small Communist fraction, the official term for a group of Party members within a larger organization, into depression and panic. Bail believed the situation could be saved, however. He recommended that an experienced Communist from the New York Carpenters Union be sent to Baltimore to hold a meeting with the six fraction members, both to cheer them up and to help them overcome their most serious handicap, the fact that none of them spoke English.[18]

In March of 1927, Charles Ruthenberg, the head of the central Party, died suddenly from a ruptured appendix and was buried with honors in the Kremlin Wall. His death triggered a factional fight in the Party between a group supporting Jay Lovestone and one promoting the leadership of William Weinstone. Although the Political Committee appointed Lovestone as acting Party secretary, Weinstone's backers, most prominently William Z. Foster and James P. Cannon, thought they had a majority on the Central Executive Committee and appealed the decision to the Comintern. Comintern head Nikolai Bukharin preferred Lovestone because the two men had worked closely together in the past. Although Bukharin left the final composition of the Party leadership up to a convention, he made it very plain which way the delegates should vote.[19]

The Weinstone group did not get the message and continued to organize itself in the weeks before the convention. Several faction supporters visited Baltimore hoping to bring the city into Weinstone's camp, but their efforts failed because Chatty solidly supported Lovestone. Alex Bail, also a Lovestone partisan, faced strong opposition in Philadelphia, forcing him to send a divided delegation to the New York convention. In contrast, the Baltimore Party held a city conference that elected a three-person delegation unanimously committed to Lovestone. The Weinstone group challenged the results, claiming Baltimore was entitled to more delegates. Bail, however, produced figures showing that between February and May, the period on which convention representation was based, Baltimore averaged just seventy-three paid-up Party members and was not entitled to additional delegates.[20]

The vote at the national Party convention, held in New York City on 21 August, overwhelmingly endorsed Lovestone as Party secretary and gave his faction large majorities on both the Political Committee and the Central Executive Committee. The convention also provided the Baltimore Party delegation with a platform to vent their frustration over the national organization's inability to provide requested speakers. William Wilkens, one of the Baltimore delegates and a local Party organizer, read a memorandum detailing the Party's complaints. It listed the five most important speakers who had canceled engagements in the last two years and castigated them for inflicting "moral and financial failures" on the city as well as retarding Party growth.[21]

All of this had been said before, but the combination of the complaints and firm support for Lovestone finally produced results. Lovestone began paying his political debts in District 3 by fulfilling a promise to his longtime supporter Alex Bail to reassign him to more congenial work. So eager was Bail to go that he left only a few days after Herbert Benjamin, his replacement as District 3 organizer, arrived in the city.[22]

Lovestone rewarded Chatty by coming to Baltimore himself and delivering a speech at the Hippodrome, which drew a crowd of over fifteen hundred "Communists and sympathizers." Ernest B. Fielder, a prominent local Socialist, introduced both Lovestone and his warm-up speaker, Herbert Benjamin. Lovestone gave a dramatic address, predicting a chain of Soviet states across the world by 1937 and complete worldwide victory for communism in the next world war. One of the factors bringing about the Communist victory, Lovestone declared, would be a wholesale defection of American workers, who, when they realized the benefits of the Soviet system, would "know where their interests lie and in the next world war will know upon whom to turn their guns." Lovestone left the platform accompanied by enthusiastic applause and cheers.[23]

The Maryland Party's situation continued to improve in the months after Lovestone's visit. Pat Devine, a national Party organizer, traveled to Baltimore to speak at the Baltimore Open Forum on the evening of Christmas. Devine reported that his speech on the causes of unemployment was well re-

ceived and inspired five people to join the Party at smaller meetings held after his public appearance. A few weeks after Devine's visit, the Party began
publishing the *Sparrows Point Worker*. The May 1928 issue scoffed at plant
owner Charles Schwab's claim to have never turned a profit in the steel industry and compared the mill to a battlefield because of the high rate of accidents
and deaths. Other articles denounced the Coolidge prosperity as a fairy tale,
warned of a coming world war, and recruited members for the Young Workers League. Several "letters" from workers, actually miniature editorials written by Party members, denounced the speed-up of production and rallied
against the twelve-hour workday. The six-page mimeographed paper sported
on its masthead a crude drawing of workers laboring at a forge and projected
a militant but engaging attitude.[24]

On the Fourth of July, members of the Communist Party gathered at Cooperative Beach in Stony Point, Maryland, to celebrate the holiday with pic-
nics, swimming, and a speech by Robert Minor, the famed radical artist who
had become a major Party spokesperson. Cooperative Beach was a jointly
owned resort that provided left-leaning Baltimoreans with a vacation spot.
Minor forfeited a five hundred dollar bail bond, resulting from his arrest at a
demonstration in front of J. P. Morgan's New York office, to appear before the
festive crowd of six hundred. In the spirit of the occasion, Minor focused his
speech on George Washington, exhorting his listeners to learn from the example of a man who gained world fame only after entering into "a criminal
conspiracy in the eyes of the law." Minor concluded by predicting a second
American revolution, but this time by a democratic majority instead of the
small group that had established the capitalist dictatorship in 1776.[25]

Minor's appearance coincided with the convening of the Sixth Comintern
Congress, which signaled a sharp turn in global Communist policies by announcing the beginning of the "Third Period" of world capitalism. Nikolai
Bukharin introduced the concept of the Third Period in his keynote address
to the Sixth Congress. He defined the time from the Russian Revolution to the
defeat of the German radicals in 1923 as the First Period, characterized by acute
revolutionary crises. The Second Period, up to 1927, saw capitalism recover and
regain some of its former vitality. Now, however, capitalism had entered its
Third Period, a time of continued recovery but of increasing internal contra-
dictions that would, according to Bukharin, eventually lead to revolution.
Joseph Stalin, general secretary of the Communist Party of the Soviet Union
(CPSU), agreed with Bukharin on all but the last point. Stalin thought that
instead of developing gradually, the conditions necessary for revolution would
manifest themselves explosively and that the Comintern's member parties
must be ready to seize the moment.

Politically astute as always, Stalin used the divergence of opinion to eliminate Bukharin as a threat to his authority. The Kremlin power struggle spilled over to the international parties as well and had a particularly dramatic impact on the American Party. Under Comintern pressure, the major European parties had begun moving toward the tactics of militancy, sectarianism, and aggressive anticapitalism advocated by Bukharin and Stalin even before the official adoption of Third Period policies. In April of 1928, some months before the Sixth Comintern Congress, this leftward shift prompted John Pepper, the Comintern representative to the American Party, to write a lengthy article for the *Communist* questioning the wisdom of following similar tactics in the United States. Pepper noted that American capitalism was the most robust example of the species in the world and that the American working class was the most privileged and inherently conservative group of workers in the industrialized nations. Given these circumstances, Pepper argued, American Communists should avoid radical tactics and continue their policy of cooperation with other left-wing groups.[26]

Pepper and Lovestone are often thought of as believers in American exceptionalism. In its most extreme form, exceptionalism held that America's lack of an aristocracy, its early conversion to democracy, and its abundant resources allowed the nation to develop outside of the Marxist principles governing European history. However, neither Lovestone nor Pepper advocated pure exceptionalism. They simply believed that because of America's unique conditions, moderate tactics worked best in the United States. Stalin disagreed and recalled Pepper to the Soviet Union, where he disappeared in the purges of the 1930s.

Lovestone adapted his rhetoric to suit the change of line but was suspected of harboring reservations. As a result, the Comintern demanded that he step down as Party secretary and accept an overseas assignment. Lovestone turned the top Party post over to his close supporter, Benjamin Gitlow, but refused to agree to the overseas posting and hastened to Moscow to defend himself. Stalin detained Lovestone in Moscow, along with several important supporters, while the faction backing William Z. Foster reorganized the Party. Foster and his backers changed its name to the Communist Party of the United States of America (CPUSA) and then began a purge of Lovestone's supporters, expelling Lovestone himself in June of 1929.

The fate of the "rightists" has sharply colored most writing on the subject of the Third Period, which is often dismissed as a misguided Stalinist detour into sectarianism. Some historians, however, have praised the Third Period as a time of great enthusiasm in the Communist Party that produced both an expanded membership and a seasoned cadre of leaders who guided the movement for decades. Others go even further, criticizing the Popular Front of the late 1930s for betraying the rank and file who had joined the Party in the Third Period to create a revolution. In Baltimore, the Third Period produced mixed results. Initially, Third Period militancy did build a strong disciplined Party and brought in new members. But the demands of constant activism over-stretched its resources, exhausted its members, and contributed to a near collapse in 1934.

While Lovestone languished in Moscow, Herbert Benjamin, who had allied himself with the Foster faction, sent twenty-five-year old Dominic Flaiani to Baltimore to reorganize and purge the local Party. Flaiani arrived in Baltimore on 23 April 1929, called a meeting of the Baltimore Central Committee, and was elected chair without opposition. The young activist then introduced a series of detailed resolutions on the organization of men's clothing workers and made arrangements for a committee to assist the newly established Marine Workers Progressive League in renovating its Fells Point headquarters. The meeting concluded with the establishment of a committee to print signs and leaflets for a public May Day meeting and celebration, which took place a week later.[27]

On 3 May, Flaiani chaired another meeting, which elected him to the post of city organizer and created an agitprop (agitation and propaganda) committee. The committee doubled as the *Daily Worker* committee and was headed by Louis Berger, a lawyer already in charge of the city's Inter-Racial Workers Forum. The Central Committee then created a series of smaller committees to oversee specific aspects of the Party's reorganization. The short meeting concluded with a motion to retain a portion of the proceeds from literature sales to finance organizational activities and the creation of still another committee, this one to find a way to pay Flaiani's salary.[28]

Five days later, Flaiani reconvened the Central Committee for a lengthy session in which he laid out his plans for carrying out the policies of the Third Period. He began by stating that in the two weeks since his arrival, he had visited each of the Party's street units and shop nuclei and was pleased to report that the Party was drawing "new and proletarian" elements, including a number of black workers, into its ranks. The Party had begun to properly implement the decisions of the Comintern by concentrating its efforts on shop work, as demonstrated by the reactivation of the Sparrows Point unit and the distribution of over a thousand copies of the *Daily Worker* on May Day. But, Flaiani continued, much more remained to be done.[29]

He illustrated his point by reading into the minutes a lengthy report on the makeup of Baltimore's working population, which he seems to have compiled from copies of *The Sun Almanac* at the Pratt Library. The purpose behind the report is somewhat obscure since Flaiani never referred to it again. Instead, he hurried on to make arrangements for improved fund-raising, a stepped-up schedule of Party meetings, and increased support for the International Labor Defense (which every Party member was instructed to join). The meeting ended by making the final preparations for a trade union conference to elect delegates to attend the founding convention of the Trade Union Unity League (TUUL), the new and improved version of William Z. Foster's Trade Union Educational League.

The TUEL had been dedicated to working within the mainstream AFL unions to gradually bring them around to a militant revolutionary stance. However, the ideology of the Third Period denounced the AFL as an unredeemable "social fascist" organization. Instead of attempting reformation of existing unions, the Comintern now demanded that Communists establish competing revolutionary, or "red," unions. These radical organizations would provide a clear alternative for the working class and help support the work of the Communist Party. At the TUUL's inception, the CPUSA established three dual unions: the National Miners Union (NMU), the National Textile Workers Industrial Union (NTWIU), and the Needle Trades Workers Industrial Union (confusingly also NTWIU). The Baltimore TUUL, headed by Jacob Levinson, consisted solely of a branch of the Needle Trades Workers Industrial Union.[30]

Flaiani's plans for increased militancy and visibility began to bear fruit in early July when the Party staged a rally at Hopkins Plaza to protest the imprisonment of the Gastonia, North Carolina, textile strikers. The Gastonia strike, unlike several other work stoppages in the southern textile mills, had the distinction of being lead by Communist organizers from the National Textile Workers Union. Violent reaction to the Communists on the part of the North Carolina authorities broke the strike and deprived the union of victory. But the event still provided a great boost to Communist morale. For a moment at least, the Party had broken away from its isolation in the ethnic communities and had led a united group of distinctively American workers. More important, Party analysts believed that the Gastonia strike pointed directly to the coming capitalist apocalypse.[31]

Nineteen-year-old Irving Keith, a Young Communist League organizer recently dispatched to Baltimore from Philadelphia, made his first public speech at the Gastonia rally. Keith and Flaiani worked well together and quickly gained public reputations as Communist firebrands. On 27 July, police arrested Keith for disturbing the peace and obstructing traffic while making a speech at the corner of Collington Avenue and Monument Street. Testimony at his court hearing revealed that the arrest had been made after two neighborhood bankers complained that the crowd of several hundred people gathered around the Communist speakers made it hard for customers to enter their places of business. An additional complaint came from the Reverend Henry Einspruch, pastor of the Hebrew Lutheran Mission. He claimed that the Communists called out insulting remarks and attempted to convince people to leave the mission by making fun of the prayers and hymns accompanying Einspruch's relief efforts.[32]

Louis Berger, who in addition to his other duties worked for the Baltimore branch of the International Labor Defense, posted Keith's bail. Two days later, Keith was back in jail, this time for obstructing the sidewalk while giving a speech at Baltimore and Bond streets. Jon O'Ren, author of the popular "Down the Spillway" editorial column for the *Baltimore Sun,* felt moved to protest this cavalier treatment:

> I have read several times recently of radical speakers being arrested in this city for obstructing free passage of the streets. . . . But yesterday about the noon hour I walked two blocks up crowded Baltimore Street from crowded Charles Street, and there was a gentleman in a black suit having nothing less than a seizure of some sort. He was talking religion, but to do that it seems he had to bounce from the curb into the street and then make a standing broad jump back onto the pavement again and so forth. . . . But of course he was not obstructing traffic; he was not a radical. Then after noon I walked about three blocks up crowded Charles Street from crowded Baltimore Street. In that distance I met, besides a lot of strangers, a man selling pencils; one selling a cure-all ointment; one playing a musical instrument and two girls dressed in humiliating uniforms, distributing some form of confection. But they were not obstructing free passage of course. Those things you put down to advertizing and charity.[33]

O'Ren's column so rankled Thomas Mooney, the police officer in charge of the northeastern district, that he wrote a lengthy letter to the editor defending the actions of his men. Mooney then asked the presiding judge to drop the charges against Keith and his codefendants as a conciliatory gesture.[34]

With the consent of Police Commissioner Charles Gaither, Mooney worked out an arrangement with the Communist Party. Mooney promised that his officers would not interfere with Party speakers as long as the Communists kept the sidewalks clear and moved along when politely requested. Flaiani made good use of the treaty with the police department and the sympathetic public reaction by throwing the Party into a flurry of sidewalk speaking. In August alone, he organized four major rallies, mostly focusing on the plight of the Gastonia workers, although the largest rally, on 6 August, had an antiwar theme. The August rallies also featured a series of black speakers, mostly Party members from New York City. The Baltimore Communists, although fully committed to the Third Period policy of reaching out to the nation's African American population, had yet to recruit any prominent blacks.[35]

Although the Party tried very hard to bring African Americans into the organization, estimates of national black membership in the CPUSA during the 1920s range from two or three hundred to as few as fifty. Shortly after unification, the Party attracted a small black nationalist group, the African Blood Brotherhood. However, the Brotherhood's emphasis on racial nationalism proved to be a poor fit with the Party's ideology of class struggle and internationalism. The group was dropped in favor of two Communist-created and controlled organizations, the American Negro Labor Congress and the Tenants League. Branches of both organizations existed in Baltimore, but neither made any headway in the African American community.

As a result, at the 15 September 1929 Baltimore Central Committee meeting, Flaiani decided that the Party could no longer afford to fund the position of "Negro organizer." Flaiani and George Mink, the national organizer of the Marine Workers Progressive League who attended the meeting, then had a lengthy discussion about releasing the African American organizer, Comrade Welsh, to work on the waterfront. Flaiani refused and insisted that Welsh continue to hold the position of (unpaid) Negro organizer.[36]

The relative importance of marine and Negro work occupied only a portion of Flaiani and Mink's attention. Their major task was to complete the purge of the Lovestonites. Although the Baltimore Party had backed Lovestone unanimously during the 1927 factional fight, that support dissolved overnight once the Comintern denounced Lovestone. A small group of Party members retained their loyalty to Lovestone, however. The most active Lovestone supporter in Baltimore was Philip Labovitz, who publicly opposed the Comintern line and sought to organize an opposition group in the city's Party. The Baltimore Central Committee condemned Labovitz as an enemy of the working class, and the Communist Party and expelled him.[37]

Flaiani and Mink then took up the cases of M. Socolove, P. Miller, and Nicholas Chatty, who had refused to submit written statements denouncing Lovestone to the Communist Party and were expelled for breaches of Party discipline. In the light of the "poisonous, anti-proletarian, anti-Communist, and counter-revolutionary activities" of the Baltimore Lovestone group, the Baltimore Central Committee resolved to send letters to every member of the CPUSA and the Trade Union Unity League and to the heads of all fraternal organizations alerting them to the activities of the four men. Further, they would be denounced in the Party press to prevent them from trying to rejoin the Party in another district.[38]

The fates of Miller, Socolove, and Labovitz are unknown, but Nicholas Chatty remained a radical and either joined Lovestone in the Communist Party Opposition (CPO) or returned to the Socialist Party. He died in 1936 and asked in his will to be given a "worker's funeral" rather than a religious ceremony. The funeral, organized by the Peoples Unemployed League, a Socialist Party affiliate, was a simple affair. Family and friends assembled at his home, hosted a red flag, sang such revolutionary songs as the "Internationale," "The Scarlet Banner," and "Solidarity Forever," and listened to brief testimonials honoring the deceased cobbler. Dorothy Dare, a Communist Party member and, interestingly, secretary of Chatty's section of the Peoples Unemployed League, conducted the service.[39]

Having taken care of the Lovestonites, the Executive Committee turned to plans for a membership drive, discussed the possibility of securing a loan of a hundred dollars to move Party headquarters from Baltimore Street to Eutaw Street, and criticized the Industrial Committee for not holding regular meetings. Irving Keith described the plans of the Agitprop Committee to organize an elaborate workers school, which would include a series of public speeches. Flaiani requested that Sophie Melvin, a southern textile organizer, be sought as a speaker for an International Labor Defense "solidarity banquet" to be held in honor of the Gastonia strikers.[40]

Melvin came to Baltimore on 27 September and gave a stirring speech on southern labor conditions at the banquet held at Lithuanian Hall on Hollis Street. The eighteen-year-old Melvin raised $111.67 and captured the heart of the *Sun* reporter covering the affair. He affectionately described the recent high school graduate as a diminutive, bobbed-haired radical and concluded his article solemnly, stating that Melvin, one of the arrested Gastonia strikers, would depart the city the next day to face trial for her life.[41]

Lithuanian Hall also provided the venue for speeches by William Z. Foster, the Party chairman, and Juliet Stuart Poynitz, head of women's work for the CPUSA. Both occasions went well, but the same can not be said of a gathering of the Jewish branch on 13 October. Midway into a speech by Sol Hurwitz, editor of the *Jewish Daily Forward,* an angry mob broke into the hall and tried to disperse the crowd. The assembled Communists defended themselves with chairs until the police arrived, expelled the anti-Communists, and restored order.[42]

On 9 November, two hundred Party members and sympathizers gathered for a lively evening of songs and speeches in celebration of the twelfth anniversary of the Bolshevik Revolution. Harry Wickes, a member of the CPUSA Central Committee, gave the keynote address, and music was provided by Walter Potzuski and the Freiheit Singing Society. Potzuski, who had been admitted to the Communist Party on 8 May 1929, deserves some additional mention. Although never publicly prominent as a Communist Party member, Potzuski frequently appears in the record in supporting roles, providing musical accompaniment for Party meetings, serving as an informal speaker and Party recruiter, or fulfilling such necessary duties as appearing on the ballot in 1936 as a Communist Party presidential elector. The Reverend Joseph Nowak, a Party sympathizer in the mid-1930s, recalled Potzuski as a kind of village fool known to everyone in the Polish community as a Communist. But Potzuski is more important than that; he represents the "Jimmy Higgens" type of Party member created out of the factional fights of the 1920s, a true believer committed to unstinting service to the Communist cause.[43]

Although Potzuski and the Communists did not realize it at the time, they had more to celebrate than just the success of the Russian Revolution. A little over two weeks earlier, on 24 October, the New York stock market had crashed, wiping out personal fortunes, triggering a worldwide economic collapse, and provoking a reaction that would eventually propel Maryland's Communists to their greatest level of popularity and influence.[44]

3

The Third Period

Nationwide, the impact of the Great Depression was little short of catastrophic. During the depression's early years, personal incomes declined by nearly 50 percent, the New York stock exchange lost four-fifths of its total value, and unemployment climbed into the millions, claiming a third of the work force by 1932. At first the citizens of Maryland avoided the worst effects of the collapsing American economy because businesses there had already contracted during a recession in 1928. In the end, however, Maryland's early economic downturn provided little cushioning. Two large banks, the Frederick Central Trust Company and the Baltimore Trust, crashed in the first year of the depression. By 1932, the full effects of the depression idled six out of every ten Maryland factories. The resulting rise in unemployment forced the Family Welfare Association, Baltimore's largest charity, to close its doors to new families seeking relief.[1]

Baltimore businesspeople tried to remain positive, pointing out that conditions in the city were "appreciably better" than in other East Coast ports. The president of Baltimore's power company, echoing President Herbert Hoover, even claimed that the causes of the depression had completely disappeared, leaving only "fear and lack of confidence" to overcome. William Lawrence, who took over responsibility for the Baltimore Party after Flaiani and Keith returned to Philadelphia, gleefully took the opposite position and portrayed the economy in the bleakest possible terms. In late February 1930, Lawrence announced that the Party would hold an unemployment demonstration in Memorial Plaza, a public square near Baltimore's city hall, to protest the widespread hunger brought on by the depression.[2]

Three days after Lawrence's announcement, Jacob Levinson, the head of the Trade Union Unity League (TUUL), and three young Party members held a warm-up rally at the Lexington Market, one of the huge covered meat and produce markets that served Baltimore's population. At the rally, Levinson announced that the demonstration to be held on 6 March would be only one of a series of mass protests held simultaneously across the country to demand relief from the rapidly worsening depression. Preliminary marches had already taken place in many cities, and the newspapers told ominous stories of increasing levels of violence at Communist rallies in the United States and printed lurid accounts of raids on secret arsenals held by European "Reds." At the end of the short demonstration, Levinson announced that the Party intended to defy city authorities and march without a parade permit.[3]

Communists normally refused to apply for parade permits during the Third Period, partially as a matter of principle but mainly to provoke confrontations with the authorities. The protests gave the Party considerable publicity and usually resulted in figurative "black eyes" for local police departments and real ones for the demonstrators. The *Baltimore Sun,* aware of the Party's tactics, ran an editorial criticizing the actions of the New York police commissioner for allowing his officers to break up Communist Party demonstrations. According to the *Sun,* such tactics turned policemen into nothing more than "press agents of the revolution."[4]

Charles D. Gaither, Baltimore's police commissioner, did not want to promote the revolution, but the situation was complicated. Gaither checked the city code and had no choice but to insist that the Communists obtain a permit. The Communists, however, remained firm in their intention to march without one. Gaither even called Lawrence and Levinson to his office to talk things over, but neither party budged from their positions.[5]

On the morning of 6 March, Communist Party members assembled at Party headquarters on Eutaw Street. At the same time, nine hundred policemen took up positions along the route of march, a meandering path that would take the demonstrators through as many residential and well-traveled commercial districts as possible on the way to city hall. At Party headquarters, Levinson encouraged everyone to remain passive in the face of police aggression and to be particularly careful when the parade passed through the Lexington Market. At 11:33 A.M., Levinson led three hundred Communists into the street and arranged them in marching order. Before he could proceed, however, he found himself confronting the imposing figure of Sergeant Hitzelberger. Levinson braced for trouble, but all Hitzelberger did was hand him an official signed parade permit.[6]

While the marchers were lining up outside of Party headquarters, a black man calling himself George Alexander Turnipseed had appeared at city hall, identified himself as a Communist, and requested a parade permit. Police swiftly issued one and then escorted Turnipseed and his vital document to Eutaw Street in time to present it to Levinson and the police inspector at the scene. Communist officials later denied that anyone named Turnipseed belonged to the Party, and reporters discovered that no house existed at the address given on the license. George Alexander Turnipseed did not exist either. He was an invention of Police Commissioner Gaither, who pulled off a public relations coup by avoiding violence in Baltimore, saving face for the police department, and making the Communists look foolish.

The last-minute permit drained the tension out of the day and even an inflammatory speech at Memorial Plaza by Charles Alexander, a black Communist brought from New York for the occasion, failed to restore it. Alexander tried his best to enrage the surrounding police. Gesturing at the line of officers, he boasted that he and his comrades would soon march over their dead bodies. When nearby church bells rang, drowning out his harangue, Alexander claimed they were part of a government conspiracy and then declared that all religion would be banned when the Communists came to power. Gerald W. Johnson, a writer for the *New Republic,* congratulated Baltimore for dealing so gently and effectively with the potential crises. Johnson commented that it seemed that "in dealing with Red Menaces a policeman with a sense of humor is more valuable then one with a tear [gas] bomb."[7]

Nationwide, nearly a million people participated in the 6 March demonstrations. All of them faced lines of police, but only Baltimore kept the peace. Riots broke out in New York City, Boston, Detroit, Chicago, and Los Angeles, as well as Berlin, Paris, and Stockholm. In Washington, D.C., William Lawrence led over 150 pickets back and forth in front of the White House. Climbing on to the iron fence along Pennsylvania Avenue, Lawrence began a speech by calling out "Comrades." A spectator shouted back "Comrades Hell!" and dragged Lawrence from the fence, igniting a free-for-all that police dispersed with tear gas and black jacks.[8]

Lawrence returned from his beating in Washington to read headlines in Baltimore describing the Party's humiliation in the wake of the Turnipseed affair. He must have received some comfort however, from Levinson's announcement that the TUUL had enrolled over three hundred new members in the two days following the parade. District headquarters also evaluated the parade positively. E. Gardos, a Philadelphia organizer, thought the Party had gained "tremendous" prestige from the march, which could be turned into momentum to organize the unemployed, boost the TUUL, and make new headway on the Baltimore waterfront.[9]

Lawrence scheduled the Party's next public outing for May Day and announced plans for another march, ending at War Memorial Square. Harry C. Jones, chairman of the Baltimore War Memorial Commission, refused to grant the Party permission to use the square, maintaining that Communists celebrating at the memorial would be nothing short of "desecration." Lawrence denounced the memorial commissioners as capitalist lackeys, pointedly refused to apply for a permit, declined to supply the police with a map of the parade route, and remained in Baltimore to personally supervise the celebration. Despite Lawrence's efforts, May Day turned out much like the 6 March demonstration. Several days before the event, the Police Department produced another black Communist, this time one Joseph Jones whose address was an abandoned building, who obligingly applied for and promptly received a parade permit. Lawrence gave in, publicly announced the route of march, and changed the location of the rally from War Memorial Square to the area in front of the fire department.[10]

Four hundred and fifty policemen turned out to shepherd seventy-two Communist marchers as they wound slowly through the city, suffering grievously from the unseasonable heat. The columnist Jon O'Ren, who was becoming an enthusiastic amateur Red-watcher, captured the event:

> Along about 12:20 or 12:30 or so I heard faint sounds of voices as if singing. . . . I looked out my window that faces Baltimore Street. And there indeed were the marchers. I can't resist processions even if there is not a band. So as soon as I saw the head of the line appear I dashed out to the elevator and dropped four floors to the street. Very strangely, it seemed to me, there was nothing to see but the customary street sights. "Where is the parade?" I asked someone. "Oh its over and gone." Said the same one. So that is what May Day is in Baltimore, Red marchers that pass while you're coming down to see them.

The Party did not attempt another large-scale demonstration after this rather dismal showing but contented itself with organizing a series of small street-corner rallies and literature distribution campaigns.[11]

In late June, the Party suffered another of its periodic financial crunches. When the unpaid bills began mounting, the phone company discontinued service, and the electric company threatened similar action. Party leaders noted ruefully that although the unemployed had proved a fruitful source of new members, they were not the dues-paying kind. Another Communist told reporters that he hoped the reports of Russian monarchists, who claimed that the Comintern was sending a million gold rubles to the United States for use in Baltimore, Philadelphia, and Chicago, were true because they could certainly use the money. The next day, reporters returned to Party headquarters to find phone service restored and the lights still working. When asked about the timely debt relief, William Lawrence joked—or maybe not— that the bill had indeed been paid out of Soviet funds.[12]

In July, Edward Bender, a Philadelphia-based organizer who gradually took over many of Lawrence's responsibilities in Baltimore, presided over the Maryland Communist Party's first nominating convention for state elections. The day-long event featured thirty-four delegates from around the state, including Cumberland and Hagerstown. The meeting took place at Party headquarters in a room festively decorated with Russian and French Communist Party posters. After the convention, reporters were allowed to interview the newly nominated candidates. The candidate for governor, Samuel Parker, an African American longshoreman, currently unemployed, stated that he had been involved in politics for many years but had become discouraged with the mainstream parties after the 1928 defeat of Al Smith and had joined the Communists. If elected, Parker promised to work to eliminate unemployment or, if unemployment proved intractable, "at least see that all are fed."[13]

Lena Lipman, a young garment industry worker, was nominated for the position of comptroller, Maryland's somewhat archaic term for state treasurer. When questioned about her competence, Lipman fixed reporters with a reproachful stare and replied, "If the workers in Russia can handle state finance, so can a Baltimore needle trades worker." Isadore Samuelson, an artist and frame shop owner, accepted the nomination for attorney general. George Kelly, a twenty-year-old Party member, received the nomination for clerk of court. Neither men had any legal training but, like Lipman, felt that lack of previous experience was no barrier to holding public office.[14]

The Communist Party adopted a campaign platform advocating a seven-hour day and a five-day week at current pay levels, unemployment insurance, and full social and political equality for blacks. However, Party leaders took pains to emphasize that these were only short-term goals. The Party's major electoral task was to "make it clear to the working masses that only the overthrow of this system and the establishment of a workers and farmers' government can really liberate the toiling masses from capitalist exploitation and oppression." The Communists had no illusions about their chances of winning elective office. One Party leader remarked that Parker might become governor if Albert Ritchie, William Broening, and Elizabeth Gilman, the Republican, Democratic, and Socialist candidates, respectively, all dropped dead on election day. Another Communist standing nearby replied that it would take more of a miracle than that.[15]

The day after announcing its candidates, the Party learned that each nominating petition for statewide office had to be accompanied by a $270 filing fee. This came as an unpleasant surprise to Party leaders, but they recovered quickly. "After all," one quipped to reporters, "what's one thousand and eighty dollars among friends?" Other difficulties promptly followed, however. State law dictated that candidates for governor had to be at least thirty years old. Parker was only twenty-six. Maryland statute also held that candidates for attorney general must have practiced law in Maryland for at least ten years. Samuelson was not even a lawyer.[16]

Bender expressed uncertainty about both the restrictions and the fees since the filing papers he had submitted said nothing about any of them. He told reporters that "if the State refuses to allow us to put our candidates on the ballot we will tell our followers to write in the names on election day." A write-in campaign proved unnecessary, however, because the Party raised the filing fees and the attorney general of Maryland approved the entire slate of Party candidates, despite Parker's and Samuelson's failure to meet state guidelines for their offices. The attorney general's action mirrors Police Commissioner Gaither's tactics and indicates that state officials did not take the Party seriously enough to fight with it.[17]

Bender arranged for Israel Amter, a national Party leader famous for his uncompromising radicalism, to visit Baltimore as the centerpiece of the Communist election campaign there. A parade of ten cars and two trucks assembled on Greene Street and, amid much cheering and singing, drove up to Pennsylvania Station to meet Amter's train. There a crowd of nearly two hundred lifted Amter to their shoulders and carried him to a waiting auto, while ten policemen kept the line moving and maintained order. More police were on hand at the Colored Elks Hall at 1112 East Madison Street, where a capacity crowd heard Amter and several Baltimore Communists extol the virtues of the Party platform and praise the candidates for local office.[18]

A week later, on 4 November, the citizens of Maryland rejected Samuel Parker and overwhelmingly endorsed Albert C. Ritchie for a fourth term as governor. District 3 organizer Gardos noted Ritchie's unsurprising victory in his election report to Party headquarters and then turned to discussing the victory of conservative forces in Pennsylvania and analyzing the performance of the Communist Party candidates. In Baltimore, the Communist vote per candidate, Gardos reported, ranged from 450 to 784. Throughout the rest of Maryland, Party candidates averaged 400 votes apiece. The result represented a gain over the 1928 vote but compared badly with the 3,500 votes given to Elizabeth Gilman, the Socialist Party candidate, whom Gardos described as a "millionaire liberal lady." The outcome of the election, in Gardos's opinion, pointed to the need for more aggressive politicking, firmer foundations for the Party in the workplace, and much stronger local leadership.[19]

Shortly after the elections, the Maryland Party came under investigation by Hamilton Fish, a congressman from New York. In March of 1930, Fish, concerned about the rise in Communist activity since the onset of the depression, formed a special congressional committee charged with investigating radicals in the United States. Fish's efforts earned him the scorn of editors at the *Baltimore Evening Sun,* who declared that he would discover that the Communists amounted to no more than a "chemical trace" in American society and were hopelessly divided by doctrinal disputes.[20]

In November, Fish invited George G. Henry, chief inspector of the Baltimore police, to come to Washington to testify before his committee. Henry refused the invitation, commenting, "I must advise [you] that we have no Communist problem in Baltimore; hence I have no information on the subject that would be of interest." However, another Baltimorean, Ella Virginia Holloway, a well-known woman in the community, disagreed completely. Invited to appear before the committee as a substitute for Henry, she testified that on the basis of extensive clippings from the city press and her own attendance at Communist-sponsored meetings, she had concluded Baltimore had become a "little center" of radical activity.[21]

Although concerned about Party influence in all areas of American life, Holloway thought that the most insidious effect of Communist ideology was on children. Young people, she declared, no longer respected their teachers and were taught in the home such unfortunate ideas as "your bodies are your own to do with as you please." Equally destructive of public morals were the interracial dances the Party sponsored at the black Elks Lodge. "We had [previously] interracial marriages and interracial dinners in Baltimore," Holloway commented, "but not interracial dances for white and colored people, and when you get to such a time as that, you know, it is quite time for Americans to wake up." Holloway's comment on children should not be misinterpreted: to her, teaching that one's body belonged to oneself was not protection against unwanted attention but a license for immoral conduct.[22]

Holloway identified herself as president of the Children of the American Revolution; national chair of the Correct Use of the Flag, a standing committee of the Daughters of the American Revolution; and a member of the Daughters of the Confederacy. She told the Fish Committee that she first became interested in Communist activities in the wake of the Russian Revolution, which convinced her that Communist principles were an intolerable danger to America's values and way of life. Since then, she had made a career out of confronting radicals and, in the 1920s, brought enough pressure to bear on George Goetz, a Baltimore public schoolteacher, that he was forced to resign his position.[23]

Goetz, better known by his pen name of V. F. Calverton, edited the *Modern*

Quarterly, an independent radical magazine that he used to promote his synthesis of feminism and materialism. Calverton also wrote numerous pamphlets and tried to steer an intellectual path between the Communist and Socialist parties. Holloway, indifferent to Calverton's self-declared independence, quoted portions of his pamphlet *Is Monogamy Desirable?* (Calverton felt it was not) to the Fish Committee to prove Calverton's Communist tendencies.[24]

At the time of Holloway's testimony, Calverton spent most of his time in New York but maintained a house in Baltimore that he used for weekend visits. Al Richmond, a Communist organizer who lived in Baltimore, recalled the writer as a particularly colorful figure. "He roared into Baltimore, throttles wide open, with entourage and baggage that typically included: one intellectual attraction, one woman, one box of cigars, two bottles of whiskey, and the manuscript of the book on which he was then working. By the end of the weekend it was said, he had smoked all the cigars, drunk the whiskey, slept with the woman, kept open house for much of the time to display his intellectual attraction (and, not incidentally, himself) and added fifty or sixty pages to his manuscript." Richmond, who often attended the open houses, believed everything except the part about writing fifty or sixty pages, although he changed his opinion when he learned of Calverton's casual attitude toward plagiarism.[25]

A month after the Fish hearings, Calverton appeared in Baltimore as the featured speaker at a lively meeting of the Friends of the Soviet Union, and he did nothing to relieve Holloway's fears. Calverton denounced reports of the persecution of Russian clergy, tens of thousands of whom had in fact been murdered or sent to prison camps, as propaganda spread by American wheat growers who wanted to destroy the market for Soviet grain. He delighted his audience by declaring that democracies were, by their diffuse nature, unsuited to deal with the demands of heavy industrialization and would all eventually be replaced by dictatorships modeled on the Soviet Union.[26]

A week or so before Calverton's speech, Maryland's Communists took what they hoped would be a major step toward fulfilling Calverton's prophecy by establishing a local branch of the Party's unemployed councils. The Detroit Party organized the first Unemployed Council in late 1929. After the 6 March demonstrations, the CPUSA, on Comintern instructions, launched a national movement. Communist ideology held that, in a capitalist system, unemployment was a natural function of employment so the councils were placed under the administration of the Trade Union Unity League.[27]

At first the councils floundered, but, as the depression worsened, local organizers began to make headway, and in some places the councils took on a life of their own, becoming effective organizations for recruitment and promotion of the Party line. In general though, the councils played a small, although highly visible, role in Party affairs, providing warm bodies for demonstrations and acting as adjuncts for the Party's industrial unions. In Maryland, the councils remained indistinguishable from the Communist Party and required constant attention from Party leaders.[28]

Carl Bradley, an industrial organizer originally from Ohio, became the prime mover behind the Baltimore unemployed councils. Bradley held a series of meetings to promote the Party's solution to unemployment that included, among other items, unemployment insurance, reduced work hours with no pay reduction, and opposition to evictions for nonpayment of rent. The last point inspired Leroy Crawford, the unemployed head of an ill-housed black family, to actively improve his dismal circumstances. Crawford sought and found a desirable vacant house, took down the For Rent sign, and moved in with his family. When the owner discovered the Crawfords, he attempted to collect rent, but all he received from the unemployed man was a Party pamphlet outlining the "No Work No Rent" policy.[29]

The Crawford incident aside, the unemployed councils mostly worked to keep people in the houses they already had, not to redistribute surplus properties. Bradley organized flying squads to forcibly resist landlords trying to remove nonpaying tenants. In a typical January 1931 incident along McMechen Street, Bradley and several Communists moved furniture back into the house of an unemployed black man as fast as the landlord's men could move it out. The incident had a characteristic ending as well. The police appeared, arrested Bradley and two other Party members, and then completed the eviction.[30]

In the summer of 1931, Bradley decided to appeal to both the public imagination and the state government by staging a hunger march on Annapolis. Hunger marches on city halls and state capitals were a staple of Third Period activity, and Bradley had already led several small marches in Baltimore. What made this march different was Bradley's intention of actually walking the entire twenty-six miles from Party headquarters in downtown Baltimore to the Annapolis statehouse. Normally, for long marches Party members rode to the destination and then walked the last few blocks. Bradley sent a letter to Governor Ritchie informing him of the march and asking him to meet a delegation that would present demands for increased levels of relief. Ritchie received the letter in good humor and commented, "Let them come on, we'll take care of them." Several legislators, when questioned about the matter, expressed the hope that the approaching Reds would liven up a rather dull legislative session.[31]

The Communists more than fulfilled the legislators' wish. The Communist marchers, seventy-five in all, accompanied by Bradley, Edward Bender, and William Lawrence, got off to a good start, singing revolutionary songs and

shouting slogans to the spectators lining the streets and roads out of Baltimore. By the next day, however, the Communists' spirits and their numbers
had suffered grievously from the miles and a nasty rainstorm. Arriving at the
capitol drenched and in a foul humor, the radicals, with Bender in the vanguard, pushed into the House of Delegates and demanded that their petition
be read immediately. Instead, the Speaker of the House ordered the hall
cleared, and a free-for-all erupted with several legislators, in particular T. William Browne, a former Yale all-American halfback taking an active part. The
disheveled Communists regrouped in the hall, and David C. Winebrenner, an
assistant secretary of state, led four march leaders off to see the governor.
Ritchie received them cordially and listened to their demands, which ran to
three pages and were mainly concerned with diverting large amounts of state
money to unemployment relief.[32]

Out in the hall, the rest of the Communists were confronted by a squad
of Annapolis policemen and fire fighters hastily summoned to defend the
government. One of the wet and irritable marchers made an unfortunate remark about "capitalist representatives," and another fight broke out. Police
arrested nine men, and two were sent to the hospital with severe cuts to the
scalp. Despite the riot and earlier invasion of the legislative chamber, the four
individuals meeting with Governor Ritchie requested and received permission
to read their petition to the assembled House of Delegates. The arrested men
were later all released, and no charges were filed.[33]

Besides organizing local demonstrations, the Maryland Party mobilized
the unemployed councils to participate in a national hunger march on Washington. The march, conceived of as a national version of the 6 March demonstrations, took place in December of 1931. Over sixteen hundred demonstrators assembled in Baltimore under the direct supervision of Herbert Benjamin,
who left his post as District 3 head to become national secretary of the unemployed councils. The marchers rode trucks to Washington, paraded through
the city, lustily sang the "Internationale" outside the White House, and held
a three-day national convention before returning to Baltimore and dispersing
across the country.[34]

Encouraged by the success of the march, the CPUSA began to plan for a
bigger and more broadly based follow-up. One of the ideas considered was a
march by veterans of the World War to demand immediate payment of the
bonus, scheduled to mature in 1945, granted to them as part of their postwar
benefits package. The idea of a "bonus march" proved very popular, and it
quickly spread beyond Party circles. Walter W. Waters, an unemployed veteran, heard Communist speakers in Portland, Oregon, talk about the proposed
march. Waters liked the idea so much that he gathered several friends and set

out for the capital. By the time Waters arrived in Washington, he had over three hundred traveling companions, and everyday dozens more streamed into his makeshift camp on the Anacostia flats. It eventually swelled to over thirty thousand veterans and their families.[35]

The Communist Party sent Emanual Levin, head of the Workers Ex-Servicemen's League (WESL), the Communist veterans organization, and a small group of followers to Washington, where they played a small role in the tragic end of the Bonus March. Communists in Baltimore had little direct contact with the Bonus March, except for guiding some of Waters's "volunteers" through the city. Al Richmond recalled the marchers vividly: "It was toward the middle of May that we first began to notice them, these men wandering the streets in the evening, sometimes in pairs, more often in large groups, but seldom more than a dozen together. They drifted aimlessly up and down Baltimore Street, manifestly strangers in the city." Bradley, Richmond, and Oscar K. Everett, a local waterfront organizer, gathered the scattered groups of veterans together each night and directed them to Salvation Army shelters or nearby police stations, where they could find food and shelter.[36]

Much more important to the Maryland Party than the Bonus March was the unfolding of a controversial murder case on the Eastern Shore, which, for a time, held out the promise of dramatically increasing support for the Party in the region's black population. In September of 1931, Greene K. Davis, a farmer in Taylorsville, hired a black man known locally as Orphan Jones to do odd jobs around his farm. Jones, whose real name was Ewell Lee, received wages of a dollar a day, board, and the privilege of sleeping in the farmhouse kitchen, but the job did not work out. Davis's wife and daughters frequently insulted Lee, calling him "coon" and "nigger" to his face, and Davis cheated him out of a day's pay. After only a few weeks, Lee left the Davis farm and moved to a boardinghouse in Ocean City. Very bitter about his treatment, Lee complained loudly to several people and on 12 October was seen walking in the direction of the Davis farm. Later that day, a small boy saw him returning to Ocean City carrying a brown valise. The next day, visitors to the Davis residence found all four family members shot to death in their beds.[37]

Police quickly apprehended Lee and made much of various articles belonging to the Davis family found in his possession. Once in custody, Lee gave a full confession, which was never introduced in court because of the prosecution's fears that it would be thrown out because it was obtained under duress. The *Baltimore Sun* carried reports of the coerced confession, which prompted Louis Berger, head of the Baltimore branch of the International Labor Defense, to contact the Communist lawyer Bernard Ades and ask him to look into the matter, with a view toward defending Lee.[38]

Initially, Ades worked in association with the court-appointed lawyer, F. Leonard Wailes, but had difficulty convincing him of the necessity of moving the trial off the Eastern Shore and the critical importance of having blacks on the jury. Shortly before Wailes withdrew from the case, he did request that the Snow Hill court move the case to neighboring Dorchester County. Once in complete charge, Ades informed the court that sentiment on the Eastern Shore was so hostile to Lee's case that a fair trial there was an impossibility. Ades presented affidavits stating that threats had been made on Lee's life and asked the court to reconsider its initial change of venue and remove the case to central Maryland.[39]

Lee was not the only person being threatened. Ades also received thinly veiled warnings. One day in early November while conducting business at the courthouse, Ades was visited by a citizens committee that advised him to leave Snow Hill. When Ades and his assistant investigator, the Communist Party member Helen Mays, attempted to leave the building, a mob pressed so tightly around them that police officers had to surround them while the judge walked directly behind to ensure safe passage to their car. The mob, however, had destroyed the auto, and Ades and Mays, who started carrying a handgun after the incident, took refuge in the jail until police could spirit them out of town.[40]

A week after the assault on Ades and Mays, a mob stormed the jail at Chestertown, Maryland, and tried to lynch George Davis, a black man arrested in Delaware and extradited to Maryland on charges of attempting to rape a white, Kent County woman. The leaders of the mob forced their way inside the jail, but Davis had already been removed to an undisclosed location. Despite such dramatic proof that the mood of racial violence on the Eastern Shore prevented a fair trial, the Snow Hill court refused to consider a second change of venue. Ades took his plea to the Maryland Appellate Court, but his appeal was refused, and the case was set to come to trial in early December.[41]

The week before the trial, Ades spoke at an International Labor Defense rally in Salisbury, which was well attended by the black population. Ades and the other speakers protested the refusal of the appellate court to move the case and then launched into general criticisms of the condition of blacks on the Eastern Shore. Matthew Williams, a thirty-five-year-old, reputedly developmentally disabled Salisbury resident attended the demonstration and listened very intently.[42]

The next day, the fifth of December, witnesses saw Williams pacing back and forth in front of his place of employment, a crate factory owned by Daniel J. Elliot. After an hour or so, he entered the building, found Elliot, shot him to death with a pistol, and then turned the weapon on himself. James Elliot, Daniel Elliot's son, heard the shots, ran to the scene, picked up the gun, and shot Williams a second time. Elliot then called the police, and Williams was taken to a nearby hospital, where it was initially reported he died. However, a local radio station learned that he had survived both gunshot wounds and announced Williams's condition over the air. Unknown individuals posted flyers in downtown Salisbury, and a mob quickly formed. The throng descended on the hospital, a committee "distracted" the police guards and doctors, while others threw the injured man out a window to the waiting crowd.[43]

The mob took Williams, who appeared to be unconscious, to the center of town, selected a strong tree at the side of the courthouse, threw a rope over a limb, and hanged Williams as the crowd of over two thousand whites cheered. Willing volunteers pulled Williams high into the air and let him drop at least three times before tiring of the sport and letting the body swing quietly. While Williams was dying, the fire department arrived and watched as mob leaders cut the body down and dragged it a few blocks to a lot near the black section of town, where it was doused with gasoline and set on fire. The police reclaimed the body several hours later and dumped the smoldering remains in the woods.

The next day, police officers discovered the body of an unidentified black man with a smashed skull lying in a ditch, possibly a second victim of the mob that killed Williams. The *Salisbury Times* published a front-page statement deploring the violence and urging a swift return to "absolutely harmonious and normal conditions." The mayor of Salisbury called together leading black citizens, recommended that blacks stay off the streets for a few days, and issued a statement denying that there had ever "been any trouble between the races here." No one was ever arrested in connection with the Williams lynching.[44]

The horrifying events shocked the entire state. Governor Ritchie instructed the attorney general to arrest the mob leaders and ordered postponement of the Lee trial. The appellate court then reconsidered its earlier ruling and granted Ades's request for a second change of venue. The trial was rescheduled and moved to Towson, a small community directly north of Baltimore.[45]

Before beginning proceedings, Ades announced that he would insist that black men be included on the jury hearing the case. On 18 January 1932, the morning the trial began, Ades and David Levinson, the Philadelphia attorney who assisted him and conducted much of the case, discovered that no blacks were included on the jury panel, the group from which the trial jury would be selected. The two attorneys asked three times for qualified blacks to be brought from the spectators gallery and placed on the panel. On each occasion, the bailiff returned with a group of white men and responded that because of the crowd, he "just couldn't get over as far as where the colored gentlemen were seated."[46]

After the seating of an all-white jury, the trial began with the testimony of witnesses to whom Lee had complained about his treatment at the hands of Davis and those who had seen him coming and going in the direction of the Davis farm. Other witnesses testified about the state of the bodies of the Davis family. The Worcester County sheriff had to be reprimanded several times for reminding the jury the "he had the right man."[47]

Ades and Levinson based their defense on the inability of prosecution witnesses to place Lee any closer than a mile to the Davis farm on the day of the killing and on the highly irregular tactics of the Ocean City police. The police not only had failed to take fingerprints at the murder scene but also had refused to pursue any further investigation once Lee had been arrested. In their closing arguments, Levinson and Ades accused the police of framing Lee and suggested that a single individual could not possibly have killed all four members of the Davis family. After thirty-two minutes of deliberation, the jury returned a guilty verdict.[48]

Ades appealed the verdict on the grounds that the lack of blacks on the jury panel was a violation of the Fourteenth Amendment. Had Baltimore County court officials followed common practice and selected the jury panel from lists of eligible voters, Ades's appeal probably would not have succeeded. However, Judge Duncan assembled prospective jurors from among individuals who had previously impressed him while on the witness stand or from people he met socially. When asked if he deliberately excluded blacks, Duncan replied that he never even considered them because jury duty was not something he thought blacks were capable of performing. The court found that Duncan's system amounted to an "unconstitutional exclusion of Negroes" and granted Lee a second trial, but it refused to allow another change of venue.[49]

On 26 September 1932, the second trial opened in Towson. Three African Americans were conspicuously featured on the panel, but all three were excluded from serving on the jury by the prosecution's use of its right of challenge. Despite the setback, Ades and Levinson conducted a strenuous defense, which earned Ades disbarment proceedings for improper conduct in the courtroom. The future Supreme Court justice Thurgood Marshall, then a civil rights lawyer for the NAACP in Maryland, acted as Ades's attorney, and the charges were dismissed after a public reprimand. Ades did not enjoy similar luck with Lee; the jury returned another guilty verdict. Levinson and Ades appealed the case a third time on the grounds that because of the atmosphere of discrimination in Baltimore County, as indicated by the segregation of public toilets among other things, no black man could get a fair trial there. The court of appeals dismissed the plea as being without merit, and Lee was executed in October of 1933.[50]

Despite Lee's conviction and execution, the case had a wide impact. Levinson, in later trials, continued to insist that blacks be present on juries sitting on cases with black defendants. Samuel Lebowitz borrowed elements of the *Lee* case for his defense of the Scottsboro Boys before the Supreme Court. Thurgood Marshall thought that the Lee defense created a feeling of solidarity among blacks in Baltimore and elsewhere that greatly aided him in raising funds to bring other civil rights suits to trial. He also believed that the case inspired blacks to give much more support to the NAACP.[51]

The *Lee* case inspired the Young Republican League to sponsor a series of monthly rallies held at black churches in Baltimore designed specifically to counter recent "Communist agitation," which it feared would lead blacks to defect from the Republican Party. Their efforts were in vain; the GOP, which once had an almost complete lock on the black vote, lost it all by the middle of the decade. But the defectors went to the Democrats, not the Communists.[52]

The editor of the *Afro-American,* Maryland's major black newspaper, publicly thanked the Communist Party for its work on behalf of Ewell Lee. The editor believed the Party had helped expose the practice of Jim Crowism in Maryland's courts, aroused the civic interests of the state's black citizens, inspired the introduction of antilynching measures in the state legislature, and "reassured colored citizens that they have rights which must be respected." All this, the editor stated, had been done by the International Labor Defense— the "dangerous" Communists, the radical Reds. "But these Reds have contended the Euel Lee case against a trial in a mob atmosphere, against third degree police brutality. . . . These Reds, supposed enemies of the Bible and the United States Constitution, have contended for the rights of a humble black citizen to a fair orderly and impartial trial. If that be dangerous, Communistic and radical, it is nevertheless patriotic Americanism to which all thinking citizens can well subscribe." Henry McGuinn, in a 1936 article on the case for the *Journal of Negro History,* spoke warmly of the work of the Party in general and particularly praised the contributions of "the brilliant communist lawyer, Bernard Ades."[53]

Despite the praise of the *Afro-American* editor and McGuinn, the *Lee* case did little for the Communist Party. The press publicity and the Party's continual work raising funds and staging rallies certainly improved the Communist image in the black community, but black Party membership did not increase in either Baltimore or on the Eastern Shore. In fact, the Party's influence on the Shore declined after the trials. In 1930, Samuel Parker, even though he never visited the region, received 130 votes from Eastern Shore counties in his bid to become chief executive of Maryland. But when Bernard Ades ran for governor on the Communist ticket in 1934, he garnered only 65 Shore votes, despite his frequent visits, public speeches, and strenuous work for Lee's defense. Two conclusions can be drawn from Ewell Lee's case. Black interest in communism coincided only with Party involvement in racial issues, and blacks would vote for one of their own they had never met before they would vote for a sympathetic white.

4

The Communist Party and the New Deal

In the early autumn of 1932, the residents of Maryland and the nation turned their attention to the presidential election. Despite his tattered reputation, Herbert Hoover, with the reluctant consent of the Republican Party, choose to run for a second term. In contrast to Hoover, his Democratic challenger, New York's Governor Franklin Delano Roosevelt, exuded energy and self-confidence. Roosevelt flew to Chicago to accept the Democratic nomination in person and pledged to give Americans a "New Deal." Although the expression was only a variation on his cousin Theodore's 1904 promise of a "Square Deal," the slogan resonated with Americans desperate for action. It also helped distinguish FDR's rather pedestrian campaign platform, with its emphasis on sound money and a balanced budget, from Hoover's, which supported more or less the same thing.

The Communist Party ran its own candidates, William Z. Foster for president and James Ford for vice president, in the 1932 elections. Fifty leading intellectuals and writers, including John Dos Passos, Sherwood Anderson, Malcolm Cowley, and Edmund Wilson, endorsed the Communist ticket. But their support did not translate into votes. Foster and Ford received only a little over 100,000 votes nationally and just 1,031 in Maryland. In contrast, Franklin Roosevelt polled over 300,000 votes in Maryland and enjoyed a victory margin of 130,000 in the state. The low tallies did not overly concern Party leaders since they regarded the election as primarily a public relations vehicle and made no secret of their belief that only a violent revolution could free the working class from capitalism. The Communist Party saw no distinction between Hoover and Roosevelt and greeted the Roosevelt's election as a triumph for capitalism and another step toward the destruction of American liberties and enslavement of the working class.[1]

Sometime during the late summer or early fall of 1932, the post of Maryland state organizer passed to Paul Cline, a Lenin School graduate who came to Baltimore from Kansas City. Cline, described in police reports as a "short, dark complected, extremely profane" individual, divided his time between electioneering and preparing the Baltimore Party for its role in the Second National Hunger March. National Unemployed Council leaders revealed plans for the second march in the fall of 1932. This demonstration would be much larger than the 1931 march and would capitalize on both the public outrage over the crushing of the "Bonus Army" and the gloomy mood of the country during Hoover's lame-duck presidency. The final plans called for three thousand demonstrators, organized into eight columns, to advance across the country and converge in Washington on 4 December.[2]

The 1932 march posed special problems for the Party in Maryland because all the marchers, with the exception of the tiny southern column, which was not expected to number more than a hundred demonstrators, were due to pass through the state. To complicate matters, the members of the combined western columns, over fifteen hundred people, would stop not in Baltimore but in Cumberland, a mining and industrial center in the western panhandle of the state, where the Maryland Communist Party was virtually nonexistent.[3]

Cline decided that mobilizing four hundred local marchers and providing for the two thousand others expected to stop in Baltimore was as big a task as the Party could manage so he handed the Cumberland problem to District 3 headquarters in Philadelphia. The reduced responsibilities still overstretched the Party's resources. Cline requested that Baltimore be exempt from the 33.3 percent tax levied on all money raised locally for the national demonstration, because of the "much more difficult task here than obtains elsewhere." By depression standards, the exemption saved the Party there a considerable amount of money, because the final cost of arranging for food, lodging, transportation, and sundry other matters totaled over six hundred dollars.[4]

The march itself went well in Baltimore. The advance guard arrived at Golden Ring, a small community (now a shopping mall) northeast of Baltimore, where police stopped them to wait for the remainder of the column. Once the entire group had assembled, the police led them to the corner of Lakewood and Fayette streets. There the demonstrators dismounted and marched eight abreast in a line four blocks long to the Fifth Regiment Armory, where dinner and a lively evening awaited. The efforts of the Baltimore Party did not go unappreciated. Carl Winter, leader of the eastern column, remembered the Baltimore stop as the most comfortable of the entire journey.[5]

The comfort enjoyed by the eastern column in Baltimore was not shared by the members of the western column in Cumberland. In the mountains, organization had been handled by the Philadelphia Communist and International Labor Defense organizer Jennie Cooper. Cooper traveled to Cumberland, formed a delegation, ostensibly representing the local Unemployed Council, and called on Mayor George Henderson to demand public assistance for the protesters. In 1931, the city of Cumberland had allowed members of the first, much smaller Hunger March to spend the night at a converted factory, which housed the municipal skating rink. In 1932, however, the mayor refused to allow the marchers to stop in Cumberland and mobilized the police and local militias to prevent any resistance.[6]

The evening of 3 December, the combined western columns, traveling in a caravan seven miles long, reached the outskirts of Cumberland. A barricade of hay bales stopped the lead car. Michael Morrisy, a Communist from Chicago who was in charge of the entire column, got out to see what was wrong. Behind the barricade, Morrisy found uniformed police and a dozen men armed with rifles. The column, broken up into units of three or four vehicles, inched through Cumberland under the watchful eyes of more armed citizens. It reassembled itself on the farm of T. Grant Mooreland, where Cooper's volunteers served a watery stew to the exhausted demonstrators. Police and militia encircled the camp and kept watch throughout the night.[7]

The next morning, stiff and sore from the damp, the march leaders awoke and began to consider their next move. Three of them, suffering from various ills, rested in Cumberland's Memorial Hospital, and the mayor of Hagerstown, Maryland, a town lying astride the main highway, announced that the marchers would be forbidden to stop there. National Unemployed Council chairman William Reynolds, who had driven to Cumberland from Washington the night before, decided to avoid the state of Maryland altogether. Instead, the column would head south through West Virginia and east across northern Virginia. Reynolds appointed a contingent of Communists under Jennie Cooper to stay behind, look after the injured marchers, and prepare for the return trip.[8]

The same morning, Carl Winter assembled the members of the eastern column and prepared to descend on the national capital. Winter's reception in Washington, however, had much more in common with the situation faced by Morrisy in Cumberland than the relaxed, hospitable treatment given the demonstrators in Baltimore. At the intersection of New York Avenue and Florida Avenue, Winter found his passage blocked by a squad of fifty policemen, who informed him that the demonstrators would be allowed to go no further. Instead, they were to be interned in a narrow cul de sac bounded by low hills and railroad tracks for the duration of their stay in the capital. When the western column reached Washington, it, too, was greeted by police and escorted to the impromptu camp on New York Avenue.[9]

There, the marchers languished while Communist Party officials, International Labor Defense lawyers, and members of a variety of left-wing groups debated with Washington authorities to resolve the issue. Eventually, District of Columbia officials gave in and allowed the marchers to parade through Washington on Tuesday, the fifth of December. Two small delegations even visited the Capitol, one meeting with Vice President Charles Curtis and the other with Speaker of the House John Nance Garner, soon to be the vice president. As soon as the demonstrators returned to New York Avenue, they began preparing to depart. Carl Winter's eastern column left just after dark and reached Baltimore at 9:00 P.M., where the marchers were served a hearty meal, made up of mostly donated goods, and then bedded down at the 104th Medical Regiment Armory, Finn Hall, and Tom Mooney Hall.[10]

The western column did not get under way until midmorning on Wednesday, when it left the capital the same way it had arrived, crossing the Key Bridge from Georgetown into Arlington, Virginia. Once in the Shenandoah Valley, the column broke up to avoid a second mass descent on Cumberland. Those who could stayed on Route 50, crossed West Virginia, and spread out into Ohio. For those who could not avoid the mountain city, Cooper and her assistants worked to prepare a warm reception at the Mooreland farm. One group of demonstrators stopped only long enough to eat a quick meal and depart; a second group, traveling in trucks and autos in bad repair, remained overnight. Both groups together constituted only half the number of individuals who had arrived from the West four days earlier.[11]

The excitement of the cross-country trip and the confrontation with the police inspired the Communists who had participated, and local Party demonstrations took place all over the country in the early months of 1933. In Baltimore, the Party had another confrontation with long-suffering Police Commissioner Gaither. Since the late 1920s, as Ella Virginia Holloway had pointed out to the Fish committee, the Party had occasionally sponsored "interracial" dances. The social events were particularly popular with members of the Young Communist League and generally took place at the black Elks Lodge. In the wake of the Hunger March, however, the dance organizers decided to move the soiree to the waterfront neighborhood of Fells Point.[12]

International Workers Relief, a long-standing Party organization, hired a hall at 435 South Broadway and hosted a dance for three hundred people. Youths from the predominantly Polish and Ukrainian neighborhood learned of the interracial nature of the gathering, and about one hundred of them assembled outside the hall. At midnight, when the dance ended, the revelers poured out onto Broadway, and two hostile crowds formed. In the resulting riot, Roosevelt Coleman, a twenty-two-year-old black man, stabbed nineteen-year-old Edward Kleczkowski, who was taken to Johns Hopkins Hospital in critical condition. Police reinforcements broke up the mob, arrested several seamen, who had attended the dance and enthusiastically participated in the riot, and prevented about fifty neighborhood youths from attempting to kidnap and lynch Coleman. Police Commissioner Gaither took the incident very seriously and was horrified to learn that the Communists planned to hold another mixed-race function at the same location the following week.[13]

To forestall another riot, Gaither had the health department declare the Broadway Hall unsafe for large crowds. The Party responded by rescheduling the dance and changing the location to the Tom Mooney Hall on Lloyd Street. When dance guests begin arriving at around 6:30 P.M. on 21 January, they found the entrance to the hall blocked by a squad of twenty policemen, who informed them that it, too, had been declared unsafe for large crowds. Louis Berger, a Communist Party lawyer and head of the Baltimore chapter of the International Labor Defense (ILD), declared that he would fight Gaither's actions, which were nothing less than an attempt to deprive Baltimore citizens of the rights of free speech and assembly.[14]

Bernard Ades, famous for his role in Ewell Lee's case, filed an injunction on behalf of Sarah Berger, Louis Berger's wife. Sarah Berger had signed the lease on Mooney Hall, the Party's name for the general purpose facility, on behalf of the Women's Cultural League. The injunction, swiftly granted, prohibited police officers from interfering with meetings at Mooney Hall until they showed just cause for condemning the structure. Under cover of the injunction, the ILD held a small rally in the hall naming Police Commissioner Gaither, the Chamber of Commerce, and the realty company that owned the hall as participants in a "capitalist conspiracy" intended to destroy the ILD and the Women's Cultural League.[15]

The *Baltimore Evening Sun* commented that it could see "no justification" for preventing the Communists from meeting and talking because "that is how they have their fun." The editorial continued by criticizing the police for interfering with the dances, saying that police officers "have shown a disposition lately not to protect the Communists in their constitutional rights." On 28 January 1933, the Women's Cultural League hosted a mixed-race dance at Mooney Hall. No rioting resulted, Gaither relaxed, and the health department dropped its attempt to condemn the building. The Party declared that the easing of official opposition to the dances had nothing to do with the restoration of civil order and that the police had retreated because "there was too much dynamite in . . . Mooney hall not to let the dance go on."[16]

Paul Cline did not take a public role in the dance controversy. Instead, he spent the first six months of 1933 dealing with internal problems in the Party and, after FDR's famous first hundred days, trying to craft a Communist response to the New Deal. The internal problems stemmed from a series of long-standing issues, but they seem to have been triggered by Cline's appointment of Clara Speer as head of the Washington, D.C., branch of the Party. Speer, a twenty-five-year-old Russian-born Jew who immigrated to the United States as a child, accompanied Cline from Kansas City to Maryland and may have been his lover. Once installed in Washington, she became embroiled in a fight with the members of the Washington Party's Jewish section, whom she treated arrogantly and, on at least one occasion, called horse manure.[17]

Speer targeted J. A. Rinis, a former member of the Soviet Party and 1927 Lenin School graduate, for particular harassment. At one point, she even asked Israel Amter if Rinis's lack of activity was the result of his engagement in "special work." Rinis responded to the slight by sending a three-page letter to the Central Committee detailing his work for the Party. Among his list of responsibilities were financial secretary of Unit 2, former financial secretary of the Washington Central Committee (until demoted by Speer), Party representative to the Friends of the Soviet Union, and member of the *Daily Worker* subscription and fund-raising committee. Rinis also worked for International Labor Defense, attended AFL fraction meetings, and pointed out that "on top of that I still have to drive nails (I am a carpenter) in order to live." The letter concluded by accusing Speer of squandering Party funds and spending most of her time sequestered in a Party-financed apartment recovering from an unspecified illness.[18]

Cline backed Speer, writing that she had done good work in the Washington section and, despite her battle with illness, had managed to establish a new unit of government employees. He characterized the Jewish elements in the Party as "petty-bourgeois" and prone to opportunist-sectarian tendencies, which he implied were dangerously close to Lovestonite beliefs. Not only had the Washington section not held a public demonstration for over three years, but, Cline noted, when one was staged in March 1933, none of the twenty Jewish branch members attended. During discussions after the demonstration, District 3 leaders from Philadelphia praised the effort as a step toward broadening and deepening the struggle against unemployment. Rinis and his supporters disagreed strongly and, pointing to the arrest of thirty-eight demonstrators, accused the Party of leading the workers into a bloodbath.[19]

Although Speer's personality certainly exacerbated the situation in Washington, the substance of the problem was a generational conflict between Party members recruited in the 1920s from the original radical and ethnic groups and Party members who had joined since the Lovestonite expulsion.

The problem was widespread and even interfered with Party work among blacks, where the militant atheism of the old guard clashed with African Americans' deeply held religious beliefs. Older Party members frequently asserted that a religious, church-going worker could not join the Party. They ridiculed the religious sentiments of black sympathizers and tried to convince them to abandon their faith.

Cline condemned this attitude as un-Leninist and sectarian and urged the old guard to carry the struggle into the churches. He even took care to make certain that no Party members interfered with "Comrade Jones," a black Communist who was also a lay minister and occasionally preached in Baltimore area churches. Cline did not believe that Rinis and the old guard could be rehabilitated and several times stated that they would have to be expelled. However, no purge occurred and the controversy died temporally when Speer left to seek medical treatment in Chicago. She was replaced as Washington section organizer by Sophie Minkin.[20]

Similar trouble erupted in Baltimore between Cline and H. K. Shore, the Baltimore representative of the *Jewish Daily Forward*. The Jewish buro of the national Party's Central Committee sent Shore to Baltimore to build up circulation for the *Freiheit* so that the Party could expand into Baltimore's Yiddish-speaking population. Shortly after his arrival, Shore wrote to the Jewish buro protesting his treatment at the hands of Paul Cline and Carl Bradley. According to Shore, Cline, Bradley, and several other comrades constantly demanded that he neglect his work with the paper and concentrate on organizing and raising funds for work among steel and maritime workers. Cline responded that he did not want Shore to neglect his work but wanted him to develop it in concert with the Party's official policy of concentrating its work in basic industries. Cline accused Shore of sharing the petit-bourgeois outlook of Washington's Jewish branch and collaborating with its members in their opposition to the Party leadership.[21]

By May, however, Shore and Cline had seemingly resolved their differences. Cline wrote a letter to New York praising Shore and the members of the "left wing" for leading a successful bakers' strike. The strike had inspired the bakers and opened up possibilities for organizing in the Jewish-dominated needle trades. Besides giving Shore credit for the successful strike, Cline added his voice to Shore's plea that the Party send Ben Gold, a Jewish Communist prominent in organizing the fur and leather workers, to Baltimore to speak at a mass rally organized by the bakers.[22]

While Cline defended Speer and fought with Shore, the attention of the country at large was captured by the events of Roosevelt's first hundred days in office. Roosevelt's whirlwind of reform legislation during the spring of 1933 momentarily disconcerted Party leaders, and even the hard-line ideologue Israel Amter grudgingly admitted that at least a "temporary" improvement had taken place. Earl Browder, the future head of the Party, conceded the improvement but condemned the centerpiece of the New Deal, the National Industrial Recovery Act (NIRA), as the "militarization of labor" and the first step on the American road to fascism.[23]

Cline felt that simple criticism of the New Deal was not enough and sought to craft a Communist alternative. He called his scheme "Labor's Public Works Plan for Baltimore" and presented it as a radical alternative to a proposal advanced by Baltimore's Mayor Harold Jackson. Jackson's plan called for the use of federal funds to put unemployed individuals to work on urban renewal projects and to build a regional airport. Cline denounced Jackson's proposal as an exercise in graft and corruption. For proof, he pointed out that condemned property along Gay Street, part of a proposed street extension, had an assessed value of only $17,895 but was being purchased by the city for $54,250.[24]

Cline conceded that some men would be put back to work by the mayor's plan but argued that the tasks they would be employed on—street extensions, viaducts, and the airport project—would provide them no long-term benefits. In contrast, Cline boasted, his plan would take half of the $16 million budget and devote it to slum clearance and the construction of workers' apartment buildings that would be fully equipped with "electric lights, bathtubs and furnaces" and would rent for no more than $8 or $10 a month. The remaining money would be for additional school buildings, public baths, swimming pools, and playgrounds, half of which would be located in black neighborhoods. Precise allocation of the funds would be decided by referendums held in each of the city's councilmanic districts.[25]

Cline proudly reported to Party headquarters that he had mobilized the entire Baltimore organization behind the plan and intended to do the same in Washington. Cline suggested that the plan could be adopted on a nationwide scale and that it might provide the basis for a genuine united front with the AFL. Unfortunately for Cline, he had developed the plan without consulting the central Party apparatus, and reception of the pamphlet was decidedly cool. In July, Cline wrote a letter to the Organization Department complaining about the superficial coverage given his plan in the *Daily Worker* and asked why he had never received any official comments about its substance. Shortly afterward, he left Baltimore under a bit of a cloud.[26]

Ed Williams, a somewhat shadowy figure, replaced Cline. His first mention in the Party records is in a blistering letter from H. Baxter, a maritime organizer. In November, Baxter and several members of the Marine Workers Industrial Union (MWIU) organized a ministrike by the crew of a Munson Line ship. The crew struck for twenty-four hours, won recognition of the ship's committee, and received a promise of reforms in line with NIRA guidelines. All of this pleased Baxter, but he was livid about the role Williams played:

> This goddam section laid down on us, he made statements to Duncan and Mac that he could do nothing, however, when I went up the last time he got his ass on the job and after the strike was over he scared up the big sum of three bucks to feed the pickets. . . . If this kind of stuff is going to continue we may as well close up. I will tell you now that threats were made against this bird William's life before he agreed to do anything and either this bird leaves or he will be put on the spot. . . . All possible funds including *Voice* money was spent to feed the pickets and after the strike when this Williams was cornered he functioned a little in order to keep on living.[27]

Many other Party members echoed Baxter's complaints about Williams, although in less blunt terms. Jack Roth, a national organizer for the Furniture Workers Industrial Union, found the situation in Baltimore completely "chaotic," which he blamed on a lack of organization. Although in Baltimore for less than a month, Roth was the only person local Party members could find to nominate as TUUL organizer to replace Louis Berger, who was serving a six-month jail sentence in Annapolis. Once in charge of labor work, Roth discovered that no connections existed between the various trade union organizations and that no attempt had been made to establish strong active Communist Party fractions within either the revolutionary unions or those belonging to the AFL.[28]

Williams's failure to fulfill his duties stemmed partly from his careful, plodding personality, but the most important reason was the amount of time he spent working for Alexander Goldberger, better known by his Party name, J. Peters. Peters, a participant in the short-lived Hungarian Soviet, arrived in the United States in 1924 to assume responsibilities as the director of the Party's Hungarian Bureau. In 1930 and 1931, he worked as the organizational secretary for the New York district, leaving in 1932 to attend the Lenin School in Moscow. After his return to the United States, Peters took control of the Party's secret apparatus, which he used to channel internal communication, improve security, and set up clandestine avenues to raise funds for secret work. The only major shortcoming of the secret apparatus under Peters's direction was that, in the words of Rudy Baker, "everyone found out that Peters was in charge."[29]

In 1933, Peters began laying the foundations for a covert network in Baltimore but found some of the local Party members reluctant to support his work. Angered at the "impermissible situation which exists in Baltimore," Peters sent a strongly worded letter to A. W. Mills, the Philadelphia official responsible for the oversight of the Baltimore subdistrict. Peters reminded Mills of the importance the Central Committee placed on his endeavors and commented that "this is one of the few places in the country where we succeeded to build up [an] organization and this place is one of the most important place[s] for us because of its location [near Washington, D.C.]." Peters concluded his letter by instructing Mills to remind the "Manager of our business in this city" that in secret-work comrades were not "agitated" but subject to strict instructions and expected to obey without hesitation or discussion. Although Peters named no names, the "manager" could be no one but Paul Cline. The disagreement with Peters may partly explain Cline's departure from Baltimore.[30]

Peters kept a close watch on Williams. When Cline had communicated with the national offices, he directed his letters either to the Central Committee or to William Wiener. Williams's replacement, Joseph Gaal, reported directly to Fred Brown, a member of the Central Committee. During Williams's tenure, however, every major communication dealing with Baltimore went through Peters. The context of Williams's correspondence with Peters indicates that he was helping the Hungarian establish a secret communication network. On 25 April 1934, for example, Williams wrote to Peters advising him not to use 35 South Front Street for any further messages. Regular Party mail went to Communist Party headquarters on Bond Street; the Front Street address was clearly for "special purposes."[31]

David Carpenter, a native Baltimorean known outside the Party by his real name, David Vernon Zimmerman, entered the underground during Williams's tour of duty. Acquaintances described him as "small, lean, and wiry, with long dark hair." Carpenter dressed casually, had an air of Bohemianism about him, and possessed a sardonic sense of humor, characteristics that allowed him to circulate freely among Baltimore's avant-garde and intellectual set. Born in 1906, Carpenter came from a left-wing family, leading FBI agents to describe him as having "grown up in the movement." In 1924, he attended the University of Virginia as a chemistry major but soon had to leave. Despite the brevity of his college career, Carpenter frequently recalled it with pride to acquaintances. After returning to Baltimore, he found employment at the *Baltimore Sun,* where he worked until 1930. He left the newspaper to become a paint chemist and became active as an organizer in the Federation of Architects, Engineers, Chemists, and Technicians (FAECT).[32]

By 1933, Carpenter had become the organizational secretary for the Baltimore section of the Party. Roth mentioned him unflatteringly in the same report in which he blamed Williams for the inactivity and chaos of the Baltimore Party. Roth related that many Party members criticized Carpenter because he did not actively participate in "workers struggles." Such behavior, Roth strongly believed, was incompatible with holding a leading Party position. However, keeping a low profile and not becoming publicly known as a Communist was very compatible with the underground work with which Carpenter increasingly occupied himself by late 1933.[33]

Peters controlled a secret network of underground Communists in Washington. The group, made up primarily of government employees, began as a Marxist discussion circle under Hal Ware and evolved into a clandestine influence group seeking to favorably shape American policy toward the Soviet Union. In 1934, Peters began a campaign to convince his Moscow superiors that the Washington underground apparatus could be used for intelligence gathering. Peters intended to monitor American knowledge of German and Japanese activities, not to operate against the United States. To ensure greater security, he expanded beyond the original Ware group and established a second network, organized around Carpenter and a woman, most likely Jane Foster, who worked in the Party bookstore in Washington, D.C. Carpenter's most famous recruit was Henry Julian Wadleigh, an Oxford-educated employee of the Department of Agriculture.[34]

All open Party work in Baltimore suffered during Williams's stay in the city. Roth described the Party as being in "turmoil"; the section office was rarely open, attendance at unit meetings dropped sharply, and the unemployed councils disappeared. Although most of the problems can be laid at Williams feet, the unemployed councils had collapsed during Cline's administration. The councils had never been self-sustaining but depended on support from the Party section and on the energy of Carl Bradley. When Bradley, following Party orders to concentrate Communist efforts in basic industries, turned to steel organizing, the councils rapidly fell apart.[35]

Bradley's main task as steel organizer was to revive the branch of the Steel and Metal Workers Industrial Union (SMWIU) at the Sparrows Point steel mills. The sprawling complex, located on a peninsula or "point" of land southeast of Baltimore, employed seventeen thousand men but operated at such a low capacity that everyone endured irregular hours, and some men worked as little two days a week. Such severe job insecurity made the mill's employees reluctant to jeopardize what little income they had, and, not surprisingly, the Party had only a very small foothold. At one time, the SMWIU local had operated openly and even issued a shop paper, the *Sparrows Point Worker,* but by the summer of 1933 the paper had ceased publishing, the union had stopped meeting, and the Party unit itself had stagnated.[36]

Bradley attacked the problem as best he could despite the fact that as a known Communist, he was forbidden to enter the sprawling Sparrows Point complex or the nearby company town. Instead of a workplace campaign, Bradley held public meetings and conducted leaflet campaigns in Dundalk and Highlandtown, where many mill workers lived. By September of 1933, Bradley had reorganized the union and enrolled nearly two hundred members. However, they were largely paper members. Bradley confessed that half of them had not paid the minuscule dues and initiation fees, and the remainder could hardly be considered reliable. The genuine level of Bradley's accomplishments can be better measured by the fact that only twenty-three SMWIU members belonged to the Communist Party and only seven to the Young Communist League.[37]

In the autumn of 1933, the factionalism that marred Paul Cline's work in Baltimore exploded again, this time in response to the publication of an "open letter" from the Party's head, Earl Browder. Browder issued the open letter in the wake of an extraordinary national Party conference that met in New York City in July of 1933. The conference convened to deal with several crises, most notably Hitler's rise to power in Europe, the enthusiastic response to Roosevelt's New Deal, and the failure of the CPUSA to transform itself into a revolutionary mass party. Browder's manifesto recommended a number of changes: smaller Party units, concentration of effort on specific targets, and cultivation of disciplined cadres. The changes were designed to "Bolshevize" the Party and make it into a revolutionary army capable of deploying its forces with military precision and efficiency.[38]

The open letter split the Baltimore Party along the usual fault lines and inspired a vigorous factional fight. Military intelligence officers noticed the split and dubbed the two groups the "Regulars" and the "Opposition." The officers reported that the Regulars wanted to continue the Party's earlier methods, such as staging openly Communist demonstrations, distributing radical publications, and building the Red trade unions. The Opposition group supported the more moderate tactics recommended by the open letter. The terminology makes sense from the intelligence officers' point of view since those they called Regulars had been in the Party longer than the Opposition. However, the newer members represented the official line from New York and the larger trends in the international movement. Those in the old guard were really the "oppositionists."[39]

The factional fight ended in December of 1933 when Browder's supporters in Baltimore, among them Carl Bradley and Albert Blumberg, a professor at Johns Hopkins University, held a conference and overwhelmed the old guard. The conference generated an official Party document, entitled a *Two*

Month Plan of Work, designed to implement Browder's open letter. The plan called for an ambitious reorganization of the Party's network of clubs and concentration of the Party's resources on civil rights work, steel, the waterfront, and three designated neighborhoods, two in Baltimore proper and one in Highlandtown. David Howatt, although a Party member since the mid-1920s and, generationally, a member of the old guard, wrote an article for the *Party Organizer* praising the plan, which in his words had "placed the Baltimore Party on its feet." Howatt exaggerated somewhat. Party membership remained well below one hundred, no lasting results came from the plan, and the Baltimore Party coasted through the early months of 1934.[40]

Although the inland Party floundered, Communists on the waterfront enjoyed a series of spectacular, though brief, successes. Communist organizing among sailors and dockworkers in Fells Point, Baltimore's main waterfront district, dated from 1928, when organizers established a chapter of the Marine Workers Progressive League (MWPL) on Thames Street. In 1930, in response to the Third Period's policy of establishing revolutionary unions, the MWPL transformed itself into the Marine Workers Industrial Union (MWIU). Although officially a part of the TUUL, the MWIU was also directly affiliated with the Profintern and enjoyed virtually complete independence of action.[41]

Marine work in Baltimore struggled along fitfully after the founding of the MWIU until the summer of 1932, when Oscar K. Everett, a former upholsterer from Philadelphia and self-described "roughneck organizer," joined forces with Joan Hardy, a diminutive but fiery member of the Young Communist League. Together Hardy and Everett launched a series of demonstrations in support of the MWIU, beginning with a rally on 27 June 1932 at the foot of Broadway and continuing throughout the summer. After Everett's reassignment to the New Orleans waterfront, work continued with slow but measurable success, largely the result of a series of brief strike actions conducted throughout 1933.[42]

The organizers of the ministrikes targeted highly specific complaints, such as more water buckets for washing, which would directly improve shipboard life. Equally important, the strikes were directed as often as possible at either the Orr Steamship Company or the Munson Line. Munson teetered on the brink of bankruptcy, while the Orr Steamship Company ran iron ore from South America to the Sparrows Point mills and adhered to a tight shipping schedule. Since neither company could afford a lengthy tie-up in port, they tried to settle strikes quickly and usually gave in on the small points raised by MWIU organizers.[43]

While the MWIU struck ships and agitated up and down Broadway, the Roosevelt administration sought a way to ease the impact of unemployment through the Federal Emergency Relief Administration (FERA), headed by Harry Hopkins, one of Roosevelt's closest advisers. The FERA dramatically expanded Herbert Hoover's rather cautious unemployment relief program and enlarged the scope of local initiative through grants to both state and municipal agencies. One of the primary targets of FERA relief efforts was the maritime industry, stricken with unemployment levels of 25–30 percent. Lacking any established government agencies on the waterfront, the FERA directed its funding toward private institutions. In Baltimore, the FERA designated the Seaman's YMCA to receive and distribute federal relief funds. On 1 January 1934, money began to reach the nearly a thousand unemployed seamen on the beach in Baltimore. Unfortunately for FERA, the officials of the Seaman's YMCA handled their duties very ineptly. They regularly broke up political meetings at the Anchorage Hotel, which earned them the opposition of the Communists, and distributed their funds parsimoniously, which turned even conservative seamen against them.[44]

Sensing an opportunity, the MWIU organizers sent several delegations of sailors to the FERA offices in Washington to complain about the behavior of the YMCA officials. In mid-January, Communists representing the Waterfront Unemployed Council, which was maintained and controlled by the MWIU, rallied the beached seamen to march on the Anchorage Hotel. The sailors occupied the building, threw out the YMCA staff, and sent a delegation to Washington to request that the FERA recognize the Unemployed Council as the new relief agency. The Unemployed Council representatives backed their request with proposals demonstrating that the council could administer relief much more efficiently and cheaply than the deposed YMCA officials. The FERA administrators, fearing a riot and intrigued by the proposals, agreed with the petitioners and allowed a three-man council elected by the Unemployed Council to determine the distribution of FERA funds.[45]

The Communists were as good as their word. Not only did the FERA save money, but more funds found their way to the unemployed seamen of Baltimore than in any other U.S. city. The Unemployed Council directors improved food quality, opened up a recreation hall, stocked a small sick bay, and paid seamen with barbering skills a stipend to provide haircuts free of charge. In February of 1934, Roy Hudson, the national secretary of the MWIU, visited Baltimore and proposed that the seamen create a centralized shipping bureau, which would assign men to ships on a rotating basis and eliminate the corrupt "crimpers" and company hiring officers. Over seven hundred seamen voted unanimously to establish the bureau, which was housed in the new MWIU headquarters at 702 South Broadway. Within weeks, the bureau was placing nearly 90 percent of the men shipping out of Baltimore.[46]

Ironically, the publication of Howatt's glowing testimonial on the benefits of Browder's open letter coincided with the collapse the MWIU's gains on the Baltimore waterfront. In March, Joseph P. McCurdy, president of the Baltimore Federation of Labor, addressed a meeting of the barbers union at St. Johns Hall at Paca and Saratoga streets:

> Probably the State Relief Administration is unaware of it, but it is true that the handling of all funds for relief for seamen is in the hands of Communists. The situation has grown to such an extent that Baltimore is known among Communists as the chief communistic center for seamen. Word is being sent out by local waterfront Communists to all ports in the country that Communists control this waterfront, as far as relief goes at least. . . . These seamen would not work if they were given a few hours of labor each day. And why not? I know they had a dinner of turkey and cranberry sauce last Sunday. They have everything paid for them. They even have their own barbers to shave them.

Sailors at the Anchorage Hotel vigorously denied Communist control of relief distribution. One individual hotly replied, "Communist Hell! I'm a Republican. . . . Look at me I got a haircut ain't I," while others pointed out that McCurdy had never even been to Fells Point.[47]

Shipowners inundated the FERA with letters claiming that by allowing the MWIU to control unemployment assistance, the agency encouraged "communism, mutiny, voluntary idleness, and violence." In March, in response to union and shipowner pressure, Maryland relief officials met with the Unemployed Council and suggested that it give up control of relief funds in exchange for employment of its members. The officials promised all the beached sailors permanent stand-by jobs tarring bilges, chipping paint, and cleaning out laid-up ships at the wage of three dollars a day, with two days of work a week guaranteed. The Communists in turn insisted on a thirty-hour work week at union wages. The two sides tussled back and forth for over six weeks, but the MWIU was eventually forced to give way and accept the state-sponsored plan.[48]

The Central Shipping Bureau quickly followed the relief project into oblivion. Rather than attack the Communist-run hiring hall directly, shipowners destroyed its effectiveness by importing crews from Philadelphia and New York on the pretext that certain vital job categories were underrepresented in Baltimore. The MWIU may have contributed to the success of its enemies, because many seamen resented the use of the shipping bureau as a distribution center for Communist Party literature. Hard feelings also existed over the practice of dragooning sailors between ships for marches on Washington to promote such causes as the defense of the Scottsboro Boys, which had little to do with maritime issues.[49]

While the MWIU's gains on the waterfront faltered, the national Party organization sent M. Zeibel to Baltimore to try to reverse the damage caused by the factional fight and Williams's neglect of his official duties. Zeibel arrived in the port city in June of 1934 and found a barely functioning section that held no regular meetings and conducted no political work. Zeibel observed that Williams "does not do anything at all . . . he very seldom shows up." Zeibel felt overwhelmed by the job facing him and confessed in his first report to Fred Brown that he did not believe he was physically up to the task:

> As I told you on my visit [to New York] Baltimore needs *one* who is strong politically, organizationally and also physically. I shall not discuss the first two qualifications, but I certainly do not posses at present the third one. At the present moment one is needed here who is a good mass speaker, one who can arouse the enthusiasm of the Party membership and the masses. Do not delay sending an organizer in. While I am still on my feet I will be able to acquaint him with Baltimore. But I assure you that it is not possible for me to continue much longer.

Despite his protests of ill health, Zeibel worked very hard. He tried to develop a campaign for the release of the imprisoned German Communist Ernest Thaelmann and cultivated the Party's election campaign, which he thought was hampered by the lack of a proper platform. A very bad one, in Zeibel's estimation, had been drawn up by Bernard Ades, who was running for governor. Unfortunately, the committee assigned to rewrite the platform included Ed Williams and proceeded sluggishly.[50]

Williams's tour of duty ended in late July of 1934 when he received train tickets and a letter from J. Peters reassigning him to Detroit. Shortly after Williams's departure, Joseph Gaal arrived in Baltimore to take up duties as Party chief. After ensuring that he would continue to receive the customary section organizer subsidy of five dollars a week, he conducted a survey of conditions in Baltimore. Gaal reported that despite its setbacks, the MWIU remained strong on the Baltimore waterfront, where between eighty and a hundred mariners attended union meetings. The marine workers had also created a longshoremen's local; however, its membership was predominantly black and represented only a fraction of the longshoremen working the Baltimore docks, and it suffered from poor leadership. In Norfolk, Virginia, which fell under Gaal's supervision, the Party actually controlled two International Longshoremen's Association (ILA) locals, and the situation looked much more promising. Gaal's major criticism of MWIU work centered on its neglect of political indoctrination in favor of "pure unionism." In an attempt to correct the situation, Gaal planned to hold waterfront classes on the fundamentals of communism.[51]

Other areas of Party work received much less favorable comments. Gaal found steel organizing very weak. Despite a paper membership of over two hundred, only fifteen to twenty workers ever attended union meetings, and most of the Communists at Sparrows Point were Finns or Greeks who had trouble speaking English. Gaal characterized Bradley's leadership efforts as a "one man show" and noted that considerable friction existed between Bradley and the rank and file.[52]

Party activities among the unemployed and the city's black population verged on nonexistent, and the Party seemed unable to establish fractions, even in those AFL locals that harbored open sympathizers. Party sections, Gaal reported, performed only the most basic functions, such as dues collection, and members resisted attempts to engage them in political agitation or literature sales. The election campaign, faltering under Zeibel, had not improved after Gaal's arrival, and the sixty-member Young Communist League was underappreciated and underutilized by the parent organization.[53]

Gaal actively sought to revive the Baltimore section by calling meetings, making speeches, and holding classes on every subject, from Marxism-Leninism to Party building. He assigned several Communists the task of infiltrating the Peoples Unemployed League, a Socialist Party affiliate, and sought to reactivate the Baltimore chapter of the League against War and Fascism. The Comintern had launched the league at a conference in Amsterdam in early 1933. An impressive rally at New York's Madison Square Gardens inaugurated the American branch, called the American League against War and Fascism. Although the league would become an important mass organization for the Party during the Popular Front period, it remained small and inactive in its early years. Gaal planned to send twenty delegates from Baltimore to a league conference in Chicago in the hope that it would inspire them and broaden the Party's base among sympathetic liberals.[54]

Gaal also worked closely with the MWIU as it sought to rally Atlantic Coast seamen in support of their fellow workers on the Pacific Coast. In May of 1934, a strike by San Francisco longshoremen accelerated, first shutting down the entire port and then, for a few heady days in July, stopping the entire city during the first general strike in the United States since the 1919 IWW strike in Seattle. Elements of the MWIU figured prominently in the opening stages of the "Big Strike" in San Francisco and set up their own strike and relief committees. Gaal and the MWIU in Baltimore hoped to stage a sympathy strike by the small group of MWIU longshoremen in Baltimore and the two Party-controlled ILA locals in Norfolk, but neither work stoppage materialized.[55]

Despite the failure to organize sympathy strikes, the events in San Francisco had a profound impact in Baltimore. On 22 August 1934, the Comintern received a confidential report entitled "Lessons of the San Francisco General Strike." The unnamed author of the report praised the militant nature of the strike and the leading role played by the both the Communist Party and the MWIU. However, he noted, the most significant Communist successes did not come from the "revolutionary unions." Since "the middle of 1933," the author reported, "when the majority of the workers showed their desire to belong to the AFL, we [have] actively participated in the organization of the AFL local union among the longshoremen." The writer concluded by recommending the consolidation of Communist gains in the ILA and the establishment of opposition groups in every local of the AFL, to be followed by a federated merger of the ILA, the International Seamen's Union (ISU), and the MWIU.[56]

In November of 1934, the Comintern issued a directive ordering the liquidation of all the Red trade unions, including their umbrella organization, the TUUL. All of the members of the revolutionary unions were instructed to join the appropriate AFL locals and establish opposition groups and Party fractions. The termination of the Party's union movement had a mixed effect in Baltimore. Bradley's work at Sparrows Point suffered greatly from the loss of his main organizing vehicle, the SMWIU, and all of his modest gains evaporated. In contrast, Gaal and Roy Hudson, the former MWIU secretary, cooperated on the waterfront to ensure the presence of a strong Communist fraction in the ISU. Hudson instructed Gaal to retain the MWIU hall in preparation for its conversion into a branch of the International Seamen's clubs, and the Central Committee sent all of its available marine organizers into Baltimore to ensure Communist control of the union merger. In return, Gaal asked for permission to retain the services of Comrade Drummond, the MWIU organizer, as a general section organizer after the merger of the MWIU and the ISU.[57]

Besides overseeing the transition of the Party's labor efforts, Gaal devoted considerable time to improving the Party's work among Baltimore's black population and making overtures to other left-wing groups. One of the barriers Gaal faced in improving minority outreach was the existence of racism, called "white chauvinism" in Party jargon, among members of his subdistrict. White chauvinism in Washington had become so pervasive the previous year that Richard McAlister, a Communist, felt compelled to write to the *Daily Worker*. McAlister sharply criticized the Washington Party's Jewish branch for refusing to admit blacks, including black Party members, to a dance held in support of the International Workers Order (IWO), a fraternal society organized by the Communist Party in 1930. The Jewish Communists defended themselves rather weakly on the grounds that the hall they had hired did not admit blacks. McAlister blamed the slow pace of minority recruiting on such attitudes and accused Jewish branch members of speaking "sneeringly of the negroes," conducting their meetings in Yiddish, and criticizing all opposing views as "naive idealism." The *Daily Worker* forwarded McAlister's letter to Max Bedacht, the general secretary of the IWO, who promised the distressed Communist that action would be taken.[58]

In Baltimore, the worst problems with racism were in the Russian branch of the Party, whose members often refused to work with blacks. Gaal, like McAlister, found it necessary to request outside assistance. The Organization Commission of the Central Committee took Gaal's problems very seriously. It planned to bring the issue before a general meeting of the Party's Russian groups and to send the secretary of the Russian Bureau to Baltimore to deal personally with his recalcitrant compatriots. The commission believed that white chauvinism ran "rampant in the mass organizations in Baltimore" and hoped that by making an example of the Russians, the entire situation could be improved.[59]

During his time in Baltimore, Gaal succeeded in reversing some of the problems that had built up during Cline's and Williams's terms of office. Gaal did particularly well in strengthening the Party's ties with the Socialist Party and mainstream liberal groups, as attested to in a letter Edward S. Lewis, the executive secretary of the Baltimore Urban League, sent to Earl Browder in April of 1935:

> I was certainly disappointed to learn that Mr. Joseph Gaal had been re-moved from this area as Communist Organizer and returned to New York. He has certainly done a magnificent job and was quite successful in mak-ing friends. I have heard some of our Socialist friends say the following: "Gaal is the one Communist that I can work with." Indeed I think if he had been allowed to stay here longer he would have bridged some of the gaps which exist between the two working class Parties. I am glad therefore to add my humble testimony to the effectiveness of Mr. Gaal's work and to express the hope that you may find it possible to send him back to Balti-more in the near future.

Browder did not, however, reassign Gaal to Maryland. Instead, the Party sent Earl Reno, a Michigan organizer.[60]

5

"Let's Make Baltimore a Union Town"

By 1935, it had become clear not only that capitalism was not in danger of imminent collapse but also that Third Period policies had produced ambivalent results at best and a disaster at worst. In the United States, the demonstrations and angry rhetoric increased Communist visibility and generated some membership growth, but reaction to the Party's militancy was often hostile and the new membership highly unstable. The CPUSA's most ambitious Third Period project, the creation the TUUL's revolutionary unions, trained a small cadre of very effective organizers but drained Party resources, divided the national union movement, and in the end proved ineffectual.

In Europe, the Comintern had believed that the growth of fascism would benefit communism by polarizing public opinion and driving huge numbers of people leftward. To ensure that the Communist parties would be seen as the only viable political alternative, the Comintern reserved its most violent rhetoric for the "social-fascists" in the German Socialist Party and even occasionally secretly cooperated with the Nazi Party against them. The tactics backfired horribly, dividing the European Left in the face of an implacable enemy and resulting in Hitler's destruction of the German Communist Party, once the greatest of the international parties.

In response, the Comintern leadership developed a new set of policies, collectively called the Popular Front, which it introduced at the Seventh Comintern Congress in the summer of 1935. The Executive Committee declared that fascism had temporally replaced capitalism as the greatest threat to the world proletariat. The change compelled Communist parties to seek allegiances with their former class enemies and to exchange sectarianism for more subtle, broad-based anti-Fascist and progressive coalitions. Although often characterized as an abrupt shift, a general evolution toward the Popular Front strategy had begun as early as 1933. In the United States, signs of the shift can be seen in Earl Browder's 1933 open letter and the 1934 decision to abandon the dual union movement.[1]

The briefing Earl Reno received in New York before traveling to Baltimore had little to do with the coming changes. Instead, his instructions concerned ways to continue reviving the demoralized Party section. Because factionalism had played an important role in the Baltimore Party's troubles, officials in New York advised Reno to use the name Earl Dixon while in the city. The alias would prevent the local Communists from knowing anything about his background or previous experiences. Reno, who had always used his own name for Party work, was somewhat bothered by the request but obeyed instructions. The precaution may well have been justified, because Reno, who had joined the Party in Michigan after working in the unemployed councils, was a classic example of a depression-era recruit and his open appointment could have created needless difficulties with troubled veteran Party members.

Once settled into Baltimore Party headquarters at 209 South Bond Street, Reno put an end to the problem of factionalism, which he termed "monkey business" in his official report to New York, through pointed meetings with individual Party members. He then conducted a quick survey of the tiny Party and began a round of speaking engagements. Reno's survey of the Party revealed fifty-two dues-paying members and no more than sixty registered Communists. By mid-May, however, dues payments had risen to the equivalent of 150 members, largely because many had paid their back dues, and Party membership had risen to 96. The increase pleased Reno, but he believed it was only a beginning and predicted a membership of 300 by October.[2]

During his first few weeks in Baltimore, Reno concentrated on reorganizing the Section Committee, the body responsible for oversight of the subdistrict. He broke up the committee and assigned its members to one of three committees: Organization (called the Org Committee by Reno), Agitprop, and Trade Unions. The action had the benefit of reducing the threat of factionalism and centralizing authority in Reno's hands since each committee reported directly to him. Reno also recommended that Maryland be made an independent district because District 3 was far too large to be properly supervised from Philadelphia and local work suffered as a result. Reno's suggestion was the second time such a plan had been put forward. In 1934, Party leaders had submitted a proposal for a new district around Maryland and the Virginia cities of Richmond and Norfolk. The only result was further confusion. Philadelphia promptly dropped Baltimore, but a new district was not formed, and the section drifted along without a home for two months. This time the proposal would be implemented, creating District 34, composed of Maryland and the District of Columbia.[3]

With organizational affairs in order, Reno turned to the task of increasing the influence of the Communist fractions Joseph Gaal had created within the AFL locals. Reno ordered them to organize a united front conference in protest of unemployment relief cuts and to prepare for the upcoming Maryland AFL convention by nominating Party members as delegates and convincing union locals to present Party-inspired resolutions at the convention. Initially Reno's plans unfolded smoothly. The AFL, along with several independent unions, needed only a little urging to support the idea of a citywide conference on relief. Even better, the organizing committee of the AFL met on 7 May and invited the Communist and Socialist parties, as well as the Peoples Unemployed League (PUL), which was well seeded with Communists, to openly participate. Party efforts to nominate Communists to the AFL convention also went well, allowing the Party to control 15 out of the 150 delegates.[4]

On 1 June 1935, however, Reno wrote to New York informing them that all of his plans for the AFL convention had collapsed because of the inaction of Comrade Powers, the leader of the Communist fraction within the Amalgamated Association of Iron, Steel, and Tin Workers (AA). Powers had replaced Carl Bradley as the Party's steel organizer after the dissolving of the SMWIU, but he was never happy in the role, did not get along with other Party members, and constantly claimed he had insufficient funds to support himself. Reno tried to smooth over the problems by warning his colleagues against ganging up on Powers and advancing the steel organizer eighteen dollars a month from section funds to supplement his normal stipend of five dollars a week from the steel unit.[5]

For a time, Reno's solution seemed to work. Powers convinced the AA to introduce several Party resolutions at the upcoming AFL convention and was elected to one of the three slots in the AA's convention delegation. Placed in charge of the entire Communist fraction at the convention, Powers received additional good news: the other two steel delegates could not attend so Powers would have three votes to himself, and his trip would be funded by the AA. Everything appeared ready until Powers appeared at Reno's office at 11:00 P.M. on the night before the convention and announced that he could not go. The Communist fraction floundered without leadership and accomplished none of Reno's goals. Reno demanded that Powers explain himself, but the steelworker only repeated his complaints about finances and claimed that the money advanced by the AA was insufficient to attend the convention. Reno threw up his hands and asked the national Party to transfer Powers to another district.[6]

Powers vigorously protested the transfer, citing his efforts in building the AA, which had "resulted in winning over a broad group of leading American workers." Powers also claimed that union officers, recognizing his contributions, had arranged a farewell dinner for him and had asked him to delay his departure from Baltimore by at least a week. Powers devoted half of his four-page protest letter to heaping abuse on Pete Sturgeon, a fellow Communist who, Powers believed, had conspired in his removal. According to Powers, Sturgeon had failed to assist with the merger of the SMWIU and the AA, had not recruited a single worker for either the union or the Communist Party, and, whenever criticized, threatened to tear up his membership book. In addition, Sturgeon, a single man, did not subscribe to the *Daily Worker,* pleading poverty, even though many steelworkers with large families managed to subscribe. The Central Committee turned a deaf ear to Powers's arguments and ordered him to take up new duties in Pittsburgh.[7]

Since the death of the TUUL, the CPUSA had called for unity of labor within the AFL. However, an eight-hundred member independent union, called the United Building Trades Federation, stoutly resisted every attempt to convince it to merge with the larger organization. Baltimore Communists branded the United Federation a scab union and refused to allow it to participate in united front activities. All of these actions followed the official Party line but were complicated by the fact that the United Federation's chief organizer was a secret Communist. Before Reno's arrival, he had been ordered to refuse to recruit new members or to establish more union locals.

Naturally, the organizer's inaction raised a storm of protest, and he was in danger of being removed from his job and expelled from his local. Reno thought that the Baltimore comrades had interpreted the united front line too strictly and did not want to waste such a well-placed Party member. He reported to Jack Stachel, CPUSA's organizational secretary, that he had ordered the organizer to stay in the union and in his job, at all costs. "There is a certain group," Reno wrote, "that will give him . . . support. He is also arranging a meeting of several leaders of locals with whom I will have a talk (they understand who I am), and where I will discuss the question of union policy as it concerns them and will also try to draw them into the Party." Reno added that while he fully supported the unity policy, the issue should be put off in this case until the Party had built a secure fraction within the United Federation. The incident reveals a streak of independence and pragmatism in Reno that contributed to his successes during his stay in Baltimore.[8]

Reno, like many before him, also sought the elusive goal of mass black support for the Party. He frequently spoke at black churches and cultivated black leaders, such as Carl Murphy, the editor of the *Afro-American*. In July of 1935, he established a Baltimore branch of the Ethiopian Defense Committee. Created by black nationalists in New York who saw the Italian invasion of Ethiopia as a racial issue, the Ethiopian Defense Committee had appeared spontaneously earlier that year. Communists in New York helped organize the first committee, gained control of the organization, and sought to expand its focus from racism to antifascism, which they hoped would attract Italian Americans opposed to Mussolini. Reno never tried very hard to bring Italians into the Baltimore branch and made their recruitment even less likely by locating the committee's office in a storefront on Pennsylvania Avenue, in the heart of Baltimore's black neighborhoods.[9]

Reno gave the task of staffing the Ethiopian Defense Committee's new office to Leonard Patterson, a Young Communist League (YCL) organizer who had graduated from the Lenin School and was a well-known figure in national Party circles. Patterson, who arrived in Baltimore in 1934, divided his time between YCL activities on the waterfront and at Johns Hopkins University and "antimilitary" work directed against the Maryland National Guard. Patterson identified suitable members of the YCL, trained them in clandestine propaganda distribution, and turned them over to Stanley Bloomberg and his "secret committee." Bloomberg's committee arranged for the YCL cadres to infiltrate the National Guard, where they distributed propaganda designed to demoralize the guard units. By 1935, Bloomberg and Patterson controlled squads of Communists at Fort Meade near Maryland City, at Fort Holabird in Baltimore, and at the Aberdeen Proving Grounds near the head of the Chesapeake Bay. In 1936, the national Party reviewed the "antimilitary" work, decided it put the distribution squads at great risk for too little return, and discontinued the program.[10]

In July 1935, however, Patterson's combination of open and covert work kept him quite busy, and he asked Reno for assistance with the Ethiopian Defense Committee. Patterson's help arrived a little over a month later in the form of Joseph Nowak, a Presbyterian minister. Reared in the Polish neighborhoods on Baltimore's East Side, Nowak had graduated from Johns Hopkins University in 1932 and then had entered Union Theological Seminary in New York City, graduating in 1935 with a bachelor of divinity degree. While at Union, Nowak became a part of an informal circle of students around Harry Ward, a philosophy professor, who believed that the church needed to reach out to the growing radical movement.[11]

Years later, Nowak summed up his own feelings as well as those of his friends:

We were coming to this conclusion—I can speak for myself, but I know we discussed it among the students—that the great world depression was going to wind up eventually in the struggle of the classes. . . . We believed that this movement which we called communism was going to lead and head up the masses and that the church was not going to be able to hold them back. . . . Therefore it [was] up to those individuals who believed in the Christian ethics of the New Testament to go out on their own and identify themselves with the masses so that if and when these things should happen . . . there would be those Christian individuals who were part of the masses who could then show that they as Christians did not abandon [the] masses, but stayed with them and helped to bring the new order.

After his graduation, Nowak's superiors assigned him to a small mission, St. Paul's Presbyterian Church, in east Baltimore.[12]

Once established at St. Paul's, Nowak began visiting union halls and attending street-corner meetings in an attempt to find places where the seeds of revolution might be germinating. Near the end of August, he met Walter Potzuski, a longtime Communist, who invited the young cleric to a meeting of the Ethiopian Defense Committee and, a week later, introduced him to Earl Reno. Nowak liked Reno from the moment he met him and soon convinced the Reverend John Hutchinson, a fellow Union College alumnus, to come with him to Communist Party headquarters. The two ministers inquired about the work of the Ethiopian Defense Committee, spoke proudly of their association with Harry Ward, and then asked a somewhat bemused Reno what they could do to help. Reno, after a few days' thought, suggested that the two men work with both the Ethiopian Defense Committee and the Baltimore chapter of the American League against War and Fascism.[13]

Hutchinson soon transferred all of his efforts to the American League. Nowak, however, threw himself into the work of the Ethiopian Defense Committee, helping to plan and organize a series of outdoor meetings that ranged from soapbox-style speeches to small street fairs. The larger occasions required a police permit allowing the Ethiopian Defense Committee to rope off a block or so in the chosen neighborhood and set up lighting, a stage, and a public address system. The evening usually began by cruising through the selected neighborhood in a sound truck that gradually circled back to the stage, where several speakers would address the crowd while others would take up a collection and sell Ethiopian Defense Committee and Communist Party literature. At the height of the committee's activity, Nowak conducted two or three meetings a week, with attendance ranging from four hundred to two thousand.[14]

Although able to attract large crowds, the Ethiopian Defense Committee remained a small organization with little appeal outside the black community. The American League against War and Fascism, however, had the potential of appealing to a very broad audience. Reno appointed Sam Swerdloff, a professional artist originally from Madison, Wisconsin, to chair a committee charged with increasing the league's membership and outreach. Swerdloff's assistants included Walter Bohannon and Edith Bohannon, both public schoolteachers; Albert Blumberg, a philosophy professor at Johns Hopkins; the Reverend Hutchinson; and a shifting group of YCL members.[15]

Swerdloff and his colleagues held an organizational conference in Swerdloff's loft apartment and began to promote the anti-Fascist goals of the American League. By October of 1935, the American League enjoyed the endorsement of the Baltimore locals of the Amalgamated Clothing Workers of America and the International Ladies Garment Workers, as well as numerous churches, peace societies, the NAACP, and the Urban League. Several leading members of the Baltimore Socialist Party, including Broedus Mitchell and the Reverend Paul Schilling, also supported the organization. In contrast to the informality of the Ethiopian Defense Committee rallies, the American League specialized in conferences and panel discussions, a format that appealed to its middle-class membership.[16]

After the outbreak of the Spanish civil war, the American League devoted most of its energy to condemning the Franco rebellion, staging demonstrations in support of the Republican government, and clandestinely recruiting volunteers for the International Brigades. In Reno's opinion, the height of American League activity occurred in the summer of 1936, when word reached Baltimore that the German battleship *Emden* planned to make a courtesy call at the port. Such a solid and tangible example of Nazi Germany's military might presented the American League with a tailor-made opportunity to rally public support. In the weeks before the ship's arrival, the American League peppered Governor Harry W. Nice with letters protesting the visit and conducted a vigorous campaign of open-air speeches denouncing Fascist aggression.[17]

A few days before the ship's docking, a group of Young Communist League members dressed up in makeshift German army uniforms, climbed in the back of a truck, and rode through the city shouting Nazi slogans. A crowd of nearly two thousand greeted the battleship at Recreation Pier in Fells Point with jeers and speeches. The meeting began with an invocation by the Reverend Nowak, who thought a prayer was a foolish way to begin an anti-Fascist meeting, and advanced through a series of short speeches by representatives of the sponsoring labor, political, and church groups. Thurgood Marshall, legal counsel for the Baltimore NAACP, delivered the keynote address.[18]

Reno's accomplishments in Maryland would not have been possible without the dedicated assistance of Mary Himoff. The Ukrainian-born Himoff accompanied Reno from Michigan to Maryland to assume the official roles of Party educational director and head of women's work. In actuality, Himoff, who was Reno's lover, functioned as his chief assistant and troubleshooter, responsible for a wide variety of tasks. Among other duties, she compiled ward election statistics to guide future Party campaigns, established a workers school for 111 Party members and sympathizers, oversaw the publication of shop and neighborhood papers, and helped organize the "open forums." The forums, a series of lectures by Communist and progressive speakers, proved very popular and received broad endorsement from Baltimore's liberal groups. Roy Hudson, the maritime organizer, spoke to a crowd of two hundred at the first forum in October of 1935.[19]

Himoff aggressively looked after Reno's personal interests, often making requests on his behalf or arguing for favors. On one occasion, she asked Fred Brown for a pair of tickets to the Thanksgiving Day debate between Earl Browder and Norman Thomas at Madison Square Gardens:

> For the last five years I have worked out of [meaning away from] New York, I haven't seen one of our large Madison Square gardens for that period. Comrade Dixon has never seen a large NY meeting or demonstration. We would both like to be at that debate very much. We will be able to get away for that day and there will be comrades going to NY then so we will be able to manage with the fare. Any kind of tickets will do, as long as we are able to hear the debate. I am sure that some way, 2 tickets will be able to be found for us.

On another occasion, Himoff added a handwritten note to an official report vigorously suggesting that she and Reno be sent to Party school because they would not be "young" elements forever. Reno, she continued, was "just the American proletarian type" while she was a young woman, and they would both work hard and be greatly improved by the experience. She included an underlined plea in her note to say nothing to Reno about her request.[20]

In March of 1936, for reasons never made clear in the relevant correspondence, Robert Ray, the section organizer for Washington, D.C., abruptly left his post. Ray's sudden disappearance deeply disconcerted the Communists in Washington, prompting Pat Toohey, the organizer for all of District 3, to send Himoff to the capital as temporary replacement. Himoff approached her new responsibilities with the same energy she devoted to everything she did. She immediately called a section convention to reassure the Washington Communists and reorganize the District of Columbia's two street units (one for blacks and one for Jews). Himoff also established a neighborhood paper in the black unit, reorganized dues collection, and formalized a system of regular section meetings, all the while still teaching a class at the Workers School in Baltimore. The Washington assignment put a great strain on Himoff, who wrote "I haven't the physical energy to do anymore, since I've been working at full speed for six years with only 2 'vacations' and both times when I was sick in bed with no time after to recuperate."[21]

Besides subjecting Himoff to tremendous strain, her reassignment to Washington created serious problems in Baltimore. Carl Reeve visited the city a few weeks after Himoff's departure and reported that most political and organizational work was in a state of "lethargy and absolute inactivity." Reeve noted that the Workers School, the open forums, and trade union organizing were in particularly bad condition. The most pressing problem, however, was that only two weeks remained for the Party to collect the 1,500 additional signatures needed to get its candidates on the fall election ballot.[22]

Toohey bluntly informed Fred Brown that "Dixon is heavily burdened and in many respects without Mary is slipping." Reno's condition also worried Himoff. She informed Toohey that "Earl is in a nervous state where he will be out physically damn soon." On 3 April, Toohey turned Washington over to a promising local Communist and sent Himoff back to Maryland to ensure completion of the signature drive. Himoff wrote a farewell letter to Washington Party members praising their efforts, stressing the importance of her work in Baltimore, and assuring them that a new section organizer would arrive soon.[23]

Mary Himoff's brief stay in Washington coincided with changes in the tightly sealed Maryland underground. Henry Julian Wadleigh, David Carpenter's agent in the Department of Agriculture, had received a transfer to the State Department. The move made Wadleigh much more valuable as a source and may have prompted J. Peters to merge part of Carpenter's circle of government employees with the larger Ware group. Whatever his motivation, Peters introduced Carpenter to Whittaker Chambers, the regular courier of the Ware group, and instructed them to work together. The two men disliked each other on sight. Chambers suggested in his memoirs that Carpenter was jealous of his position in the salaried underground. Wadleigh, who knew and liked both men, implied in his *New York Post* exposé, "Why I Spied for the Communists," that Carpenter thought Chambers was unbearably pretentious. Peters found the personality conflict irrelevant and instructed the two men to cooperate in collecting new material from their sources for transmission to Moscow.[24]

The efforts of the three men paid off, and Peters was able to transform the secret apparatus into a full-time espionage network by late 1936. By the early months of 1937, the dramatic increase in material overwhelmed Chambers's former system of typing copies of selected documents at Washington-area safe houses. Searching for a solution, Carpenter approached William and Anna Spiegel, an artistic couple on the fringes of left-wing circles, told them he was trying to write a novel, and arranged to share their rent in exchange for occasional use of their apartment. Carpenter left a suitcase full of film-processing equipment in the Spiegels' apartment, which the Spiegels thought was a typewriter, and arranged for the couple to be absent whenever he and Chambers photographed documents. William Spiegel, who had just started a new novelty business, appreciated the extra money and asked no questions. However, he later related that he found Chambers, whom he knew as Carl and believed to be a European, very mysterious and intriguing.[25]

Upon Himoff's return to Baltimore, Reno regained his composure. The Party completed the signature drive placing Earl Browder and James Ford on the Maryland ballot, and Reno turned his attention to plans for the annual AFL convention. The convention looked very promising that year because of a new feeling of militancy inspired among several unions by the founding of the Committee for Industrial Organization in November of 1935. At first, the committee attempted to work with the AFL, and a strong progressive minority in the Baltimore AFL formed around J. Fred Rausch, the secretary of the United Building Trades Federation. The Baltimore Party controlled a strong fraction within the progressive group and believed it could use the group's support to push for resolutions favoring a farmer-labor party, industrial unionism, organization of black workers, and a variety of local relief measures. Doubtless mindful of the 1935 disaster with Powers, Reno decided to lead the Party delegation to Hagerstown himself.[26]

The Hagerstown convention opened with a vigorous floor fight over the credentials of delegates from militant unions, such as the Textile Workers Union from Cumberland. Conservative unionists followed the credential battle with a series of filibuster speeches designed to give Maryland AFL president Joseph P. McCurdy time to devise his strategy for the next day. That evening, the progressive caucus met and, sensing the weakness of the conservatives, engaged in vigorous political horse-trading in an attempt to put together a slate of officers that might overturn McCurdy. The naked fight for votes at the expense of principles disturbed a number of the younger Party members, but Reno gently straightened them out at the Communist Party fraction meeting held later the same night. Reno reminded them that they answered to the Communist fraction, not the progressive caucus, and that the creation of an opposition group based on clear principles was far superior to an election victory by a hopelessly diffuse coalition.[27]

The next day, the progressives scored several victories over the conservatives. They defeated a resolution supporting government regulations mandating the firing of married women before any other layoffs might take place and only narrowly lost a vote in support of increasing union efforts to recruit and organize blacks. The only bleak spots were when the Communist fraction let a blatantly anti-Communist International Seamen's Union resolution pass unopposed and failed to speak against a convention vote endorsing Franklin Roosevelt's New Deal policies. Reno, in contradiction to his early advice, criticized his colleagues for their silence, instructing them not to throw away principles for votes. He then prepared two young Communists to deliver speeches opposing both measures at the next session.[28]

Although occasionally upset with his own comrades, Reno had only praise for the progressive caucus when it nominated its slate of officers on the last day of the convention. Ulysses DeDominicis, manager of the Joint Board of the Amalgamated Clothing Workers of America, made the nominating speech presenting Rausch and his fellow candidates not as individuals but as representatives of the progressive caucus selected to lead its members in their struggle for vital principles. McCurdy retained his post as president of the Maryland AFL, but only by an 88-vote margin. Reno felt it was an excellent showing and a strong beginning for the progressive caucus, which would doubtless "temper the whole attitude of the State Federation in the coming year." The convention demonstrated the correctness of the Party's united front line, although, Reno cautioned, carrying out the line constantly exposed comrades to the temptations of right-wing opportunism. The Communists participating in the convention had given in, in small ways, to such temptations, but overall, Reno declared, they had been strengthened organizationally and politically "100%" by the experience.[29]

The left-wing block Reno hoped for never developed. Instead, most of the AFL progressives, including Rausch and DeDominicis, became disgusted with the intransigence of the old guard and abandoned the AFL for the Congress of Industrial Organizations (CIO), which had replaced the Committee for Industrial Organization. The defections did not upset Reno because the CIO was much more attractive to the Communist Party. Its promotion of industrial unionism matched the Party's own philosophy much better than did the AFL's reliance on craft unionism, and John L. Lewis had already begun to informally recruit CPUSA members as CIO organizers. One of these recruits, a young man known variously as Mike Smith, Mike Silver, or Smitty, arrived in Baltimore in early 1936 to help organize a local of the CIO's Steel Workers Organizing Committee (SWOC).[30]

Smith found work in the Eastern Rolling Mill, a part of Bethlehem Steel's vast industrial empire, and applied himself to learning the job and discovering the attitudes of his fellow workers. He succeeded at both tasks, coming to deeply enjoy the challenges of rolling hot steel and organizing a strike in the rolling mill in June of 1936. Reno closely supervised Smith's work and was delighted with the strike, which not only succeeded but so impressed the AA leaders that they openly thanked the Party for its efforts.[31]

Outside the plant, Smith joined in the SWOC organizing drive, personally going door-to-door in east Baltimore to promote the union and spread the slogan "Let's Make Baltimore a Union Town." The Party's efforts to promote the union got an extra boost from the arrival in Baltimore of thirty to forty Finnish families from Warren, Ohio, where they had been blacklisted as radicals. The newcomers supported the Communist Party faithfully and significantly increased the level of radical activity at Sparrows Point. SWOC needed all the help it could get because Bethlehem Steel used every available tactic to break the organizing drive. Smith recalled the mid- to late thirties as "a low, low, time."[32]

To give Smith a break from the grind of steel organizing and possibly to reward him for the rolling mill strike, Reno selected Smith to help create a Party branch in western Maryland. Reno hoped to establish a permanent Communist presence there by sending Party members to Cumberland to recruit among the coal miners in the nearby Georges Creek area. He began the project by writing a series of letters to Communist Party officials in Pittsburgh, who were organizing among striking miners around Uniontown, a Pennsylvania city only forty miles from Cumberland. The letters requested the names of regional contacts, local subscription lists to Communist journals, and advice on coordinating Maryland's efforts with the ongoing strike work of the Pittsburgh district. Reno also hinted that since Baltimore was nearly a 150 miles from Cumberland and the Party did not have a car, he would not be offended if the Pittsburgh district chose to take over organizing in western Maryland.[33]

Pittsburgh declined to accept Reno's offer, and he began sending small groups into the region. In 1954, at his testimony before the House Committee on Un-American Activities, Reno spoke proudly about the accomplishments of his teams and singled out a recruiting expedition led by Tom Pinkerton in the summer of 1936 as the most successful. Reno may have remembered Pinkerton's group less for its organizational success than for its romantic results. Among the Communists journeying to Allegheny County that summer were Evelyn Howard, a member of the psychology department at Johns Hopkins University, and Mike Smith. Howard and Smith met on the trip west, took a liking to each other, and eventually married. After the wedding, Smith took his wife's name and became Mike Howard. The Cumberland trip yielded other results besides romance. Pinkerton's people stabilized the western Maryland branch of the Party and increased its membership to fifty people, divided unevenly between Cumberland and Frostburg.[34]

Almost none of the western Maryland recruits came from among the coal miners in Georges Creek. Instead, most of them were employed at the Celanese Mill, an artificial silk plant, in Cumberland. Working conditions in the silk mill were very difficult, the weaving machines were incredibly loud, the chemicals used to create the silk smelled terrible, and fibers from the silk clogged the lungs of the workers, often resulting in "brown lung" disease later in life. A group of Celanese Mill employees had tried to organize a union at the plant in early 1935, and it was among these activists that the Party found sympathizers and recruits.

In the fall of 1936, Party members intent on raising funds for a seamen's strike in Fells Point visited the Celanese Mill. The leader of the group, Patrick Whalen, a Communist seaman who had recently arrived in Baltimore, fell into conversation with a young mill employee named George Meyers. Meyers, a native of Lonaconing, Maryland, had worked at the Celanese Mill since 1933 and, except for a brief period tramping about looking for employment in the early depression, had never strayed far from his home in the Georges Creek valley. Whalen fascinated Meyers; his seagoing, nomadic existence represented a way of life entirely different from what Meyers had known growing up in the isolated mountains of western Maryland. Whalen introduced Meyers to the Communist vision of a greater purpose to union organizing than simple economic benefit and eventually recruited him into the Communist Party.[35]

The waterfront strike that brought Whalen to western Maryland arose from the discontent of sailors in the Atlantic, Gulf, and Great Lakes regions over the disparity between their wages and working conditions and those of West Coast seamen. In March of 1936, Joseph Curran, a thirty-year-old bosun's mate, led a sit-down strike on the USS *California,* demanding West Coast wages for the crew before the vessel would be allowed to sail. Shipowners declared the strike a mutiny, and the International Seamen's Union (ISU) agreed, branding the strikers "outlaws" and expelling the leaders from the union.

The incident, together with ISU acquiescence to a very weak labor contract, triggered a two-month strike on the East Coast by the "outlaws" and their supporters, who organized themselves as the Seamen's Defense Committee (SDC). Curran denied receiving any but the most modest support from the Communist Party, but in fact Party members flocked to his side and came to dominate positions of leadership in the SDC. The outlaw strike ended in a compromise, but resentments continued to smolder. After the liquidation of the MWIU, its members had joined the ISU and organized themselves as the Rank and File Committee. The Rank and Filers tried to capitalize on the discontent by bringing a series of legal actions against ISU officials in an attempt to replace conservative union leaders with more radical individuals.[36]

The Baltimore public remained largely unaware of the Communist Party's success in integrating itself into mainstream labor organizations. Most people continued to regard the Party as a fringe element in the business of providing comic relief from the grim realities of the depression. Jon O'Ren, the *Baltimore Sun*'s amateur Red-watcher, reflected the feelings of most Baltimore residents. In 1934, O'Ren good-naturedly criticized the *Sun* for reporting that Jay Lovestone was to address a Party meeting. Lovestone, O'Ren informed his readers, had been thrown out of the Party and now was about as popular with the Communists as J. P. Morgan was. When local union leaders complained that the Communist Party employed pretty girls to distribute the radical paper *Shipmates Voice* in Fells Point, O'Ren devoted a column to analyzing the offending periodical. He pronounced it no more radical than many mainstream dailies and speculated that the Communist papergirls did less harm then the women sailors normally met on the waterfront.[37]

In June of 1936, O'Ren noted that although Earl Browder regarded the election of the Republican Alf Landon as a disaster that would bring fascism to the United States, he could not bring himself to endorse Roosevelt. Instead, Browder criticized the president as an opportunist who fought reactionaries only "to the degree necessary to retain the loyalty of the leftist forces." O'Ren felt that trying to "take votes away from Roosevelt without driving them to Landon" would put the Party into a ticklish situation and force the "faithful through frightful dialectical contortions."[38]

Curious to see such intellectual gymnastics for himself, O'Ren, along with sixteen hundred other interested individuals, filled the Lyric Theater in October to hear Browder speak about the upcoming elections. Earl Reno served as master of ceremonies, introducing Browder and several warm-up speakers to the cheering crowd. The *Afro-American* editor William N. Jones praised the Communist Party as the only group advocating complete equality and full economic opportunity for blacks. Rather ironically, Jones went on to say that "the colored people this year will demonstrate they have received another emancipation—from the Republican party. This year a large number of them will vote the Democratic ticket." Pat Toohey, the head of District 3, followed Jones to the podium and launched into a tirade against the Detroit priest Charles Coughlin, whom he accused of being a follower of William Randolph Hearst, who in turn followed Hitler.[39]

Browder enlarged on the theme by accusing the Catholic church of promoting fascism worldwide. Browder assured his listeners that the CPUSA posed no danger to the United States and tried to demonstrate that the contest between Roosevelt and Landon mirrored the much more violent struggle in Spain. Browder concluded his speech with just the verbal gymnastics O'Ren had hoped for by accusing Landon of fascism, Roosevelt of lukewarm compromise, and the Socialists of intransigence. At the same time, Browder discouraged the audience from voting Communist by modestly claiming that his Party only sought to educate the American public and pave the way for a future farmer-labor party.

The real excitement occurred after the rally when a policeman assigned to traffic control reported he had assisted a federal agent in taking down the license numbers of all District of Columbia cars parked outside the theater. While Browder spoke, the agent had confronted the theater manager and demanded to see his records regarding the individuals and organizations sponsoring the Communist chief's speech. Both the head of the Secret Service and J. Edgar Hoover, who personally wrote an angry letter to the *Baltimore Sun,* denied that their agents had been involved. Both denials were true. W. J. Cruickshank, a Baltimore-based employee of the Bureau of Customs, came forward and admitted responsibility. Customs spokesmen defended Cruickshank, stating that he had behaved strictly in line with his duties. An official at the Treasury Department, of which Customs formed a part, denounced the entire affair and promised a full investigation. However, nothing further was ever heard of the scandal except for a comment by the *Sun* cartoonist Richard Yardley, who speculated that Browder must have been suspected of trying to import communism duty free.[40]

Shortly after the license plate scandal, maritime contract negotiations broke down on the West Coast. Seven maritime and longshoremen's unions, temporarily united as the Maritime Federation of the Pacific, voted to strike. All along the East Coast, the Rank and File Committee rallied sailors for a sympathy strike. In Baltimore, over eight hundred men volunteered for picket duty the first day. They were inspired by the desire to demonstrate solidarity with their West Coast brethren and to gain some of the advantages enjoyed by Pacific Coast seamen, such as union-controlled hiring halls and cash, rather than in-kind, overtime pay.[41]

Leadership of the Baltimore strike fell to Patrick "Paddy" Whalen, a man blessed with an infectiously engaging personality and earthy ability to communicate with fellow seamen. I. Duke Avnet, a Baltimore labor lawyer called in to assist with legal aspects of the strike, recalled his speaking style: "He ran sentences together. He mispronounced words; he committed malapropism. He cussed profusely. His grammar was a classic of mistakes. But his thinking was clear; and he knew the seamen and their problems." Whalen stood only a few inches over five feet tall and weighed around 120 pounds. Born in the

American West in 1884, Whalen learned unionism at his father's knee and followed him into a career as a locomotive engineer. However, wanderlust and conflicts with railroad owners caused Whalen to abandon the Great Plains for the sea.[42]

Charles Rubin, a Communist mariner and author of *The Log of Rubin the Sailor,* encountered him on board one of the ships of the Merchant Line in the early 1930s. Impressed by Whalen's extensive knowledge of such American radical groups as the Knights of Labor, the Molly McGuires, and the Wobblies, Rubin convinced him to join the MWIU. Shortly afterward, despite his inclination toward anarchism, Whalen joined the Communist Party and, after the break-up of the MWIU, became prominent in the ISU's Rank and File Committee.[43]

The strike on the West Coast developed into a battle of wills as shipowners docked their vessels and locked out the strikers. On the East Coast, however, the strike turned violent, and gangs of thugs roamed the waterfront. Sailors in their path were severely beaten, if they were lucky; in Baltimore, eight less fortunate individuals were found floating in the harbor. For their part, striking seamen quickly learned not to go about by themselves and viciously turned against nonstrikers. Angry mariners forced one man to run a gauntlet at the Anchorage Hotel in Fells Point, and another had his ears cut off. Throughout the escalating violence, Whalen served as a moderating influence. One day, three picket captains brought a sailor to Whalen's tiny office and demanded that he be thrown out of the Anchorage Hotel for refusing picket duty. The accused man defended himself on the grounds that he was in intense pain from an advanced case of gonorrhea. Whalen rebuffed the picket captains for lack of sympathy, asking who among them had not risked the disease, and he arranged for the man to receive medical treatment.[44]

In an attempt to end the strike by judicial means, the shipowners filed an injunction against the strikers that would have compelled them to fold up their picket lines. Avnet, the labor lawyer, countered with a recently passed state law guaranteeing the right to strike and forbidding antipicket injunctions without a preliminary hearing. The injunction failed, and by the end of November the numbers of striking seamen had increased to nearly twenty-eight hundred.[45]

On the Pacific Coast, Harry Bridges defied the national leadership of the International Longshoremen's Association (ILA) by supporting the seamen's strike. Along the Atlantic, however, the ILA locals remained loyal to Joe Ryan, the national leader. Whalen, knowing that the strike could not succeed without ILA support, made repeated overtures to the two ILA locals in Baltimore. Local 858, made up of blacks anxious to retain their hard-won privileges and suspicious of the motives of the largely white ISU, refused to be drawn into the strike. For a time, however, it looked as if the white longshoremen in Local 859 could be won over.

Longshoremen from the West Coast arrived in Baltimore to launch a series of street-corner orations and meet with Local 859's leadership. The visiting westerners capped their campaign with a rally at the Fifth Regiment Armory on 16 December featuring Harry Bridges and Joe Curran. Carried along by the powerful feelings of solidarity, the longshoremen voted to strike on 19 December. Joe Ryan rushed to Baltimore to bring his renegade local in line but was turned away from St. Stanislaw Church, where the local was meeting to vote, by thousands of jubilant dockworkers. The celebration proved premature, however. Local 859 could not sustain its momentum and voted to return to work two days later.

The collapse of longshoreman support doomed the strike. It also raised the possibility that the National Labor Relations Board, scheduled to meet in Washington in January 1937, would vote against the petition of the Rank and File Committee to become the collective bargaining agent for the port of Baltimore. Whalen attempted to salvage as much of the situation as possible by calling for volunteers to assemble in Baltimore on 17 January for a march from Baltimore to Washington to demonstrate the amount of support the Rank and File Committee enjoyed. Whalen led several hundred seamen and supporters down U.S. Highway 1 to Washington on what became known as the Midnight March of the Baltimore Brigade.

Once in the capital, pickets paraded in front of the Department of Commerce, and small delegations visited government offices, including the White House, where Roosevelt spoke to the demonstrators personally. The seamen returned to Baltimore, claimed a "moral victory," and on 25 January voted unanimously to call off the strike. In February, the National Labor Relations Board acted in favor of the seamen by recognizing the Rank and File Committee as a collective bargaining agent. In May of 1937, Curran announced the creation of a new CIO affiliate, the National Maritime Union (NMU), made up of members of both the Seamen's Defense Committee and the Communist Rank and File group. Whalen became the Baltimore NMU's first president.

In December of 1936, while Whalen tried to salvage the collapsing seamen's strike, Earl Reno delivered a report to the national Communist Party Congress on his achievements in Maryland. Reno spoke highly of the Party's work with relief issues and the antiwar campaign, both of which he felt were leading steadily to the establishment of a united front in Baltimore. His highest praise, as well as the major portion of his report, was reserved for Mike Howard's victorious strike at the Eastern Rolling Mill. The strike not only had made a dent, albeit small, in mighty Bethlehem Steel but also had seen non-Party labor leaders acknowledge Communist leadership and credit the achievements of Party organizers. Reno clearly felt that the strike was one of his finest moments in Baltimore.[46]

Reno was being far too modest. He and Mary Himoff had built on Joseph Gaal's work to completely restore the Maryland Party and successfully establish it as District 34. The Maryland Party now had a solid core of over 185 dedicated Communists surrounded by a fluctuating group of fellow travelers and a very large number of people who could be counted on to support this or that specific Party activity. Twenty-four people had joined the Party in Allegheny County as a result of the 1936 election-year membership drive, bringing membership in the Cumberland clubs to nearly fifty. The increase allowed the section to claim the title of Communist Party of Maryland in fact as well as in name. A few months after his report, Reno, along with Himoff, returned to Michigan to oversee Party work in the United Auto Workers Union. He turned leadership of the Maryland Party over to the Baltimore native Albert Blumberg, who would benefit tremendously from Reno's guidance of the Party from the turbulence of the Third Period to the calmer and far more productive waters of the Popular Front.[47]

6

The Popular Front

Born to a comfortable, middle-class family, educated at Yale, the Sorbonne, and the University of Vienna, and employed as a professor of philosophy at Johns Hopkins University, Albert Blumberg projected an image of urban liberalism well suited to the tone of the Popular Front. Blumberg joined the Communist Party in 1933 and served as chair of the Agitprop Committee for the next four years. He did not conceal his Party membership but did not flaunt it either; he had never been identified as a Communist in the press. Shortly after finishing the 1937 spring semester, however, Blumberg resigned his faculty position, publicly announced his Party membership, and assumed the newly created position of district administrative secretary for the Communist Party of Maryland.[1]

Blumberg took over a well-functioning Party section, which, for the first time in its history, had a solid base in labor. Reno had cultivated the young leaders of the progressive block in the AFL, many of whom had, by 1937, assumed leading roles in the CIO. Mike Howard's dedicated work on behalf of the Steel Workers Organizing Committee and his strike leadership had gained him tremendous respect, and he was now the liaison between the CIO and the Communist Party. Patrick Whalen's leadership of the seamen's strike earned him, by May, the presidency of both the Baltimore local of the National Maritime Union and the citywide Maritime Union Council.

Whalen interpreted his presidency of the Maritime Union Council very broadly and held forth on a wide range of issues, from making seamen eligible for social security benefits to criticism of Franklin Roosevelt. The president came under fire for allowing cuts in the Works Progress Administration bud-

get, which Whalen was convinced would condemn "millions of families . . .
to hopeless starvation." Popular with the rank and file, Whalen frequently ran
into trouble with local union leaders because of his blunt tactics and domi-
neering presence at committee meetings. Whalen's independent streak also
got him into trouble with the Communist Party, although his care in staffing
the Baltimore NMU office with Party members kept such criticism relatively
mild. Benjamin Fields, the chairman of the Maryland Party, called Whalen a
"good comrade despite some mistakes and a frequently poor attitude." Years
later, George Meyers reflected that "Paddy held the Party at arms length."[2]

Besides continuing their efforts in the steel and maritime industries, Mary-
land Party members successfully planted Communist clubs at the Glenn L.
Martin Plant in Middle River, where the Communist Party Opposition, the
splinter group loyal to the ousted Party leader Jay Lovestone, was also trying
to establish a foothold, and among the auto workers at the Broening Highway
Factory. Both clubs put out newsletters, and members actively recruited for the
CIO and the Party. The Party also maintained its long-standing fraction in the
International Ladies Garment Workers Union of America, had five energetic
new recruits in the Amalgamated Clothing Workers of America, and, at the
time of Blumberg's appointment as Party head, was setting up a club of Communist restaurant employees. In addition, virtually all of the Baltimore organizers in the United Electrical Workers local belonged to the Party.[3]

In July of 1937, CIO activists in Baltimore called for a conference to establish an industrial union council in Baltimore. The CIO strongly encouraged
the formation of state and local councils because they provided a forum for
establishing common policies and gave labor a united voice. The Communist
Party also approved of the councils, and Baltimore Party members were under orders to "talk up" the need for a council in their locals and to nominate
Communists as council officers. Seventy-seven delegates, representing twenty-
four unions, met on 21 July and established the Baltimore Industrial Union
Council (BIUC).

On 29 July, Mike Howard reported on the meeting. Out of fourteen officers elected, he was pleased to say that five were Party members and seven others close sympathizers. Patrick Whalen had been elected first vice president,
while Howard became BIUC secretary. Six months later, new elections would
make Whalen president of the council. Benjamin Fields congratulated everyone on a job well done but cautioned that the most difficult task, properly
guiding the council, still lay ahead. Albert Blumberg also thought that the
Party had done well but criticized the Communists in the steel and maritime
unions for nominating Party members for every office.[4]

Conditions in Washington and western Maryland remained much more conservative than in Baltimore. In those areas, the Party continued to try to expand within the AFL unions, particularly among building trades and railroad workers. In January of 1938, the CPUSA held a conference of Communist AFL members in New York City. District 34 sent ten delegates from Washington and five from Baltimore, making up the largest group at the conference. The conference established a national committee to oversee AFL work and mandated the creation of official AFL fractions in each district, which would regularly correspond with the national committee. After hearing a full report on the conference, the officers of District 34 voted to appoint Joe Rinis, the Washington carpenter and former opponent of Clara Speer, as secretary of the district's AFL fraction.[5]

One of the problems arising from the rapid expansion of the Party was the low level of ideological awareness among many of the new members. Blumberg hoped to correct the problem by expanding the Workers School begun by Mary Himoff. He moved the school to a suite of second-floor rooms at 322–24 West Franklin Street, just around the corner from Party headquarters on North Eutaw Street, and arranged for an annual budget of two thousand dollars. One hundred and twenty-five students enrolled for the school's 1937 fall semester and paid a fee of two dollars for each twelve-session course. The students chose from a wide range of offerings, including classes in English, history, and politics, as well as courses on progressive trends in drama, historical materialism, principles of the class struggle, and communism. Blumberg thought the school was a great success and urged Martin Chancey, head of the District of Columbia Party, to establish one in Washington.[6]

Blumberg also planned to use the three-hundred-member Baltimore chapter of the American League for Peace and Democracy (formerly the American League against War and Fascism) to reach out to the city's working class. Blumberg believed that the league concentrated too exclusively on the middle class and needed to broaden its scope, possibly by creating chapters in Cumberland and Highlandtown. The proposed expansion encountered resistance from league members, who preferred things the way they were, as well as union members, who found league speeches on the crises in Spain irrelevant to their immediate needs.[7]

Blumberg found union members' attitude confusing because the league had recruited working-class volunteers for the International Brigades. But virtually all of the thirty-five Baltimoreans who eventually signed up to fight in Spain were relatively footloose seamen, members of the Communist Party, or usually both. The names of most of the volunteers are unknown, with the notable exception of Carl Bradley, the former Unemployed Council chief and steel organizer. Bradley left for Spain in 1936 and served with the Abraham

Lincoln Battalion. He participated in the Aragon offensive, fighting from house to house in the cities of Quinto and Belchite. In Belchite, Bradley and his men built mobile barricades out of grain sacks, inched them forward under sniper and machine-gun fire, and captured nearly seven hundred nationalist troops. The exploit earned Bradley a promotion to captain and a commendation in the pages of the *Volunteer for Liberty,* the journal of the International Brigades.[8]

The Communist Party was not the only organization to take an active interest in the Spanish civil war. By the late summer of 1936, almost every issue of the *Catholic Review* carried vivid accounts of bishops, priests, and members of religious orders who had suffered atrocities at the hands of the Loyalist government. The war inspired the archbishop of Baltimore, Michael J. Curley, to launch a national crusade against communism. On 3 January 1939, he wrote a letter to be read in all the churches of his diocese urging the faithful to attend a mass meeting at Constitution Hall in favor of retaining an arms embargo against Spain. When the Spanish ambassador invited Curley and others to go to Spain to see for themselves that there was no persecution of churchmen, Curley refused to go, remarking, "He is a common, ordinary Liar."[9]

By late 1937, Archbishop Curley was elated, and the Communist Party distressed, by the retreat of the Republican armies, the revelations of treason in the Moscow "show trials," and the defeat of the CIO in a series of strikes against midwestern steel mills. At a District Committee meeting in September 1937, Party chairman Benjamin Fields urged Party members to try and see things from a Communist perspective. True, Fields said, the war in Spain dragged on, but the American Civil War had lasted four years, and although Hitler still raged against the Soviet Union, he had moderated recent statements. The CIO setbacks, Fields reasoned, were only temporary, the result of a new and inexperienced membership. Overall, the CIO continued to expand, and, according to Fields, it was the Party's duty to help stabilize it.[10]

As for the Moscow trials, Fields felt they had benefited the Soviet Union, not weakened it: "The Soviet Union has been strengthened, and it is clear how correct was the Comintern line on the struggle against Trotskyism, and that the extermination of the Trotskyites in the Soviet Union, upon whom Hitler relied so much to carry out his plan of conquest, was needed and greatly successful." The victory over subversion in the USSR, Fields continued, was an advance for "the working masses" the world over and of great significance for the Party's work in the United States.[11]

Not all of the Party members in Maryland agreed with Field's opinions about Stalin's purge of the Soviet Party. One man who began to harbor particularly strong doubts was the underground Communist Whittaker Chambers, who, together with David Carpenter, controlled a sophisticated, smooth-ly functioning espionage network. The operation processed several batches of documents a week and had long outgrown the temporary arrangements in the Spiegel apartment. Instead, Carpenter established his own workshop in Wash-ington, while Chambers, assisted by Felix Inslerman, a technician from New York, had a microfilming station on Callow Avenue in Baltimore.[12]

Despite an outwardly calm appearance, Chambers was a deeply disturbed man. In his autobiography, he describes listening intently as the Soviet secret police "padded like ferrets through the underground," eliminating less visi-ble threats to Stalin's power than prominent old Bolsheviks and their luckless companions. The disappearance of the American Communist Juliet Stuart Poynitz, apparently a victim of the purges, deeply affected Chambers and may have been the decisive factor that pushed him to flee from the underground. Chambers procured a car, located a hiding place, and manufactured a "life preserver" in the form of samples of government documents collected by his espionage ring. Early one morning in April 1938, his preparations complete, Chambers and his family simply drove away from their Mount Royal apart-ment. Chambers's defection rattled his Moscow handlers so badly that, two months later, they replaced J. Peters with Rudy Baker as the head of the Amer-ican underground and ordered a reevaluation of the entire network.[13]

Maryland's above-ground Communists remained unaware of the panic caused by Chambers's disappearance. Instead, they focused on the Democratic primary elections, which marked the Party's transition from opposition to Franklin Roosevelt to unqualified support. Roosevelt, deeply disturbed by crit-icism of the New Deal from within the Democratic Party, had determined to "purge" it of conservative members, one of whom was Maryland's Senator Millard Tydings. The president declared in a radio broadcast that the only thing that prevented Tydings from joining the Republican Party was his de-sire to profit from the prestige of the New Deal. Roosevelt urged Maryland Democrats to vote for Tydings's opponent, Congressman David J. Lewis.[14]

The Communist Party supported Roosevelt's bloodless purge, pledging to do all it could "with our very limited means of reaching the voters of the State . . . to clarify the issues and thus help defeat Tydings." Aware that too much unqualified support for Roosevelt damaged the Party's image as an al-ternate to capitalism, Communist leaders promised to run their own candi-date in the general election if Tydings was not defeated in the primaries. Ty-dings did win the primaries, and the Party ran Jack Straw, who was most likely as real as George Alexander Turnipseed, against him.[15]

Buoyed by membership growth and encouraged by growing public accep-tance of the Party as a legitimate part of the political scene, the Party clubs in

Maryland began publishing openly Communist newsletters. The small, normally four-page, publications combined political commentary on national and global affairs with matters of purely local interest and worked hard to portray the Party as a member of the New Deal coalition. One issue of the *Good Neighbor,* put out by the Twenty-sixth Ward Club in Highlandtown, juxtaposed front-page stories about the successful efforts of the New Deal Democratic Club to build a neighborhood children's playground, the meaning of May Day, and a plea to support the Communist Party candidates in the upcoming election. The July 1939 issue of *Your Neighbor,* put out by the Druid Hill branch of the Communist Party, condemned anti-Semitic attacks on Jewish schoolchildren in Druid Hill Park, discussed racial and ethnic problems in Palestine, and promoted the establishment of a free junior college in Baltimore.[16]

The newsletters presented communism as an integral part of American society. Carl Breen, editor of *Your Neighbor,* assured his readers that Communists were just the "people who live next door to you." Several journals, in their inaugural editions, printed a passage from the preamble to the Communist Party constitution that began by identifying the Party with the traditions established by Thomas Jefferson, Thomas Paine, Andrew Jackson, and Abraham Lincoln. Because of the ravages of capitalist exploitation, the passage continued, the founding fathers' collective dream of "life, liberty and the pursuit of happiness" could be achieved only by "establishing common ownership of the national economy."[17]

The *4th District News* amplified the preamble with a popular Party slogan dedicating the Communists to "Jobs, Security, Democracy and Peace" and emphasized that these things could be fully realized only after the building of a socialist America. William Taylor, editor of the *Liberty Bell,* published by the Seventeenth Ward branch, thought the issue of Soviet-style socialism was so important that his paper featured a regular column on the historical inevitability of socialism in the United States.[18]

The Baltimore municipal elections of 1939 illustrate the degree to which the Party saw itself as a constructive part of the New Deal coalition. Where once the Party used elections to call for the destruction of the capitalist, the candidates now ran on a platform advocating slum clearance and the use of federal funds to build modern, low-cost housing. Blumberg, who was running as the Communist candidate for mayor, called for increased levels of unemployment relief, equal job opportunities for blacks and whites, the construction of more hospitals and schools, and a reduction in the cost of gas and electric services. The Communists also endorsed three Baltimore City charter amendments advocating the establishment of a city planning commission, a recreation department, and a regional airport.[19]

The Maryland Party prospered under the policies of the Popular Front, but its successes remained hostage to events abroad, and a sudden shift in Soviet foreign policy in the fall of 1939 nearly cost it everything it had gained. Previously the most vocal critic of Nazi Germany, the USSR unexpectedly began to send out peace feelers toward its European rival and, on 23 August, signed a nonaggression treaty, popularly known as the Nazi-Soviet Pact. The pact caught the American Party off balance, forcing Earl Browder to confess to inquisitive newsmen that he had exactly the same information they had—none. Maryland Communists quickly staged several meetings urging American neutrality on the grounds that the United States required peace to attain the level of security and prosperity needed to pull it out of depression. Involvement in a European war, they cautioned, would be economic suicide.[20]

On 11 September, just after Hitler's invasion of Poland, the Party announced a series of five meetings that would explain the developing events. Benjamin Fields, the district chairman, spoke at the first meeting, telling his listeners that the Soviet Union remained Germany's enemy because communism and fascism "can not exist together permanently." Fields denounced as a big joke the idea, later known as "Red Fascism," that nazism and communism were virtually identical. As soon as it was possible, Fields predicted, the Nazis would attack the Soviet Union. Fields ended his speech with the claim that the Non-Aggression Pact had strengthened world forces for peace by sowing divisiveness and confusion among the Axis powers.[21]

Fields's speech had much to recommend it as an effective way around the dilemma created by the start of a European war with the Soviet Union on the wrong side. The pact could be seen as pure expediency; nothing had really changed, and both sides would soon be at each other's throats again. Fields's interpretation also had the virtue of being true. Stalin signed the Non-Aggression Pact out of pure utility and was rapidly building up the Red Army in preparation for war. However, Stalin could not afford to have the international parties going about saying that Soviet cooperation with Germany was a sham, because it might hasten a German invasion. Stalin instructed the Comintern to correct the situation, and sometime between 10 September and 12 September Earl Browder received a shortwave radio message informing him that the war was an imperialist conflict that did not concern the Soviet Union.[22]

On 2 October 1939, William Weinstone, a Central Committee member, came to Baltimore for the CPUSA's twentieth anniversary party armed with a speech based on the six-hundred-word radio message. The Soviet-German alliance, Weinstone declared, was a humanitarian move on Stalin's part: "Soviet Russia took advantage of the fact that capitalism could not unite and saved peace for herself and a good part of the world." The Soviet invasion of eastern Poland was an act of liberation that saved 11 million people, including 1.5 million Jews, from domination by both Nazis and Polish lords. Weinstone dismissed the French and English claim that the current war was one between freedom and barbarism and firmly asserted that it was nothing more than a battle between two bandits for the loot of the world. In fact, Weinstone continued, the perfidious British still fervently hoped for the destruction of the Soviet Union. They had stabbed Republican Spain in the back and allowed Ethiopia, China, Czechoslovakia, and now Poland to fall, all to strengthen the Fascists for a war against Russia.[23]

The new line on the European war placed the Party in a difficult situation. Fields had been able to blame questionable Soviet actions on grim necessity, but now the Party had to demonstrate that the USSR was engaged in a righteous struggle for peace and freedom. Painting the Soviet Union as the champion of the oppressed in light of the occupation of eastern Poland was quite difficult. The task became almost impossible after the annexation of the Baltic states and the start of the winter war against Finland.[24]

The West greeted the Soviet attempt to seize the Karelian region and reduce Finland to the status of a client state with great outcries but little concrete action. The *Champion,* the voice of the Twenty-second Ward branch in south Baltimore, sneered at the crocodile tears shed over Finland. Where, it asked, were all these supporters of national independence when Austria, Ethiopia, Czechoslovakia, Spain, and Albania were crushed under the Fascist boot. The author of "The Truth about Finland" concluded by claiming that the only reason the USSR was coming under such criticism was that it was a workers' government bent on liberating the Finnish people from their capitalist bosses.[25]

Gilbert Green, the national president of the Young Communist League, appeared at a meeting sponsored by the Baltimore Communist Party and the Maryland YCL and carried the *Champion*'s logic a step further. Green, speaking before a crowd of three hundred Party members, called Finland an international gangster and justified the Soviet invasion as an act of self-defense. "Suppose," Green declaimed, "that a gunman had been hired by a gang of cutthroats to attack you. He approached you and stood there loading his gun bullet by bullet, eyeing you and sizing you up as he made ready to shoot. You pleaded with him, offered him concessions and told him it would be worthwhile to drop that gun. . . . Then you struck the gun out of his hand. Would you be the aggressor? No, absolutely not . . . and that is exactly what the Soviet Union did." Green justified this fanciful metaphor by stating that Germany had been readying Finland for use as a staging area for an assault against the

USSR in the spring of 1940. He ended his speech with an attack on Roosevelt, who, he asserted, had betrayed everything he once stood for by scuttling the New Deal as "surely as the Captain of the *Graf Spee* had scuttled his ship."[26]

The Party deserved tremendous credit from Moscow for its adherence to the Comintern line on Finland and the European war, because its rhetoric cost it dearly in lost friends and emboldened enemies. Although slowly growing throughout the 1930s, Maryland anticommunism outside of the Catholic church lacked cohesion and was dispersed among unconnected groups and individuals. Baltimoreans, exemplified by the columnist Jon O'Ren, showed an amused tolerance of their homegrown Reds and were quick to defend the Party's right to present its case. However, the Party's defense of the Hitler-Stalin Pact and the Soviet invasion of Finland increased the ranks of local anti-Communists and subjected the Maryland Party to a series of legal attacks by the Dies Committee.[27]

The Dies Committee, officially the House Committee on Un-American Activities (HUAC) but initially named after its creator, Martin Dies, a Republican congressman from Texas, came into being in 1938. In August of that year, the committee held a series of hearings, which, widely reported in the Maryland press, condemned the CIO for harboring hundreds of Communist organizers. J. B. Matthews, a minister and former fellow traveler, testified that the Party was a Moscow-controlled instrument of subversion and that the members of Communist-controlled mass organizations were nothing but "stooges and dupes."[28]

The national Party roundly castigated the Dies Committee for both unconstitutional probing into private beliefs and for unjustly accusing the CPUSA of being un-American. Over the next two years, the Communist Party and the Dies Committee continued to attack each other publicly, but the fight never moved beyond verbal sparring. In the wake of the winter war, however, the Dies Committee adopted much more direct and threatening tactics. On 28 March 1940, committee agents Charles A. Randal and I. H. O'Hanion appeared at Party headquarters on North Eutaw Street. The two men presented subpoenas allowing them to seize Party records and then handed Sam Banks, the director of the Young Communist League, and Dorothy Rose Blumberg, the wife of Albert Blumberg, summonses requiring them to give testimony before the committee.[29]

Banks pleaded a scheduling conflict and had his testimony deferred to a later date. Dorothy Rose Blumberg agreed to appear the next morning. When she entered the committee chambers the next day, Blumberg, a very attractive and poised woman, created a stir among reporters covering the hearings, who requested several photos of her with her lawyer, Leo Alpert. J. B. Matthews, who had become an investigator for the Dies Committee, suggested to Blumberg that her husband might wish to appear before the committee with her. Albert Blumberg, who was sitting in the audience, politely declined and stated that he would wait for a formal summons.[30]

Alpert then informed the committee that his client would answer no questions regarding the material illegally seized from Party headquarters. Matthews ignored the attorney's warning and inquired directly about letters, Communist Party membership cards, and handwritten personnel records that had been seized the day before. Whatever response Matthews might have expected, he was disappointed. Blumberg refused to discuss any documents, claimed to know only a few top Party officials, and insisted she had no in-depth knowledge of Party affairs. The defense of ignorance proved very useful in defeating Matthew's attempts to pry Party secrets out of her. It was also completely untrue.[31]

Blumberg, Dorothy Rose to her friends both in and out of the Party, was an exceptional woman by any standards. Two years older than her husband, she traced descent from the Oppenheims, a prominent and wealthy Jewish family of long standing in Baltimore. An early marriage to Harold B. Cahn, a broker, ended in divorce in 1932, and the following year she married Albert Blumberg. A 1934 military intelligence report commented that she had shown no leanings toward communism before her marriage and that her activities were believed to be "largely uxorial and sentimental rather than from personal political conviction."[32]

By 1940, however, Dorothy Rose Blumberg was deeply involved in Party work. She helped run the headquarters office, maintained Party files, attended Executive Committee meetings as recording secretary, collected signatures for election petitions, spoke at Party gatherings, and took a personal interest in the welfare of other Party members. When Joan Davis, a Party member, became pregnant, she could not afford proper prenatal care. Blumberg, appalled at the risks Davis was running, "arranged" for her to see the Blumberg family doctor regularly. She did the same for Mary Himoff when she became pregnant by Earl Reno out of wedlock. She did not formally accept Party membership, however, until December of 1939.[33]

HUAC agents served Albert Blumberg with an official summons, and he appeared before the committee the day after his wife's testimony. He stated that he had no intention of testifying about any documents seized in the committee's illegal raid and that he would not discuss any member of the Communist Party except himself. Blumberg based his refusal to speak about any of his comrades on the fact that such questions were outside the purview of the Dies Committee and violated the First Amendment right of freedom of association. He also feared that the information obtained from his answers might be used for blacklisting or threatening Party members.[34]

Matthews, who chaired the session, ignored Blumberg's statement and devoted several hours to questions based on the seized material. He showed particular interest in penciled notations on membership slips, which implied that some people had entered the Party under assumed names. Shortly before the end of the session, Martin Dies took over the questioning. Dies sharply asked Blumberg what he would do if the United States should be drawn into the current war on the side opposite that of the Soviet Union. Blumberg replied that he had faith that the American people would never allow themselves to be drawn into a war for profits, and nothing Dies could do prompted Blumberg to speculate further.[35]

Blumberg could congratulate himself on defying the Dies Committee and comporting himself with restraint and dignity. In contrast, Phil Frankfeld, the New England Party chief, who testified the same day as Blumberg, ranted and raved when the committee refused to allow him to read a petition prior to his testimony. Good manners, however, counted for little; both Blumberg and Frankfeld were charged with contempt of Congress. Fallout from the Dies Committee hearings did not end with the contempt citation. Shortly after Blumberg returned to Baltimore, the Ku Klux Klan burned a cross on his lawn, and Johns Hopkins University refused to allow him to speak on campus. In Washington, Maryland's Congressman Thomas D'Alesandro asked for further investigations into Communist activities in Maryland, alleging that they were attempting to sabotage the nation's preparedness program. The Works Progress Administration, already under conservative attack, announced new legislation calling for the purging of all Nazis, Bund members, and Communists from its ranks.[36]

Martin Chancey, secretary of the Party in the District of Columbia, fought back by lodging a protest with the Justice Department. Chancey demanded that it investigate the unconstitutional activities of the Dies Committee and linked committee's trampling of civil rights with the Ku Klux Klan's renewed campaign of terror. The Justice Department did not respond, but in April a federal judge, George A. Welsh, ruled that the Dies Committee had illegally seized Party records in the raids on Communist offices in Pittsburgh. In May, Welsh declared that the committee's actions in Maryland were also illegal and ruled that the seized documents were to be returned to the Maryland Communist Party. Despite the federal court ruling, a Washington grand jury indicted both Blumbergs on contempt of Congress charges, and the Dies Committee never turned over the seized documents.[37]

Alpert attempted to fight the Blumbergs' contempt of Congress charges in a lengthy court session before Judge W. Calvin Chestnut, but his attempt failed. Chestnut closely questioned Dorothy Rose Blumberg on the nature of communism in an attempt to convince her of its basic incompatibility with the U.S. Constitution, but she remained unconvinced. Chestnut opened his questioning of Albert Blumberg by asking what conceivable reason he could have for not answering the committee's questions about Party membership. In the judge's opinion, especially in the light of the "events of the last three weeks" (the hearing took place 4 June, immediately after the Nazi invasion of France and the evacuation of the British Expeditionary Force from Dunkirk), Congress had a right to know the names of the members of all political parties in the United States. Chestnut dismissed all Alpert's attempts to defend his clients' actions on the rights inherent in the Fourth Amendment but stated that he would accept a plea based on the Fifth Amendment. Of course use of this defense, Chestnut disingenuously pointed out, implied that the Communist Party involved its members in a criminal conspiracy.[38]

In June, Dies Committee investigators acquired copies of the election petitions collected by the Party to place their candidates on the Maryland ballot. On 2 July, committee investigators sent letters to all 2,200 petition-signers advising them that the Dies Committee possessed evidence of fraud relating to the petition. The committee implied, in selective quotes from the petition's fine print, that signing the document was tantamount to admitting Party membership and requested a response if any irregularity existed. The committee received 302 replies from intimidated signers, which were turned over to Maryland State's Attorney J. Bernard Wells.[39]

Wells initiated perjury charges against signature collectors Dorothy Rose Blumberg, Sophie Kaplan, Minnie Stambler, Paul Jarvis, Benjamin Davis, and Richard Bourne. Although over fifteen members of the Communist Party had assisted in collecting signatures, these six were singled out because they had collected at least part of the contested signatures.[40]

Wells based the perjury charges on an extremely narrow reading of the Maryland election law. The law required petition-gatherers to sign an oath, printed on the petition forms, that they personally knew the signers and could vouch that they were registered voters. In practical terms, such an oath could only be an affirmation of good faith, or it would be virtually impossible for a minority Party to qualify for ballot space, which, of course, may have been the unspoken purpose behind the law's wording.

The Communist Party issued a statement attacking the charges: "The State of Maryland is now witnessing one of the worst attacks on civil liberties in its history. This attack occurs at a time when the Wall Street monopolies and trusts are attempting to jam through the Fascist conscription bill, to black out civil liberties and plunge us into the war for empire and profits now raging in Europe." The Party's belief that the election case was linked to the world situation was entirely correct. Unfortunately for the beleaguered Communists, most people felt the world situation justified the government's actions.[41]

The *Sun* columnist C. P. Ives devoted an article to discussing the election petition controversy in which he agreed with the Communists that measures intended to "publicize Communist membership or affiliation" might be intimidating. But, he continued, this was the Communists' own fault; their recent actions had stripped Stalinist communism of its "recent aura of romanticism," and even a "Party booster like Eleanor Roosevelt" had recently listed Stalin as one of the world dictators abhorrent to true democrats. The crux of the matter, Ives believed, was that a unique situation had developed: "The Communists . . . are not merely an indigenous political party with an eye to the liquidation of the capitalists and the overturning of the republic; they are agents in good standing of a foreign dictatorship which is only technically friendly with us and is in close cahoots with another dictatorship not even technically friendly." Ives's column spelled out in painful detail the problem facing the Communists. Try as they might to explain it, the Soviet alliance with Hitler condemned them in the eyes of the public.[42]

The Party's troubles spread rapidly from the political sphere to the arena of organized labor. The Maryland–District of Columbia CIO met on 15 December 1940 in Hagerstown, Maryland, and passed two anti-Communist resolutions. James Dundon, president of Local 1874 of the Textile Workers Union in Cumberland, which had an active group of Communist members, led a walkout protesting that the resolutions were far too lenient. The Maryland CIO took no action against the Communists in the Cumberland textile union, but a similar action by a waterfront union put an end to the promising union careers of Communist Party members Norman Edward Dorland and Carl Bradley.[43]

In early 1938, the Industrial Union of Marine and Shipbuilding Workers of America (IUMSWA), a CIO affiliate, had begun organizing in the Baltimore shipyards. James "Scotty" Atkins, the first IUMSWA agent in the field, signed up members to the union by the simple expedient of showing shipyard workers the pay stubs of men represented by the union in New Jersey. In the summer of 1939, workers at Maryland Drydock, a ship repair yard near the blue-collar neighborhood of Brooklyn, voted for the union as their collective bargaining agent, becoming the first IUMSWA local in the city.[44]

In October of 1939, Bradley, who had just returned from the fighting in Spain, found work at the drydock and joined the union. Dorland, a former resident of Minnesota and an established Party member, arrived in Maryland about the same time and joined the union after hiring on as a machinist. Both

Bradley and Dorland worked diligently to improve the union, which needed the help, particularly since its first business agent, William Sinclar, had been removed from office over shortages in his account books. In August of 1940, Dorland became president of the newly organized Local 31 and was elected to the Baltimore Industrial Union Council. Bradley was assigned the difficult job of business agent and also gained a seat on the BIUC.[45]

But in January of 1941, the IUMSWA passed a new bylaw mandating that any member who furthered the cause of nazism, communism, or fascism would be expelled. Bradley's career in Spain and long history with the Communist Party was well known in Baltimore. Dorland, a relative newcomer, did not have the same reputation, but his views were easily discerned, and his wife was openly active in the Party in Philadelphia. Even though IUMSWA records indicate that both men performed their jobs well, the regional director, William Smith, preferred charges and expelled them both on 21 April 1941. The IUMSWA's national office then revoked Local 31's autonomy until new elections could be held.[46]

Dorland and Bradley attempted to fight their expulsion by forming a rump union from supporters at the shipyard. They initially received help from James Drury, the Communist head of the local National Maritime Union, who allowed them to use the Maritime Hall for meetings. Frank Bender, chairman of the Baltimore Industrial Union Council, also assisted them by allowing Bradley and Dorland to retain their seats on the council. The IUMSWA complained directly to Joe Curran, the head of the national NMU, and Drury withdrew his support. Bender's action prompted Local 31 to withdraw from the BIUC.[47]

The U.S. Navy, following the affair in the press, wrote to Maryland Drydock and asked that Bradley and Dorland be fired because their continued presence was a security risk. Maryland Drydock, which held a lucrative contract with the U.S. Navy for repair of naval and Coast Guard vessels, promptly obliged. Dorland and Bradley attended the IUMSWA convention in Atlantic City in September hoping to be given a chance to plead for simple reinstatement in the union, but convention officials refused to hear them and reconfirmed their intention to expel all Communists from the IUMSWA.[48]

The combination of the Dies Committee investigations, labor setbacks, and legal assaults on the Party put a tremendous strain on Albert Blumberg and may have contributed to a sharp outburst that came back to haunt him. While enrolled at the University of Alabama, William MacLeod, a Baltimore native, became seriously interested in communism. Home on spring break in 1941, MacLeod arranged for a meeting with Blumberg in the hope that he would ask him to join the Party. The two men met at a Park Avenue restaurant near Party headquarters and began talking over current events. Much to Mac-

Leod's surprise, Blumberg became very agitated when he suggested that social change could be a slow, peaceful process. Blumberg told MacLeod that major social changes could come about only by bloodshed and cited the Spanish civil war and the American Revolution as prime examples. Blumberg then asked the shocked young man if he were "prepared to take a rifle and fight in the streets of Baltimore" when the time came for the use of force and the expenditure of blood. MacLeod's interest in communism promptly disappeared, but he remembered the encounter and repeated it at Blumberg's trial on Smith Act charges many years later.[49]

Although convicted of perjury, Dorothy Rose Blumberg and her five co-defendants continued to protest their innocence and appealed for a new trial. Alpert succeeded in getting a second hearing for three of the defendants, but his request for a retrial for Blumberg; Sophie Kaplan, who was married to Carl Bradley; and Richard Bourne was denied. At their sentencing on 12 February 1941, Blumberg spoke for all three defendants, saying that she and her companions had collected signatures in good faith. Had they known that their oath was taken at their own peril, they would have checked the signatures with the Board of Elections. She defiantly added,

> But we would have got our two thousand signatures just the same . . . for our experience shows there are plenty of people who are willing to help minority parties get on the ballot. This prosecution is part of war hysteria as generated by the administration. This prosecution was not peculiar to Baltimore alone. Wherever there was an election campaign and the Communist party was particularly active intimidations and letters followed. . . . My friends and myself . . . know in our hearts we have not committed any crime.[50]

Judge Edwin Dickerson disagreed, replying that they had committed a serious offense striking at "the very heart of good government." He then levied fines of $1,000 on Blumberg, $500 on Kaplan, and $250 on Bourne and sentenced them all to one year in jail. The jail sentence, however, would be suspended if the fines were paid within thirty days, giving the defendants a stark choice between appealing the case or avoiding jail. After a few days of deliberation, all three paid the fines. Charges against Minnie Stambler, Paul Jarvis, and Benjamin Davis, who were awaiting an appeal, were dropped.[51]

The Communist Party rallied to challenge its growing chorus of critics with some of the old fighting spirit of the Third Period. In February of 1941, William Z. Foster came to Baltimore for the Party's celebration of the birthdays of Abraham Lincoln and Frederick Douglass. He denounced lend-lease, condemned the rise of American fascism, and did wonders for Party moral. In

March, Albert Blumberg brought suit against the state of Maryland to force it to allow the names of Communist Party candidates on the ballot. Blumberg argued that even without the contested signatures, the Party still had more names than state law required. The Maryland Supreme Court agreed, and the Communists appeared on the ballot. In the fall, the Party published its legislative agenda for 1941 and distributed copies to all state legislators. Many of the Party's goals, such as extending compulsory jury duty to women and establishing infant and child care health stations in poor areas of the state, were reasonable and deserved attention. Sadly, the rising wave of anticommunism prevented their consideration.[52]

In direct response to Blumberg's successful suit to put the Party's candidates on the ballot, the Maryland House of Delegates introduced legislation designed to keep the Party out of future elections. The measure required minority parties to type up a list of all ballot petition-signers and pay a twenty-five cent fee per name to have the list published. This not only would add $125 to the cost of campaigning but also would discourage most people from signing Party petitions in the first place.

Frederick Houck, a Democratic legislator from Baltimore County, called the measure "hysterical" and said it would affect only independent and fusion candidates. L. Harold Sothoron, a Democrat from Prince George's County, violently disagreed, declaring that the CPUSA was of no use to anyone and that "we cannot permit the termites to bore from within and destroy democracy." The Party tried to fight passage of the law through a front organization, the Maryland Association for Democratic Rights, founded by I. Duke Avnet in 1940, but the bill easily passed the House of Delegates by a vote of eighty-three to thirteen. Although the Party remained willing to fight, its non-Communist allies were dwindling, and the future looked very grim. Then, in June of 1941, Hitler's massed legions crossed the Soviet border in a colossal assault, and everything changed.[53]

7

Club Convoy and the Great Patriotic War

Hitler's attack on the Soviet Union freed the Communist Party from the constraints imposed on it by the Hitler-Stalin Pact. In 1939, the Maryland Party demonstrated its loyalty to the Soviet Union by retreating from antifascism to a stay-out-of-the-war platform, but it did so reluctantly. In the wake of Operation Barbarosa, the Party's change of line came with lightening speed and visible relief. On 13 June, Albert Blumberg issued a public manifesto stating that since the European conflict had changed from a capitalist war for profits to a war in defense of the socialist homeland, the Party would now promote active U.S. involvement on the side of the Allies.[1]

In the months following Blumberg's statement, the Party gave the impression of someone recovering from a long, cramped confinement. Communists who out of necessity had been keeping a low profile began making their views public. Party leaders obtained radio time for a series of broadcasts designed to whip up support for U.S. intervention. Branch and club meetings concentrated on ways to attract new members and increase circulation of Party periodicals and pamphlets. Old organizations devoted to opposing U.S. involvement in the European conflict were disbanded or transformed, and Party members were encouraged to join or support such traditional groups as the Red Cross, Community Chest, and USO. Party leaders decided to risk exposing secret Communists in various unions by asking them to become more involved in anti-Hitler demonstrations and to push their unions to urge repeal of the Neutrality Act.[2]

As the weeks slipped by with no decisive U.S. movement toward entering the war, the Party intensified its efforts. Club members in Baltimore and western Maryland were instructed to draw up lists of individuals with radical leanings so that free issues of the *Daily Worker* could be sent to them. A letter recounting the *Daily Worker*'s history and encouraging the recipients to subscribe would follow the complimentary papers. In November, the Party held its annual celebration of the Bolshevik Revolution, recast as a "Smash Hitler" rally with the national Party leader James Ford as the main speaker. Ford begged his fellow Americans to support stepped-up war production to relieve beleaguered Moscow, "because our future is wrapped up with the Soviet Union."[3]

On 7 December 1941, the Imperial Japanese Navy launched a surprise attack on U.S. military facilities at Pearl Harbor. Immediately after Roosevelt's call for a declaration of war, the CPUSA issued a statement pledging its loyalty, its labor, and its last drop of blood in support of the United States: "In all the factories and workshops of America the voice of freedom must be heard in the quickened pace of machines producing implements of war to save our nation and increase our aid to the Soviet Union, Great Britain, China, and all nations who are resisting the Hitler-Japanese aggression. All disputes in industry must now even more urgently than before be solved without interruption of production." The Party published its pledge on a handbill, which it distributed all over Maryland and sent to the local news media as a press release.[4]

The pledge of loyalty decisively ended two years in the wilderness for the Maryland Communist Party. The intense opposition directed at the Party during the years of the Non-Aggression Pact seemed to dissolve overnight, prompting the Communists to try to regain the position they had enjoyed at the height of the Popular Front. The Party's optimistic leaders might have been more cautious had they known that several months before their pledge of loyalty, the Federal Bureau of Investigation initiated regular surveillance of Party activities in Maryland and began to send informants into the Party's ranks.[5]

Since a detailed series of reports exists recording Albert Blumberg's efforts to better organize the western Maryland comrades, one of the informants appears to have been a member of the Party branch in Cumberland. By March of 1941, the western branch had its own organizer, Samuel Deane, and its own executive committee headed by Boyd Coleman. Party activities in Cumberland focused on continued organizing at the Celanese Mill as well as ongoing attempts to establish a Communist presence among railroad workers and coal miners. The Party branch also dabbled in politics, running at least two Allegheny County Communists for public office on the Democratic ticket. Joseph Barley sought a seat on the Cumberland City Council, while Eva Chaney, a very popular Communist from the textile mill, entered the 1942 contest for the Maryland House of Delegates.[6]

Albert Blumberg frequently journeyed to Cumberland to attend meetings, lead educational sessions, and meet secretly with George Meyers. After joining the Party, Meyers kept his membership secret and rose rapidly in organized labor, holding several offices in Local 1874 and in 1941 becoming president of the Maryland–District of Columbia CIO. Blumberg met with Meyers in regional hotels but was very careful never to be seen in public with his protege. Meyers, a robust and direct individual, chaffed at the careful, clandestine arrangements, which Blumberg seemed to enjoy, but Meyers did not break Party discipline.[7]

Blumberg received considerable assistance in western Maryland from Martin Chancey, the Party chairman in the District of Columbia. Chancey sometimes accompanied Blumberg to Cumberland, but, more often, he made solo trips to conduct classes and orient new members. The job proved to be very important since the new recruits were enthusiastic but often uninformed. At a western branch meeting in February 1942, new members asked such elementary questions as whether the Party was ruled from Russia and if it was an illegal organization. On another occasion, Chancey went to Cumberland to speak to the newly activated railroad unit about international affairs, mostly the conduct of the war, and was appalled at their lack of knowledge.[8]

The same group of new members who wanted to know if they had joined an illegal organization also requested help in establishing a Party club in Keyser, West Virginia, which they thought could function as a subsection of the club in Lonaconing, Maryland. Other recruits launched a campaign to establish a Party unit among the coal miners of the Georges Creek region near Frostburg, and special efforts were directed at the Greek and Italian communities in Cumberland. In spite of these activities, Blumberg frequently criticized the western Party members and was especially unhappy with their habit of signing their membership cards with assumed names. The reluctance of the westerners to be openly identified as Communists should not have surprised Blumberg, however, because the atmosphere in western Maryland was considerably more conservative than in Baltimore.[9]

One activity in which Baltimoreans and westerners could both participate was the wave of patriotism that swept over the country following the declaration of war. The Third Ward Party Club, headquartered at 1630 Bank Street, changed its name to Club Convoy, in honor of the U.S. effort to resupply England. The Fifteenth Ward Club started calling itself the Victory Club, and, in early 1943, Party application cards changed from traditional red to red, white, and blue. So many highly placed Party members joined the armed forces that the Maryland district was forced to import cadres from other regions to make up the deficit. The most well-known wartime replacements were Baltimore

City secretary Hardy L. Scott and his wife, Verna, who came to Maryland from Atlanta, Georgia. By late 1942, 50 members of the Maryland Communist Party had volunteered for the U.S. Army, while 153 men, drawn mostly from the waterfront units, were on active duty with the Merchant Marine.[10]

Roy Hudson came to Baltimore in December of 1942 to speak at the Polish Hall on Broadway in honor of his fellow seamen. Before Hudson's speech, Dorothy Rose Blumberg presented a service flag dedicated to Baltimore's mariners. The large banner held two stars, a blue one for the 153 men in service and a gold one honoring 5 of that number who had perished at sea. One of the sailors honored was Patrick Whalen, who joined the Merchant Marine shortly after Pearl Harbor. He was serving in the engine room of the SS *Illinois* when it was torpedoed by a German submarine on 1 June 1942. He was fifty-eight.[11]

Communist Party members had mixed experiences in the military. Although the Party suspended their membership for the duration of their enlistment, military authorities treated them with distrust. William Wood, whose brother Roy Wood was a section organizer in Baltimore, found himself confined to training exercises after his enlistment. Wood tried for several months to be given a combat assignment and finally appealed to his congressman, who arranged for him to be sent to Europe. Wood landed at Normandy sixty days after the invasion, fought his way into Bavaria, won a Purple Heart, and frequently wondered why he had worked so hard to get himself shot. George Meyers joined the army airforce but, unable to overcome the suspicion of his superior officers, served out his term as a radio operator in Alaska.[12]

Communist Party support for the U.S. war effort was exceeded only by the Party's backing of the Soviet war effort. Russian films and songs were staples at Party social gatherings, Party clubs held regular discussions of Soviet war reports, and everyone contributed to Russian War Relief Incorporated (RWRI). The FBI considered the RWRI to be an important Communist front group, and the special agent in charge of the Baltimore office reported on it regularly in his monthly memos. Although the RWRI received Party support, it was not a Party organization but a private agency, like the more famous Bundles for Britain. The RWRI held a number of charity banquets to raise funds for the Soviet Union. The two most successful featured Ivey Litvinoff, the wife of the Soviet ambassador, and the Russian sniper Ludmilla Pavlichenko. Together, the two women raised nearly thirty thousand dollars for Soviet relief.[13]

Party club discussions of the war, particularly on the fighting in the Soviet Union, were much more than simple summaries of news bulletins. Party commentators subjected war reports to careful analysis and took great care to put the correct spin on events. Hardy Scott explained to a gathering of western Maryland Communists that the Soviet seizure of Bessarabia, modern-day Moldava, had prevented Hitler from invading England. Blumberg told groups of Party members that the slowing of the Soviet advance in late 1942 was not a sign of flagging Soviet strength but was due to Stalin's refusal to fight the entire war on his own. The titanic battle that raged around the Volga River city of Stalingrad attracted particular comment from Party leaders. Not content with just describing the conflict as a major turning point in the war, they held it up as an example of Soviet youth dying to defend American cities. All Communist discussions of the war ended the same way, with a call for a second European front and the sooner the better.[14]

Blumberg thought that support for the Soviet Union should come, as much as possible, from the working class and encouraged labor unions to pass second-front resolutions. Despite his urging, the response from the unions was mixed. A few impressive rallies were staged, the most elaborate an IUMSWA rally featuring the heavyweight champion Jack Dempsey, but most of them were very small. The National Maritime Union continually passed second-front resolutions, but virtually all of its Baltimore officials were Communists. In the IUMSWA, despite the success of the Jack Dempsey rally, the second-front issue provoked a campaign directed against such resolutions on the grounds that military decisions should be left to the experts.[15]

Communist support for the CIO's no-strike pledge and the Party's constant efforts to integrate blacks into defense industries also had mixed results. In Cumberland, agitation for a strike against the Celanese Mill began in the summer of 1942, when the company revealed record profits because of the skyrocketing wartime demand for artificial silk. Many workers believed the time was ripe for a strike for better working conditions, higher wages, and a union shop. After some discussion, a planning committee approached open Communists at the plant asking the Party to lead the strike.[16]

Before the war, the Party would have leapt at the opportunity; now, however, they found themselves counseling moderation and stressing the importance of maintaining production. The Communists assured the workers that they backed their goals but suggested that they apply to the War Labor Relations Board for redress. Eventually, a wage and working-conditions package negotiated between labor and management was submitted to the War Labor Relations Board and finally accepted. But, in the meantime, agitation for a strike continued, and the Communists lost considerable prestige. In January of 1943, while the strike issue remained unresolved, the Celanese management, under government pressure, hired four black workers who were to start their jobs on 1 February. When the hiring was announced at a Textile Workers Union meeting, a near riot erupted as dozens of men loudly declared they would not work with blacks.[17]

The Party condemned all racist attitudes and backed resolutions calling for both dismissal from the union and termination of employment of men who refused to accept the new workers. Unfortunately, as the Communist organizer Boyd Coleman pointed out to Albert Blumberg, the situation was going to make it very hard to elect Party candidates in the upcoming union elections. Coleman's predictions came true a few months later when Boyd Payton, who headed the list of Party candidates for union office, was defeated by Felix Walters, chairman of the Engineering Department at the mill. Walters's victory was particularly galling because he had joined the Communist Party in November of 1942 but then turned against the Party and used the Communist position on the no-strike pledge and the black workers to his benefit.[18]

Albert Blumberg, in a postmortem of the elections, blamed the loss on the fact that the Communists had openly pursued a Party line rather than cloaking their objectives in CIO policies. William Taylor, the state chairman, contradicted Blumberg and blamed the loss on the Party's small size, a situation that he believed was now ripe for change. Fortunately for the Party, Walters proved to be a weak, opportunistic leader and was latter removed for incompetence after a Party-directed campaign. During his term of office, however, some of the newly hired black workers were fired by the Celanese Mill management, and the Party was unable to convince the union to intervene on their behalf.[19]

In Baltimore, the Communist Party faced different challenges to its program of integration because the racial situation in the port city was much more complex than in the relatively isolated western part of the state. On the waterfront, a high degree of racial mixing already existed because of the cosmopolitan nature of maritime industries and the efforts of the NMU. The NMU encouraged strikes against ships refusing to sail with an integrated or "checkerboard" crew and enforced strict equality in its on-shore facilities and hiring hall. Patrick Whalen, during his tenure as NMU chief, had developed a rough-and-ready approach to integrating waterfront bars. Whalen, accompanied by a group of mixed-race sailors, would enter a bar. If the owner protested that it was a whites-only establishment, Whalen would throw a beer mug through the back bar mirror and declare, "There, you've just been integrated."[20]

Off the waterfront, the Party continued its support of the NAACP and joined campaigns launched by civic and church groups aimed at creating greater equality and opening employment opportunities for the city's black population. Albert Blumberg ordered Party members to participate in a boycott of downtown businesses, which, although heavily patronized by blacks, refused to hire African American clerks. The Party also supported petition drives aimed at forcing the hiring of black streetcar drivers on trolley routes through black neighborhoods and to convince Baltimore Gas and Electric to hire black employees. African American Communists were encouraged to apply for employment at whites-only plants in hopes of breaking the color line. Communists employed in industries already hiring blacks actively pushed reluctant bosses, and frequently racist fellow employees, to allow black workers access to higher-paying whites-only jobs.[21]

At first, the Party engaged in antidiscrimination work on a piecemeal basis, but by early 1943 it began to coordinate its demands for African American equality through the Total War Employment Committee (TWEC). The TWEC, brainchild of Selma O'Har, president of the majority-black Frederick Douglass branch of the Baltimore Party, promoted racial equality as a national policy essential for full production in the war industries and vital for victory over the Fascist powers. A number of black community leaders agreed with the Communists that the time was ripe for exploiting patriotism in the service of racial justice and became TWEC supporters. A. J. Allen, from the Baltimore Urban League, and Lillie Jackson, president of the Baltimore NAACP, served as cochairs. Jackson's daughter, Juanita J. Mitchell, organized a civil rights march on Annapolis to bring the committee's views before Maryland's lawmakers.[22]

One of the committee's most important backers was J. E. T. Camper, a black physician and a founding member of the Baltimore NAACP. Camper, a graduate of the Howard University medical school, served in France during World War I and was inspired by his experiences there to begin a lifelong fight for civil rights. Camper may not have been a Party member, but he was always willing to assist the Party whenever it called on him. In February, Camper presided over a TWEC meeting at the Union Baptist Church, attended by twelve hundred people.[23]

Camper laid out the committee's program to integrate blacks into all American industries, while James Drury, the NMU chief, and Charles Houston, a former Howard University Law School dean, heaped scorn on the Baltimore phone and trolley companies for their refusal to hire from the black population. The meeting raised $155 and was judged a big success. The TWEC itself proved to be a triumph for the Communist Party, greatly enhancing its influence in the black community. Blacks churches welcomed TWEC organizers, the editors of the *Afro-American* endorsed its policies, and it received regular free publicity from the Chuck Richards radio show, which targeted black listeners.[24]

The combination of traditional Communist goals and patriotic, win-the-war appeals seemed unbeatable. Party recruitment climbed, Communist influence in labor and progressive circles increased, and the Party became more confident about airing its views openly under the Party banner. To a casual observer, it might have seemed that the Party had finally defeated its critics and won a place in the American political spectrum. However, Maryland's anti-Communists had not disappeared. Although the alliance with the Soviet Union considerably blunted their most powerful rhetorical tools, they remained in unreconstructed opposition to Communist beliefs and goals. The openness enjoyed by the Maryland Communists actually added new, often powerful allies to the anti-Communist ranks. The most formidable of these was the Catholic priest Father John Francis Cronin.

Father Cronin came to Baltimore with a well-developed sense of social justice, an attitude he had sharpened as a student of Father John Ryan, whose course on "Distributive Justice" Cronin took while at Catholic University. Armed with Pope Pius XII's Encyclical on Social Justice, Cronin and a wide circle of other clerics who thought of themselves as "labor priests" fanned out across the country teaching the message of the encyclical and organizing labor schools. The first labor school in Baltimore opened in the spring of 1939 at the Community House on Broadway after Cronin trained a number of priests in a month-long "School of Social Action" seminar. The school offered a series of twelve-week classes that concentrated on labor history, current union issues, and the teachings of the church.[25]

Cronin's activities were possible because of a shift in ecclesiastical opinion from insistence on purely Catholic trade unions to recognition of the need for religious influence in secular unions. Cronin sought to provide such influence by becoming involved in the drive to organize the CIO in Baltimore. He later recalled, "I don't remember exactly how I got into it. I just felt there was a need. . . . At that time labor was everlastingly grateful for any help they could get from the church. They needed respectability. I just offered to go around and talk to groups and help them organize. . . . Sometimes I would even go out and pass out leaflets. I'd get out as early as 4:30 A.M. and get the early shifts at the shipyards." When the IUMSWA started organizing the area shipyards, Cronin composed an entry for their recruiting pamphlet, *The Church Speaks Out for Unions*. Cronin asserted that the Catholic hierarchy fully backed labor's right, indeed duty, to organize and then praised the IUMSWA as a truly free, "thoroughly American union." The IUMSWA's American credentials could be established in dozens of ways, but the most telling, according to Cronin, was the union's 1940 decision to block Communists from all union offices.[26]

Although Cronin began keeping track of Communist attempts to infiltrate local unions as early as 1939, he did not believe that communism was a serious problem. Instead, as he related to colleagues years later, he felt that the claims of extensive Red influence in the New Deal and the CIO were the fantasies of frustrated politicians like Martin Dies. It therefore came as a surprise to Cronin when, in July of 1942, one of his former labor school students, Francis O'Brien, came to Cronin asking for help in preventing a Communist takeover of IUMSWA Local 43 at the Fairfield Yards. Cronin initially discounted O'Brien's story, but his attitude changed completely two days later when agents of the FBI approached him requesting his assistance with the same situation.[27]

In March of 1941, Bethlehem Steel began constructing a 174-acre, state-of-the-art shipyard. The immense facility, which incorporated an entire idle pullman car factory, applied assembly-line techniques to ship construction and by the end of the war had turned out over four hundred durable, ugly, but highly functional "Liberty Ships." Fairfield Yards' astounding productive capacity required equally astounding numbers of workers. By October 1941, when the IUMSWA won a National Labor Relations Board election entitling it to serve as the yard's collective bargaining agent, thirty-two thousand people were putting in forty-eight-hour weeks.[28]

A well-organized Communist fraction existed at the Fairfield Yards. However, the Party had learned a bitter lesson from Bradley's and Dorland's expulsion from IUMSWA Local 31, and none of the Communists employed in the yards were well-known as either Party members or fellow travelers. Because of the dramatic explosion of the Baltimore work force as hundreds of thousands of people flocked to the city seeking employment in the booming defense industry, it was fairly easy to find new faces to send into the shipyards. Bernard "Whitey" Goodfriend, a particularly active Communist, came from western Maryland, while another, the controversial Walter McManamon, arrived from Chicago, seeking work and fleeing an unsavory past.[29]

While Cronin investigated the situation at the yards, Local 43 prepared for union elections to be held in July of 1942. The Communists recruited a progressive rigger, B. T. (George) Manor, to run for president as head of the "rank-and-file slate" and salted his ticket with Communist Party members. Of the seven men running with Manor, four of them—Bob Kinney, Thomas Aylett, William Jorgenson, and Whitey Goodfriend, who headed the Communist fraction at the yards—were Party members, while the other three were close sympathizers. The rank-and-file slate advertised itself as an advocate of honest trade unionism. It ran on a platform supporting full production for victory over the Axis, a 100 percent union shop for the Fairfield yards, top wages for mechanics, labor representation on rationing boards, and no discrimination against any race or creed.[30]

To oppose the rank-and-file slate, O'Brien organized the "all-American ticket," with himself as the candidate for president. Instead of a detailed list of union priorities and positions on national and local issues, O'Brien's platform focused exclusively on communism. "Brother Members of Local 43," his campaign flyers read, "There has come into our midst a Communistic element which is as deadly to our United and Democratic Union of rank and file as the Axis powers are to our United and Democratic way of living. Help us drive out this element."[31]

The weeks leading up to the election were filled with heated rhetoric and intense leafleting. Both sides signed up as many new union members as possible, under the assumption that the recruits would vote for the people who brought them into the union. By 8 July, the first day of the three-day voting period, Local 43 boasted 15,000 eligible voters. Despite the intense campaigning and the extended polling hours, only 2,200 union members cast a ballot. The rank-and-file ticket won by a two-to-one margin; not a single member of O'Brien's coalition won an office.[32]

O'Brien reacted to his decisive defeat by seeking out Father Cronin and then faded from view, leaving the active fight to Frank Tesar, who had run for business agent on the all-American ticket, and a group of his former supporters. They received assistance from individuals opposed to the changes the Communists wanted to bring to the shipyard and from an unexpected source, a loosely organized group of men led by disaffected allies of the Communist fraction. This unlikely coalition launched a program of opposition to the officers of Local 43. Rebel-controlled departments called wildcat strikes, and some shop leaders encouraged their men to withhold union dues. The most disruptive actions came from the group of former fellow travelers led by George Shriner, Milton Faircloth, Ernest Goldsmith, and Anthony Ricci, who dedicated themselves to sabotaging union meetings. They engaged in a variety of tactics, from long-winded, pointless speeches and continual procedural challenges based on obscure parliamentary points to catcalls, clacking, and, on occasion, fisticuffs.[33]

In November, the constant disruptions, wildcat strikes, and escalating violence at the shipyards prompted both the Communist-led local and the more moderate members of the opposition to take action. The union leaders determined to rid themselves of the six worst offenders by expelling them from the union. Under the terms of the maintenance of membership clause in the contract with Bethlehem Steel, this would allow them to be fired from their jobs in the yard. On Tuesday, 17 November, a union trial board convened at the IUMSWA Hall on Park Avenue and heard charges against Ray Williams, George Shriner, Philip Bowman, Milton Faircloth, Anthony Ricci, and Ernest Goldsmith. The trial proceeded with great difficulty and was marked by egregious departures from procedure by both sides. In the end, the board ordered all six defendants expelled from the union. The verdict produced such an uproar that the city police had to be summoned to restore order. The next night, a union membership meeting assembled to hear a report of the trial board's proceeding and was also interrupted by rioting. The police were once again called in, and, in the confusion, someone made off with the union records.[34]

Two days later, the situation worsened as discontent, fanned primarily by the expelled men, spread across the yard, resulting in isolated assaults on suspected Communists. George Shriner led a two-hour work stoppage by over ten thousand men to demand that the Communists be thrown out of the yard. Admitted to the company offices, Shriner and a small delegation received a lecture from a naval officer, who told them that if the yard did not quiet down, the Third Corps Area command would take over. A company representative then blandly informed the strikers that the dispute had nothing to do with communism and that the company refused to intervene in factional disputes within the union. The anti-Communists, badly divided and without outside support, would doubtless have floundered at this juncture had Frank Tesar and Philip Bowman not been working quietly with Father Cronin.[35]

Sometime after the July election defeat, Cronin started bringing selected individuals to St. Mary's Seminary, where he taught economics. There the union members received instruction in parliamentary practice, rhetoric, and the finer points of organization. Cronin's anti-Communist work received the full backing of Archbishop Curley, who regarded Cronin's efforts as a local version of his own bitter opposition to international communism. The wartime alliance with the Soviet Union forced Curley to mute his criticism, but he still gave vent to an occasional outburst, deploring governmental "kowtowing to atheistic forces." Before actively engaging the Communist Party faction at the shipyards, Cronin presented the results of his investigation to a secret clerical council, which pledged its support and gave him the use of parish facilities.[36]

With the defeat of the anti-Communists looming, Cronin wrote to IUMSWA head John Green, described the deteriorating situation in Local 43, and recommended that the Communists be cast out and the local's autonomy suspended. The same day that Cronin mailed his letter, the six expelled men appeared at the union's headquarters in Camden, New Jersey, to protest their expulsion and unmask the Communists at the yard. George Shriner summarized recent events, taking care to cast the role of the anti-Communists in the best possible light. The most stunning moment came when Philip Bowman announced that he had placed two men inside the Communist Party. Both were present and prepared to testify to the extent of Communist influence in Local 43.[37]

The two men, Joseph Poe and J. L. Stallings, presented damning testimony. Recruited into the Communist Party in August, the two attended a series of Party meetings and identified virtually all the officers and active rank and filers of the local as Party members or close sympathizers. Poe, appointed Communist Party press director in October, was invited to attend the Baltimore Communist Party convention. There, much to his amazement, he heard Lucian Koch, the IUMSWA's port director, give a report on Party membership, indicating that there were 67 Communists at the yards and 836 in Baltimore.[38]

Besides naming names, Stallings and Poe related a fascinating account of a confident, active party. In contrast to the nervous days of the Non-Aggression Pact, Party members were causal about their affiliation. Whitey Goodfriend habitually carried around a four-inch stack of membership application cards and openly signed up new recruits. Most of the meetings Stallings and Poe attended took place at Club Convoy on Bank Street and were attended by a mixture of Party members and fellow travelers. The occasions had a festive air, combining political speeches and second-front resolutions with drinking, dancing, and socializing. Stallings recalled a conversation he had with Albert Blumberg and Sam Zebit that summed up the tone of the relaxed and confident Communist Party. The three men had gone to the Owl Club, a fashionable bar in a downtown hotel, to celebrate Stallings's membership. After having a few drinks, Blumberg asked Stallings if he had ever run into any Communists at the Fairfield Yards. When Stallings said no, Blumberg and Zebit replied, "That's funny," and were convulsed with gales of laughter.[39]

Faced with the testimony of Bowman's spies, backed up by Cronin's letters and confidential reports, John Green considered taking the priest's advice and suspending the local's autonomy while he conducted a full-scale investigation. He even went so far as to draw up a letter to that effect. Dated 21 November and addressed to the local's executive secretary, Parios Fleezanis, the letter, marked *never sent,* is still in the union's archives. Green appears to have changed his mind after consulting with Philip Van Gelder, the union's secretary-treasurer, who was at the very least a Party sympathizer if not secret member. Van Gelder advised Green to take the much less drastic step of suspending the expulsion of all the trial board defendants, except the irretrievably racist and anti-Semitic Ray Williams, pending a full investigation by the national office.[40]

Dissatisfied with the measured response, the anti-Communists submitted a signed petition to the general executive board of the union. It demanded the immediate expulsion of Port Director Lucian Koch and sixteen members of Local 43 under the union's anti-Communist clause. The petition must have produced a violent reaction in Camden because it was followed two days later by a second document bearing the note that it replaced the first, rather hasty, statement in all respects. The second petition, dated 27 November, showed distinct traces of Father Cronin's subtle touch.[41]

Unlike the first communication, drafted in the form of a heated letter to the editor, the 27 November petition adopted the style of legal documents, with carefully worded grievances and respectful requests. The petition charged the local's officers with neglect of union business, unconstitutional conduct of meetings, election fraud, and policies conductive to creating racial hatred. The Communist issue appeared last in a considerably watered-down form, simply stating that "most members have been convinced that many of the officers [follow] Communist rather than union policies." All the charges against Lucian Koch were completely withdrawn.[42]

Shortly after the receipt of the second petition, Van Gelder issued a statement in a special leaflet inserted in the *Fairfield Yardbird*. The flyer announced the suspension of all the orders of expulsion until the matter could be properly investigated by the general executive board. He congratulated Local 43 for its contributions to the war effort and warned that the national offices would not tolerate any racial or religious discrimination. Van Gelder stated firmly that while no one proved to be a Communist would be permitted to hold union office, charges of communism would not be allowed to disrupt the union. More ominously, he suggested that sinister outside forces, which would not be countenanced, lurked behind the disturbances at the yard. Van Gelder pointed his leaflet directly at Father Cronin and his associates, but the evidence suggests that they failed to heed the warning.[43]

A special committee of the IUMSWA's executive board convened at the Southern Hotel in Baltimore on 10 and 11 December to consider the charges of communism. Father Cronin attended both sessions; Philip Van Gelder presided. A verbatim transcript of the proceedings ran to 571 pages. A summary of the committee's findings, however, took up only a page and a half, and its final opinion occupied even less space. "After carefully studying the affidavits, listening to testimony, and studying the written transcript of the hearing, the committee has unanimously reached the following conclusion: . . . On the whole no tangible and compelling evidence of unquestioned character was presented to prove that any one of the accused was in fact a member of the Communist Party." The committee's findings stunned Cronin's people, but they regrouped and submitted another petition on 16 December.[44]

The new petition still demanded that the officers of Local 43 be removed, but the charges against them contained no trace of the previous accusations of Communist leanings. Instead, it claimed that the officers fostered "disruptive policies." Among the specific issues cited were lack of adequate arrangements for department or division meetings, failure to bond stewards and committee chairs, lack of an auditing committee, the presence of strikebreakers in important union functions, and dissemination of vile and slanderous statements in the *Yardbird*.[45]

Father Cronin followed the petition up with a confidential letter to John Green. Cronin conceded defeat in the special committee hearing and admitted that mistakes had been made on all sides. However, he still believed Local 43 was in serious trouble and maintained that his people were the union's best hope. He now felt he understood the seriousness of the "Negro question" and offered himself as a mediator in a three-way conference between blacks, whites, and company management.[46]

The Camden offices took no immediate action, prompting the Cronin group to seek a way to demonstrate its strength. A perfect occasion presented itself in the January 1943 elections for a handful of union offices and some vacant delegate slots on the Baltimore Industrial Union Council. Cronin assembled a caucus of his adherents, nominated a slate of candidates—dubbed the "Victory Ticket"—and sent his people into the yard to organize support. Victory ticket workers put a great deal of energy into the election. Charts of supporters, broken down by job description and shift and marked "Keep This Secret," were drawn up and circulated. Father Cronin hosted numerous strategy sessions at St. Mary's and peppered John Green with letters soliciting his support. Voting took place over a three-day period in late January, and the victory ticket was soundly defeated.[47]

On 28 January, Cronin wrote again to John Green: "I write this reeling under the double impact of an election defeat and a masterful smear by the local *CIO News*. In regard to the former may I repeat that the election was eminently fair. No alibis. No regrets. In regard to the latter, I wonder what those Jews think I am. Irishmen, like Scots, are not noted for running away from fights." Cronin continued by warning Green of serious malaise among most of the second and third shift workers and the building threat of a War Labor Board election to bring in a company union. Ironically, the people behind the company union movement were none other than Frank Tesar, Ray Williams, George Shriner, and Phil Bowman, Cronin's recent allies. Cronin ruefully admitted that he felt a little foolish about being lied to so often by his colleagues, but he staunchly maintained that the true root of the problem lay in the Communist domination of Local 43.[48]

True to his word, Cronin did not take the smear campaign lying down. He circulated his own flyer that featured a letter from Frank Bender, regional director of the CIO, praising Cronin's record as a friend of organized labor, and he wrote an article for the *Catholic Review* dismissing the charges against him. He later commented that the article was rather mild, but, "they are itching to pin a libel suit on me, so I nowhere stated that it was my belief that specific individuals were Communists."[49]

The officers of Local 43, their positions secured by the election victory, submitted a detailed response to the 16 December charges of unconstitutional behavior. The national office accepted their defense and in February convened a hearing to reconsider the expulsion charges against Shriner, Williams, and the rest. After receiving numerous depositions and hearing some fresh testimony, the national upheld the local's verdict and stripped the six defendants of their union membership. Company management, however, refused to honor the maintenance of membership clause, and all six retained their jobs at the shipyard, where they continued to form the core of an active opposition group.[50]

In November of 1942, while the battle in Local 43 raged at its hottest, the Party threw a public banquet in honor of Albert Blumberg's three years as secretary of the Maryland and District of Columbia Party. John Williamson, in Baltimore as the official representative of the National Committee, made a speech praising both the Soviet war effort and Blumberg: "It is your good fortune here in Maryland to have such a man who is not only a doctor of philosophy and a good Party leader, but a fighter and an organizer and a political leader of whom you all can be proud." At the conclusion of his speech, Williamson presented Blumberg with a watch and gave his wife a pen and pencil set. Blumberg had much to be proud of: Party membership in Maryland had passed the two thousand mark, and many of the Party's cherished programs appeared to be on the way to being enacted by the Roosevelt administration. Once a deadly adversary of the U.S. government, the Party now appeared to be in the role of loyal opposition and occasional ally.[51]

On 16 May 1943, John Williamson returned to the city, this time to announce that Albert Blumberg was to be made the CPUSA's legislative representative to Congress, where he would lobby on behalf of Party goals. District 34's executive board then elected Al Lannon, a former waterfront organizer, as Party secretary for Maryland and the District of Columbia and elevated Blumberg to the largely ceremonial post of District 34 chairman. With a lobbyist in Washington, the Communist Party had arrived, if not directly in the American mainstream, at least only a short distance to the left. A few days later, the distance was shortened even further when the Comintern announced its permanent dissolution.[52]

8

The Communist Political Association

On 22 May 1943, in a gesture calculated to appease Churchill and Roosevelt, Stalin ordered the dissolution of the Comintern. The official resolution of the Executive Committee of the Comintern softened the issues of political expediency. It recommended liquidation on the grounds that the maturing of the international parties and the uniting of the Allied nations against fascism had made the old organization obsolete. Maurice Thorez, an Executive Committee member, advanced the theory that the dissolution marked the ultimate fulfillment of the Popular Front. Stalin told the Reuters reporter Harold King that the Comintern's termination proved that the Soviet Union had no plans to "bolshevize" other nations and would help unite all progressive forces in the fight against fascism.[1]

Earl Browder applauded the announcement and pointed out that the CPUSA had anticipated the development by three years when it severed its ties with the international body in November of 1940. Communist Party members in Maryland found the end of the Comintern almost as liberating as the end of the Hitler-Stalin Pact. Discussions held in Party clubs throughout District 34 concluded that the termination of the Comintern strengthened the efforts of the united nations and revealed the hollowness of "Red scare" tactics directed against Communist labor organizers. Most important, it signaled Communists worldwide to throw all their support behind their national governments and focus their energies on domestic issues.[2]

Other commentators were less enthusiastic. Martin Dies praised the move as a step forward in U.S.-Soviet relations, but he pointed out that the dissolution proved he had been right all along in insisting that significant ties existed between Moscow and the CPUSA. The *Baltimore Sun* columnist C. P. Ives caustically called the liquidation of the Comintern a "brush off" of Browder's former claims of independence. Ives made fun of Browder's contention that the activities of the Dies Committee were an affront to U.S.-Soviet relations. Now it seemed, Ives wrote, that Stalin no longer cared how radicals were treated in the United States as long as he got the military assistance he needed. Ives ended his column by dismissing Browder and the American Party as a collection of "suckers and slickers."[3]

In July of 1943, Al Lannon began to reorganize District 34 as part of a national shake-up designed to move the Communist Party fully into mainstream American politics. Lannon abolished the old network of industrial clubs and integrated the members into the neighborhood clubs. In turn, the neighborhood clubs abandoned the practice of holding closed, members-only meetings and transformed themselves into community centers where everyone of a progressive bent could come and discuss the issues of the day. Lannon adopted a similar policy regarding labor organizing, telling Party members that they should seek to influence labor through education and example instead of trying to get Communists elected to union office.[4]

Lannon also took steps to tighten internal Party practices in District 34, in contrast to the Maryland Party's more open public face. He insisted on rigorous record keeping and held Communist officials accountable for timely dues collections. Albert Blumberg had emphasized the recruiting of blacks into the Party. Lannon noted that over 90 percent of the individuals signed up during the recent membership drive were black and ordered African American recruitment stopped. Instead, Party members were to work at keeping the new black members enrolled, active, and paid up. The Party in western Maryland, however, would continue to try to attract black members, especially those in AFL unions.[5]

Lannon visited the Cumberland Party to acquaint himself with the members and to explain the new policies personally. He emphasized the need for ending industrial units because they acted as magnets for anti-Communist cliques in target unions. "The Communist Party is now fighting for its legality," he told his attentive audience, "and must reach out now, not only to the trade unions, but to the masses." The American people were very militant, Lannon asserted, and, if properly educated, they would someday demonstrate their militancy by voting the Party into office.[6]

Lannon's reorganization of the Party did not take place without difficulties. FBI reports from late 1943 and early 1944 are filled with accounts of tension between the new Party boss and Albert Blumberg. Lannon accused Blumberg of inflating membership records, being lax about dues collection, and concealing the existence of a two thousand dollar secret fund. Lannon also felt compelled to "speak plainly" to Blumberg on several occasions about his attempts to continue to run the affairs of District 34.[7]

Shortly after taking office, Lannon conducted a bloodless purge of Blumberg's appointments to Party office. He removed Roy Wood from his post as Party treasurer and *Daily Worker* agent and fired Wood's wife, Lariene, from her job as director of the Free State Bookshop. Lannon also decided to demote Hardy Scott from the office of Baltimore city secretary to head of the troubled Frederick Douglass Club. Despite his conflict with her husband, Lannon left the very popular Dorothy Rose Blumberg in her position as Central Committee member and recording secretary. The source of the conflict between the two men appears to have been rooted in personal style. Blumberg, a somewhat aloof intellectual, drew most of his support from the "white-collar" element in the Communist Party, while Lannon, a bluff, hearty, outgoing individual, was the quintessential representative of the "working class." Today, Lannon is remembered with great fondness by veteran Party members in Baltimore, while Blumberg's name is rarely mentioned.[8]

Next to reorganizing the Party, Lannon's greatest challenge came from Father Cronin and his faction at the Fairfield Yards. In July of 1943, Cronin's allies conducted an aggressively anti-Communist election campaign. The Communists countered by backing a moderate ticket containing no known Party members and won easily. Although defeated in the union elections, the anti-Communists continued to disrupt meetings. Father Cronin relentlessly bombarded John Green with letters describing the situation in Baltimore and requesting intervention from the national organization. Green had the luxury of ignoring the labor priest, but Lannon could not, and, in September of 1943, he requested a meeting with Cronin.[9]

Cronin wrote to Green to congratulate him on his reelection as IUMSWA president and discussed the meeting at some length. Both he and Lannon were concerned about the "escape clause" in the latest contract with Bethlehem Steel. The clause could potentially be interpreted to allow workers at the yard to drop out of the union or vote in another collective-bargaining agent. Lannon estimated that as a result of the constant disruptions and controversies over the last year, union membership would drop to around a thousand if yard workers were not required to join the local. Cronin concurred with Lannon's estimate, noting that "if anyone should know the condition of Local Forty-three it should be Al Lannon since he and his predecessor have been running it for some time."[10]

To avoid the very real possibility of an AFL takeover, Lannon was willing to make concessions to Cronin if he would stop his disruptive tactics. Lannon and Cronin agreed to try to establish a more democratic union through well-chosen officers and stewards and better, more orderly meetings. They also thought that Joe DiGiacomo, the national representative assigned to the local after the July elections, should have a strong voice in running the union. In return, should everything go smoothly, Cronin would cease his involvement in union affairs and publicly call for unity. According to Cronin, the deal was "all very beautiful, if not too late."[11]

It was too late. Barely a month later, a series of petitions from the Communist faction arrived in Camden demanding the removal of the national representative on the grounds that "the most militant men have lost faith with Mr. DiGiacomo." The petitions cited incidents to prove that DiGiacomo no longer had the interests of the union at heart. The Communists had organized a group of workers at Hopeman Brothers, a Fairfield Yards subcontractor, but DiGiacomo blocked their incorporation into the local. Bethlehem Steel fired Bernard Jaffe, a Communist, after he responded to an ethnic insult with his fists. Jaffe protested the action, but DiGiacomo handled the grievance himself and upheld the company's decision. The pattern of complaints made it plain that DiGiacomo had allied himself with the Cronin faction.[12]

With DiGiacomo on his side, Father Cronin believed that the situation had reached a critical point. In December of 1943, he wrote a lengthy letter to his colleagues extolling their past efforts, encouraging them to stick together, and suggesting common cause with the other IUMSWA locals in Baltimore. He concluded by saying, "We have all made mistakes. We can all be wrong. But the cause is what counts. We should not rest until every Communist is out of every union position in every shift." The international officers in Camden responded to the renewed fighting, as they had done in the past, by backing the Communist faction and ordering DiGiacomo transferred to Wilmington. DiGiacomo refused to go, resigned from his union job, and accepted a position as a salaried employee of Bethlehem Steel.[13]

On 23 January 1944, a DiGiacomo supporter stood up at a regular union meeting, quoted the passage from the IUMSWA's constitution that equated communism with fascism and nazism, and demanded the removal of all un-American individuals from the union. This development greatly alarmed Lyman Covert, the port director of the IUMSWA, and inspired him to attend the next meeting. Later he wrote to Philip Van Gelder, saying, "I am convinced now (as you stated some time ago) that of the two elements one [the Cronin/DiGiacomo faction] is definitely more dangerous."[14]

On 9 February, the anti-Communist faction began distributing flyers at the yard, urging the workers to vote out the IUMSWA as their collective bargaining agent and to affiliate with the AFL boilermakers union. The officers of

Local 43 filed a lengthy report with the Camden headquarters and then, in an executive board hearing on 27 March, expelled the men who had lent their names and support to the AFL takeover attempt. The expelled men appealed the executive board's action, but the national office upheld the decision of the local. Bethlehem Steel, as before, refused to honor the maintenance of membership clause in the union contract and allowed the ousted men to retain their jobs at the yard. The Communists launched a smear campaign against the discharged men, calling them company stooges and accusing them, not without justification, of dual unionism. Finally in January of 1945, all of them were fired or transferred to other Bethlehem Steel operations.[15]

Faced with overwhelming defeat, Father Cronin published a series of articles in the *Catholic Review* defending his actions and explaining the situation to the Catholic community. Cronin began by ruefully stating, "Communism in Baltimore has grown up," and he continued with a brief account of the Communist Party's use of the U.S.-Soviet alliance to gain legitimacy and influence. Cronin scorned the Party's recent statement that it had abandoned the class struggle and no longer sought the goal of socialism, describing it as a "temporary policy designed to attract new members." Cronin recounted the founding of "Communist cells" in the Fairfield and Key Highway shipyards and at Maryland Drydock and warned that they exercised "considerable influence on union policy, extending at times to almost unchallenged control." Only the formation of a countermovement, Cronin wrote, had prevented hundreds of skilled Communists from "directing the labor destinies of over one hundred thousand Baltimore war workers."[16]

Lyman Covert responded to Cronin's articles by accusing him of using "storm trooper tactics" and cruelly smearing thousands of CIO war plant workers. Covert denounced Cronin's labor schools, saying that Cronin's "boys" had done nothing but disrupt honest and democratic union meetings. The activities of Cronin's acolytes did not stop at sabotaging meetings, Covert continued, but had damaged the war effort as well because they had instigated many of the work stoppages and ministrikes at the Fairfield Yards in clear violation of labor's no-strike pledge. Jack Flaherty, a Communist organizer for the United Electrical Workers, challenged the priest to produce proof of Communist influence and suggested that he would be better off confining himself to dispensing spiritual advice.[17]

Cronin countered his critics by flatly stating that he had supported no unauthorized strikes and that his first loyalty, unlike that of his opponents, was to the United States. He claimed that he had become involved in the labor scene in Baltimore only "to prevent the control of labor in war industries from falling into the hands of those guided by alien loyalties." Cronin cited as proof of his accusations "no less an authority than the State secretary of the Communist Party, Al Lannon." Lannon, Cronin stated, had admitted his control of some area labor unions and had affirmed the identities of several suspected Communists. Since Cronin did not supply any details or names, however, his defense appeared strikingly weak, while his opponents benefited from their strong offense.[18]

Cronin's struggles with the Communist faction at Local 43 inspired Martin Dies to launch his own investigation. Agents of the Dies Committee interviewed a number of Cronin's supporters, particularly Peter DeGuardia and Joseph Blumenfield, who agreed to testify before the committee in Washington. Blumenfield devoted most of his deposition to discussing the extent of Communist political activity, such as second-front rallies, conducted at Local 43's expense. DeGuardia, who had once worked closely with the Communist faction, identified a number of prominent Party members at the yard and emphasized the important roles played by Sheridan Albert and Whitey Goodfriend, leading Communists. Several other men also made brief statements supporting Blumenfield's and DeGuardia's testimony. But the hearings, conducted five months after the defeat of Cronin's faction, received little publicity.[19]

Cronin abandoned his attempts to defeat the Party in Local 43 and accepted a national-level assignment from the Catholic church. However, the setback did not end Father Cronin's anti-Communist career. In November of 1944, the American Council of Bishops asked the priest to take a year off his other duties to prepare a major study of communism in the United States. The result was Cronin's "Problem of American Communism in 1945." The full manuscript remains unpublished but was widely circulated in both Catholic and governmental circles. Portions of it, in pamphlet form, were distributed by the American Chamber of Commerce. The work is moderate in tone, is careful about its sources, and presents a realistic picture of the state of the CPUSA in 1945.[20]

By May of 1944, at about the same time Cronin withdrew from union politics, Al Lannon completed his reorganization of District 34. All of the industrial units had been dissolved and the members integrated into neighborhood units. Only the Day Club, created for men working evening and night shifts; the Foster Club, made up of Communists whose membership was not public; and the Railroad Club in Cumberland remained. In turn, the neighborhood clubs abandoned their political designations, no more Eleventh Ward Club or Fourteenth Ward Club, and adopted colorful names drawn from American history, such as the Benjamin Franklin Club, the Tom Paine Club, and the Liberty Club. The New York headquarters of the CPUSA changed the designation of Lannon's district from thirty-four to four as part of the Party's national reorganization.[21]

The Young Communist League underwent an even more dramatic reorganization. In November of 1943, Selma Wiess went to New York for the YCL convention. She returned confirmed as secretary of the American Youth for Democracy (AYD) in District 34. Wiess moved the AYD out of the back room of the Communist Party offices to a new location on Lexington Street, just around the corner from Party headquarters on Franklin Street. Although the AYD office was only a block away from Party headquarters, Wiess felt the move demonstrated the separation between the two organizations. Father Cronin disagreed and warned the readers of the *Catholic Review* that the transformation of the YCL into the AYD was one of name only.[22]

In its new incarnation, the AYD strove to attract a broad range of politically engaged young people. One of Wiess's innovations was the establishment of SOS (Sweethearts of Servicemen) clubs, which mixed patriotism and civic responsibility with junior-level USO activities. As Wiess explained to Corrine Shear, a fellow AYD worker, "It's up to [the SOS] to get persons interested enough in the program of the AYD to join . . . once in it's up to us to educate them around to communism." Unfortunately for Wiess, bringing people around to communism was easier said than done. In March of 1944, Al Lannon reviewed the AYD's membership lists and discovered that only thirty-five of the nearly five hundred members were enrolled in the Communist Party. Lannon found the ratio inexcusably low and ordered Wiess to incorporate more Party activity into AYD functions.[23]

The transformation of the Young Communist League into a broad-based political club anticipated the changes the Party itself underwent in May and June of 1944. In May, the Party met for two days to select delegates to the national convention and to debate a series of resolutions, the most important of which was the issue of a name change for the CPUSA. On 4 June 1944, sixty-one Communists, the returning delegates plus representatives from all the Maryland and District of Columbia Party units, gathered at the Greek Community Center on Preston Street in Baltimore. Lannon read the following resolution: "That the Maryland and District of Columbia Communist party be, and hereby is, dissolved and that the present officers thereof are authorized and directed to take all necessary steps to effectuate such dissolution and to liquidate its affairs and to turn over all its properties to the Maryland and District of Columbia organization of the Communist Political Association." The assembled delegates voted unanimously in favor of liquidation. District 4 of the CPUSA ceased to exist, and District 4 of the Communist Political Association (CPA) came into being. The change, Lannon insisted, was more than cosmetic and marked the end of the old Party's "struggle for partisan advantage for ourselves as a separate group."[24]

In keeping with the new organization's desire to integrate itself into American life, the chief executive officer became the president rather than the secretary, an old Bolshevik term. Lannon won the new post unopposed. The convention also elected five vice presidents—three, Al Blumberg, Sinch O'Har, and Doxey Wilkerson, from Baltimore; James Branca from the District of Columbia; and Eva Chaney from Cumberland—plus a secretary and treasurer. The convention ended with a pledge by the assembled delegates to enlist all former Communist Party members into the new organization. Skeptical FBI agents observing the proceedings had little doubt the delegates would achieve their goal. The special agent in charge of the Baltimore field division was so contemptuous of the change in organizational structure that he continued to refer to the CPA as "the Party" in all of his reports.[25]

One of the members of Lannon's audience was Mary Stalcup, a twenty-one-year-old beautician from Washington, D.C. Stalcup had appeared at Party headquarters in Washington in early 1943 clutching a batch of Communist pamphlets and requesting more information. James Branca and Martin Chancey welcomed the young woman and gave her a trial subscription to the *Daily Worker*. Much to their surprise, Stalcup reappeared at the Party offices a few weeks later complaining that her paper had never arrived. Chancey promised to fix the problem and invited her to an upcoming social event. Shortly afterward, Stalcup joined the Communist Party.[26]

Once in the Party, Stalcup excelled as a *Daily Worker* distributor and was appointed literature director for the Northeastern Washington Club. By 1944, Stalcup had gained such a good reputation that she was selected to attend the New York convention that liquidated the Communist Party at the national level. Shortly afterward, Stalcup was elected treasurer of the City Committee for Washington, D.C., responsible for collecting dues, keeping the Party books, and pruning membership lists. In 1945, she would be appointed treasurer of the District 4 Central Committee. Stalcup's rapid rise pleased her and delighted the FBI agents who had recruited her as an informant before her first visit to Washington Party headquarters.[27]

Stalcup's enlistment as an FBI informant is somewhat shadowy. According to testimony given before the House Committee on Un-American Activities, a Federal agent simply called her on the phone one day and asked to meet with her. After arriving at her house, the agent explained the threat posed to the United States by Communist activities and asked Stalcup to become a spy. Although Stalcup's statement may be true as far as it goes, it seems highly unlikely that the FBI recruited its agents through random phone surveys. Some prior connection between Stalcup and the FBI or possibly between Stalcup and the Party must have existed to inspire the FBI to make its proposition.[28]

Over the course of her long career as an FBI informant, Stalcup provided the bureau with thousands of pages of information about Communist activity. Her reports during 1944, however, must have been dull reading. Instead of plotting to overthrow the government, the Communists spent all their time promoting the policies of the Roosevelt administration and working hard to ensure the reelection of the president. From January until March, when financial problems forced them to stop, the Party hosted a series of radio broadcasts combining the Communist perspective on current events with support for the war and Roosevelt's leadership. One of the first broadcasts praised Roosevelt for his role at the Tehran conference with Churchill and Stalin and discussed how the decisions reached by the three leaders would shape the postwar world. Subsequent broadcasts considered the problems of African Americans and other issues affecting the home front. In March, Albert Blumberg spoke about the upcoming elections, exhorting his listeners to reelect Roosevelt at any cost.[29]

During the transformation of the CPUSA into the CPA, Communist leaders in District 4 began laying the groundwork for their election campaign. James Drury hosted a "Fourth Term for Roosevelt Rally" at the Fifth Regiment Armory, which featured a brief appearance by Mayor Theodore McKeldin. McKeldin, a Republican, remained at the rally only long enough to present gold star flags to the families of torpedoed seamen; he refused to be in the building when the resolution backing Roosevelt was passed. Doxey Wilkerson, in charge of the reelection campaign among blacks, went to see J. E. T. Camper of the Baltimore NAACP to ask him to spearhead the establishment of an organization to be called the Non-Partisan Committee for a Fourth Term for President Roosevelt. Wilkerson felt Camper was an excellent choice to head the committee because his opinion was respected in the black community and because he was close to the CPA. As an added bonus, Camper had remained a registered Republican, making him a perfect nonpartisan Roosevelt supporter.[30]

In September, District 4 began to prepare for the election in earnest. Although Earl Browder formally endorsed Roosevelt, none of the Party leaders in Maryland thought it would be a good idea for the CPA to campaign openly for the president. Instead, Dorothy Rose Blumberg visited each of the association's branches and outlined a plan to work within the Political Action Committee (PAC) of the CIO. Al Lannon divided Baltimore into precincts and in each one appointed an individual responsible for organizing an election committee. Tom Conners, the Communist who ran the Baltimore CIO-PAC, would then make the committee chair an official precinct captain and provide the group with CIO-PAC and Democratic Party literature. Dorothy Rose Blumberg took special care to instruct all potential election workers that under no circumstances were they to identify themselves as members of the CPA. If asked, they were to say only that they represented the CIO-PAC.[31]

The message promoted by the Communist election workers was neatly summed up in a pamphlet entitled *A Word to Wise Women: What Is the World Coming To?* written by Elizabeth Searle and Dorothy Strange, two Communists from the District of Columbia CPA. The pamphlet, a very sophisticated effort, pushed hard for the reelection of Roosevelt and laid out the CPA vision of a government-managed future of price controls, full child and health care, and complete integration of women and minorities into the work force. All of these benefits would be paid for out of the profits from a thriving economy based on international trade with the Soviet Union and the emerging democratic nations of Europe. The booklet was so well received that the national CPA offices had copies made for use all across the country.[32]

The return of Baltimore area college students to school revitalized the AYD, and Selma Wiess lost no time in putting her young charges on the street to do door-to-door canvassing and distribute literature. The AYD also campaigned among servicemen, particularly the younger ones, and even staged a radio play on station WCBM. Entitled "Johnny Get Your Ballot," the miniature drama urged servicemen to register as absentee voters and support Roosevelt. The AYD sponsored several live mock debates between a Democrat, Republican, and a "non-partisan representative of labor," usually a speaker from the CIO-PAC.[33]

During a confidential meeting of the Maryland CPA State Committee, Communist leaders created the Maryland Committee for the Re-election of Roosevelt and Truman. Virtually all of this committee's officers were non-Communist members of the American Soviet Friendship Committee or Russian War Relief Incorporated, and the majority of the rank and file were individuals who approved of Roosevelt's policy of cooperation with the Soviet Union. Camper's Non-Partisan Committee also featured a largely non-Communist membership, although Thomas Aylett, the chair of the financial committee was a well-known Communist from the Fairfield Yards. Dorothy Rose Blumberg took a special, although discrete, interest in the operations of the Non-Partisan Committee. She met weekly with Alfred McPherson, another prominent black Communist at the Fairfield Yards, who would then inform Aylett of her instructions during the course of the workday.[34]

To boost the campaign in western Maryland, Al Lannon transferred one of his best organizers, Bernard "Whitey" Goodfriend, to Cumberland. Lannon regretted loosing Goodfriend, but the shipbuilder had become so well known as a Communist that his usefulness at the Fairfield Yards was severely impaired. Goodfriend chose to run an openly Communist election campaign aimed at western Maryland's black citizens. In late October, he and a group of Communists gathered outside a black Republican Party rally in Cumberland and circulated among the people arriving for the meeting telling stories about South Carolina's Senator "Cotton" Ed Smith and his ties to the Ku Klux Klan. The Communists drew a bigger crowd outside than the one inside the meeting hall, and they eventually escorted everyone to a Democratic rally on the other side of town.[35]

As the date of the election drew closer, the Maryland Committee for the Re-Election of Roosevelt and Truman planned a series of public meetings in Baltimore, to be followed by a huge indoor rally in the Fifth Regiment Armory on 3 November. Florence Schwartz, the secretary of the National Maritime Union, handled the arrangements for the rally and deserves the lion's share of the credit for its success. A particularly energetic and ambitious Communist, Schwartz not only ran the day-to-day affairs of the maritime union but also worked closely with Conners, the CIO-PAC chief, and was an active member of the American Soviet Friendship Council. Schwartz boldly called up the White House and began working her way through the president's cabinet looking for speakers. Eventually Harold Ickes, secretary of the Interior, agreed to speak after Schwartz promised him a statewide radio hookup. She also obtained the services of A. F. Whitney, an official of the Brotherhood of Railroad Trainmen; Marshall Shepherd, the federal recorder of deeds; and actor/director Orson Wells, who canceled his appearance at the last minute.

Schwartz dragooned the CPA into a massive ticket-selling campaign, selling eight hundred tickets herself, and sought sponsorship from every union with a Communist presence. On the night of the third, a crowd estimated at seven to twelve thousand people poured into the armory to cheer for Roosevelt. The official Democratic Party rally, held the following week, drew only thirty-five hundred. On 7 November, Roosevelt swept to an unprecedented fourth-term victory. The CPA, despite its outward confidence, had believed that a Dewey victory was possible and had adopted a "group captain" system to carry the association swiftly underground should the worst happen.[36]

A few days after the election, the CPA's national treasurer, Charles Krumbein, visited Maryland and congratulated everyone on a fine job of electioneering. Krumbein believed that the *Daily Worker* had directly influenced at least 5 percent of the voting public and that the work of the CIO-PAC had accomplished even more. The election, Krumbein told his audience, indicated that a Democratic Popular Front government similar to those of "certain European countries" had been established in the United States. Krumbein and the Communists had a right to be pleased with themselves. Roosevelt's victory, compared with his earlier campaigns, had been thin, and CIO-PAC help had been significant. The historian Maurice Isserman puts it more strongly: "Roosevelt might have won without PAC but by a razor thin margin. And PAC might have functioned without the Communists, but it would have lost many of its most tireless cadres as well as much of the fervor of social mission that colored its appeal that year."[37]

After praising the election effort, Krumbein turned to another issue, the district's shortfall in dues collection. Maryland's Unity Club, formed by the 1943 merger of the Third Ward Club with the Lithuanian branch, presented a typical picture. Out of a total enrollment of 83, 63 members owed back dues, a 75 percent delinquency rate. In some clubs, the situation was much worse; the 237-member Frederick Douglass Club listed 223 delinquent Communists. Krumbein suggested that the shortfall in dues collection was a result of the club members' failure to appreciate the political importance of money. The real reason was probably political exhaustion after the intense election campaign.[38]

Much to Krumbein's gratification, no one in the local Party leadership had any intention of basking in victory. Lannon began a campaign to reenroll all association members, eliminate the dues problem, and put the CPA back in the black. The Maryland CPA normally operated on a two thousand dollar a month budget. However, the election activities of October and November created a deficit of several hundred dollars, temporarily made good by "loans" from well-heeled Communists. Selma Wiess and the AYD took time off to throw themselves a victory party but then turned their attention to expanding the base of the youth organization by founding more SOS clubs. Wiess also consulted with Al Lannon about the possibility of creating an AYD political action committee that would appeal to those interested in politics but not in the AYD itself. Of course, the best of these youths would be recruited into the AYD and the best of those into the CPA.[39]

In December, Florence Schwartz, Al Lannon, and Whitey Goodfriend attended the Maryland–District of Columbia Industrial Union Council convention and successfully placed nine Communists among the organization's twenty-one officers. The Communist presence did not go unnoticed, and there were widespread accusations that the CPA completely controlled the organization. Ulysses DeDominicis, the council president, denied any Communist influence, calling any such accusation "unprincipled balderdash." But both Local 1874 of the Textile Workers Union in Cumberland and the United Wholesale and Retail Workers Union in Washington withdrew from the council, citing excessive Communist influence as their motive. Shortly after the convention, Local 33 of the IUMSWA also withdrew, citing the Communist leanings of the Industrial Union Council's secretary-treasurer Sidney Katz, coupled with his interference in union affairs, as the reasons for the local's action.[40]

Although vexing, the anti-Communist outburst did not unduly concern Lannon. The United Wholesale and Retail Workers Union's action came as no surprise because its main organizer, Nathan Klein, was a well-known anti-Communist. Local 33 was the smallest of the four marine worker divisions and also had a long history of anticommunism. The Textile Workers Union's withdrawal was potentially more serious, but it had been voted on by a minority of the organization's membership. Upon Goodfriend's return to western Maryland, he launched a campaign that brought Local 1874 back into the Industrial Union Council by January of 1945.

In all other areas, the CPA remained strong. Goodfriend created CPA clubs in Hagerstown and Frostburg, finally extending a substantial, organized Communist presence beyond Cumberland. The CIO-PAC, in response to the transformation of the national organization into the National Citizens Political Action Committee, reorganized itself as the Maryland Citizens Political Action Committee and made plans to continue its work of activism and political education. With continuing CPA control over the NMU and substantial Communist presence on the city and state industrial union councils, Lannon could congratulate himself on a solid position in labor.[41]

The Party's prestige among blacks had slipped, however. During the election, the predominately black Frederick Douglass Club enrolled over two hundred members, but by the January 1945 reregistration drive, club membership had declined to forty-three. Lannon sought to regain the association's standing by bringing Connie Jackson, a nationally prominent black Communist, to Baltimore to take over as membership director from Dorothy Rose Blumberg. At the same time, a murder case on the Eastern Shore also seemed to present the CPA with another chance to influence blacks. Early in the new year, police officers arrested two black brothers, eighteen-year-old Weldon Jones and fifteen-year-old Holbrook Jones, for killing Raynor Graham, the owner of an oyster-processing plant near Salisbury; assaulting seventeen-year-old Kenneth Willing; and raping two women. Tried only on the murder charge, the two boys were both found guilty. Weldon received the death penalty, while Holbrook was given a life sentence.[42]

The verdict and harsh sentences prompted a joint investigation of the case by the CPA and the Baltimore chapter of the NAACP. On 6 May 1945, the *Daily Worker* published the investigation's findings in an article entitled "Did Maryland Frame Negro Youths?" The article advanced the theory that Graham had been accidentally shot by white hunters, who then framed the Jones brothers as a cover-up. Juanita Jackson Mitchell, J. E. T. Camper, and Connie Jackson established the Citizens Committee for Justice, which circulated petitions and sent resolutions to Governor Herbert O'Conor requesting a new trial. But the committee was unable to generate more then casual interest beyond circles already in sympathy with Communist causes.[43]

In January of 1945, the anti-Communists in IUMSWA Local 43 rose from the dead. A ragged alliance of former Cronin protegees and right-wingers packed crucial union meetings with their supporters and passed a series of resolutions designed to eliminate Communist influence in the local. One resolution disaffiliated the local from the state-level Industrial Union Council; another dismissed I. Duke Avnet, a fellow traveler and possible Communist, as the local's attorney (Avnet's fees for 1944 had run in excess of five thousand dollars). The Communist faction under the leadership of Walter McManamon, the local's business agent, fought back by using the same disruptive tactics once employed by Cronin's loyalists.

The IUMSWA's new regional director, Charles Leone, attended several meetings of Local 43 and, disgusted by what he saw, reported to the new national secretary, Ross D. Blood: "As usual [the meeting] was boisterous and rowdy. Several fights took place. The lights in the hall went off several times. The meeting lasted from 2 P.M. to 7 P.M. The minority group tried in every way to delay, stall, confuse, or adjourn the meeting. At one point, although I hesitated because I wanted to take a hands off attitude for once, I had to go down to the rostrum to ask the assembly to get down to order and I lashed both groups for the disgraceful way of conducting themselves at a union meeting." Leone warned the feuding factions that if they refused to reform themselves, he would see that the job was done for them. Despite Leone's good intentions, the factionalism at Local 43 proved to be too much for him. After unsuccessfully trying to arrange special elections at the local, Leone wrote to McManamon that he could do anything "your little heart desires. . . . To be explicit, I am not interested in the party politics being played in your local and don't deem it necessary to lose my mind over the situation."[44]

A month after Leone's letter to McManamon, the national office finally took action and suspended the local's autonomy. Ross D. Blood traveled from Camden to Baltimore and personally assembled an interim board made up of equal numbers of members drawn from each faction. Initially, the Communist faction saw the action as a chance to regain complete control of the union and sought to cooperate with Blood. But after Blood made it plain that he lacked the pro-Communist sympathies of the recently drafted Philip Van Gelder, the Communists withdrew from the interim union board and began a vigorous and misguided campaign of opposition.[45]

The McManamon faction published a newspaper smearing the national office and accusing it of being behind every problem and factional dispute that had rocked Local 43 during its brief and turbulent history. Father Cronin and his original band of anti-Communists vanished, as did any suggestion that McManamon's faction had ever engaged in disruptive behavior. McManamon's tactics failed catastrophically. The Communists no longer had friends in high places, and the slowdown in ship building as World War II drew to a close cost many of the faction members their jobs. By April of 1945, the CPA had ceased to play a role of any significance in Local 43.[46]

Other disasters quickly followed. IUMSWA Local 24 at Maryland Drydock had its autonomy lifted, and the influence of the Communist element was blunted when Julia Katz, a Communist who had edited the local's newspaper and informally ran the union office, was fired. Ed Peters, the Communist organizer for United Auto Workers Local 738, was forced to agreed to cooperate with the anti-Communist faction for one year to preserve the positions of the Party members employed at the Broening Highway Factory. All of these disruptions paled beside the trouble that erupted in the longtime Communist stronghold of the National Maritime Union.[47]

The problem began as a personality clash between Harry Connor, Al Lannon's handpicked successor to James Drury, who left for San Francisco in the summer of 1944, and the inexhaustible Florence Schwartz. During an extended absence in New York, Connor became convinced that Schwartz was conspiring against him and fired her immediately after his return. Lannon demanded that the New York office remove Connor and reinstate Schwartz. A few years earlier, Lannon's request would have been quickly met, but by 1945 Communist influence was waning as Joe Curran, the NMU's national leader, slowly turned against his former allies. Instead of getting Connor removed, Lannon had to mend his fences. After several meetings with Connor, Lannon informed other District 4 leaders that he felt Connor could do "a good job" at the NMU.[48]

Along with his labor problems, Lannon faced difficulties in the CPA itself. In January, the District Committee of the CPA expelled Thomas Aylett, one of the most prominent black Communists at Local 43. Aylett had allowed race to take precedence over politics and, despite CPA instructions, had continued to associate with a group of pro–civil rights but anti-Communist blacks. The next month, the District Committee voted to relieve Eva Chaney from all her duties, pending executive action by Lannon and Goodfriend. The District Committee charged that Chaney had failed to properly carry out her union and CPA duties as the direct result of an irregular personal life, which included "personal misconduct prejudicial to the working class and the CPA, scandalous behavior resulting in two appearances in police court in Cumberland [and] intimate association with a man known to be anti-semitic and anti-negro." In May, Lannon and Goodfriend removed Chaney from her District Committee positions but allowed her to remain in the CPA.[49]

Among the wide variety of progressive publications in Maryland was a small paper called *People,* owned by Herbert Sugar, an independent-minded editor who employed two Communists on his editorial staff. In February of 1945, Sugar entered the armed forces and the Communists—Earl Homer, vice president of the Ben Franklin Club, and Earl Yardman, a Ben Franklin Club member—took complete control of the paper. Tom Conners, director of the Maryland Committee for the Re-election of Roosevelt and Truman, offered his financial support, and the paper was up and running as an entirely Communist organ.[50]

Albert Blumberg approved of the venture and submitted articles based on his experiences in Washington. Dorothy Rose Blumberg, however, objected strongly to the activity surrounding *People,* because it took time away from increasing the circulation of the *Daily Worker* and competed with that paper for readers. To Homer and Yardman, such criticism made little sense since under their editorship *People* hewed strictly to the Communist Party line. As long as the right message got out, they asked, what did the medium matter? Dorothy Rose Blumberg ignored such arguments and continued her outspoken opposition to *People,* which suspended publication in April of 1945.[51]

Homer and Yardman did have a point: getting the Communist message out was not as easy as it had been during the height of the war. In March, Communists in the United Office and Professional Workers of America (UOPWA), the State, County and Municipal Workers of America (SCMWA), and the Federal Workers of America (FWA) formed the Committee of White Collar and Fixed Income Workers. The members of the committee persuaded their unions to sponsor a conference on the postwar problems facing salaried workers and extended speaking invitations to a number of members of Congress. However, three of the invited legislators publicly refused to attend, and one of them, Maryland's Representative Thomas D'Alesandro, explicitly cited Communist control of the committee as the reason for his refusal. The conference took place on 11 March, but only seventy-five people, most of whom were well known in CPA circles, attended.[52]

Some bright spots existed in the difficult spring of 1945. American Youth for Democracy continued to attract new members and gain acceptance in mainstream society. The organization spent the early weeks of 1945 reenrolling its members and then devoted its energy to sponsoring a mass rally and gala banquet called a "Salute to Our Fighting Men." Wiess convinced John Coffee, a congressman from Washington State, to be honorary chairman. Richard Eaton, a well-known Baltimore area news commentator, agreed to serve as master of ceremonies. In her day-to-day organizing work, Wiess benefited from the close assistance of Barbara Woolcott Brooks, the niece of the late Alexander Woolcott, famous as the "Town Crier." Brooks's name added respectability and panache to the proposed celebration.[53]

The banquet, held 19 April at the Lord Baltimore Hotel, proved a great success and raised over six hundred dollars. Three hundred and fifty people, including fifty blacks, the maximum the hotel would allow, enjoyed an excellent dinner, accompanied by music, skits, and the presentation of awards to four winners of the Purple Heart. Receiving awards were Marine Sergeant Al Schmidt, a veteran of the fighting on Guadalcanal; Lieutenant Eleanor O. Lee, an army nurse from Cumberland who had been taken prisoner at Bataan; Captain Elwood Driver, a fighter pilot with the 99th Pursuit Squadron; and Joseph Rose, a seaman and Baltimore native who had been a prisoner of war in Germany. Mayor McKeldin sent a representative, and numerous celebrities from Baltimore and Washington also attended.[54]

Connie Jackson and Elizabeth Fields secured airtime on station WCAO for a broadcast entitled "How Communists Are Helping the Struggle for Jobs, Security, and Lasting Peace." A CIO-PAC banquet, held to erase the debt accumulated during the presidential election, sold three hundred tickets and raised enough money to clear the organization's books. The CPA's day-to-day activities continued to run smoothly, dues were collected, and regular club and citywide meetings were held as scheduled. Such national leaders as Gilbert Green, national chairman of the AYD, and James Ford, the regular Communist candidate for vice president, continued to come and go. Earl Reno's tireless assistant and significant other, Mary Himoff, stopped by to discuss the program of the Jewish Congress.[55]

Despite the sudden loss of influence in labor and evidence of the growing strength of anticommunism, Lannon remained optimistic. In March, Earl Browder, the source of Lannon's optimism, published *America's Decisive Battle*, a pamphlet that laid out his worldview. Browder stated that the world had divided into two hostile camps, one camp supported Adolf Hitler and the other the new world order of international cooperation outlined at the Yalta Conference. In early April, American and Soviet troops linked up, cutting Germany in half. Hitler committed suicide on 30 April, Berlin fell to the Soviets two days later, and Germany itself surrendered on 7 May. Unfortunately for Al Lannon and his patron Earl Browder, the fall of Nazi Germany marked not the beginning of a new world order of socialism and international harmony but the beginning of the end of American and Soviet cooperation.[56]

9

"Wallace and His Communists"

On 13 April 1945, banner headlines worldwide announced the death of Franklin Roosevelt and Harry S. Truman's elevation to the presidency. Roosevelt had tolerated support from American Communists and believed that Stalin could be managed with a moderate but firm approach. In contrast, Truman viewed homegrown Communists with dark suspicion and entered office determined to "get tough" with the Russians. During his first meeting with Vyacheslav Molotov, the Soviet foreign minister, Truman spoke so roughly and plainly that Molotov, a veteran of the blood purges, turned a little pale. The change in attitude at the top of the government would disastrously affect the American Communist Party, but the first, quite unexpected, upheaval came not from Washington but from Moscow.

After the German defeat at Stalingrad and Kursk, Stalin began making plans for the postwar world, a world in which the Soviets would have an immense zone of security in Eastern Europe and an aggressive political arm in the "bourgeois West." The transformation of the CPUSA into the CPA made the organization unsuitable to the task, and Stalin arranged to let the Americans know that a change was necessary. In December 1944, when Maurice Thorez returned from Moscow to assume his duties as head of the French Communist Party, he brought with him a number of American Communist Party documents that Stalin had given him.

Thorez turned the material over to his lieutenant, Jacques Duclos, who used it as the basis for an article that appeared in the French journal *Cahiers du communisme*. The essay criticized the liquidation of the CPUSA and called for the return of an independent working-class party. A French Communist on his way to the founding convention of the United Nations in San Francisco hand-delivered the article, thereafter known as the Duclos letter, to Earl Browder. Browder responded cautiously, admitting that the Duclos letter "reflected the general trend of opinion of European Marxists" and conceding that a political inventory on the part of the American Communist movement was needed.[1]

The publication of the Duclos letter, along with Browder's remarks, in the 24 May issue of the *Daily Worker* came as a complete surprise to the members of the Maryland CPA. Al Lannon canceled his plans for a medical check-up, expressed his opinion that the letter was the work of an anti-Browder clique, and stated that he would "go down the line with Browder." Whitey Goodfriend, the Communist organizer in western Maryland, loyally voiced his support of both Lannon and Browder. But the two men were alone. A group led by Albert Blumberg embraced the criticisms of the Duclos letter and threw its support behind Browder's rival, William Z. Foster. Elizabeth Fields, a Communist in Blumberg's camp, summed up the group's attitude: "The article is not just . . . from either Duclos or the French Marxists. It is actually the opinion of all the European Marxists and they raise the question seriously that we have deviated from the science of Marxism."[2]

Despite Lannon's growing isolation in District 4, he remained loyal to Browder and only reluctantly agreed to support Foster should he be elected head of a revived Communist Party. In June, Lannon and Goodfriend attended a hastily called National Committee meeting in New York, and both sought personal interviews with the embattled leader. Lannon emerged from the meeting with his admiration for Browder still intact, but Goodfriend began to reconsider his position.[3]

On 19 June, the *Daily Worker* published a letter from Goodfriend calling on Browder to renounce his past ideas and listen to the instincts of the working class. Goodfriend claimed that he changed his mind about Browder at a Cumberland CPA meeting when an older Communist asked him how he stood. "Well I'm still with Tehran," he had replied. "Listen," the veteran responded, "If you get up . . . and take Browder's position, I'll throw you out of the hall." Goodfriend declared that such intensity and lack of ambiguity from someone he regarded as the embodiment of working-class sentiment erased his own doubts, and he aligned himself with Blumberg and the anti-Browder faction.[4]

On 22 June, the National Committee met and voted unanimously to call a Party congress for 26 July. The National Committee then absolved itself of the blunder of liquidation by passing a resolution holding Earl Browder alone responsible for the CPA's mistakes. District 4 representatives met in early July to elect delegates to the upcoming convention and pass resolutions for submission to the national organization. Some of the resolutions, such as one calling for a reconstructed Communist Party, were most likely dictated by the national organization. However, other motions, such as one abolishing the large, unwieldy neighborhood units in favor of restored industrial clubs and another requesting the reestablishment of a Communist youth organization, seem to reflect local dissatisfaction with Lannon's policies.[5]

The Baltimore Communists had gone along with the changeover to residential clubs somewhat reluctantly, and despite Lannon's frequent insistence that everything was running smoothly, the new configuration was plagued with problems. The elimination of the industrial clubs caused such a falloff in attendance by union members that Lannon had to appoint strong labor figures as club presidents in an effort to restore worker interest in the weekly sessions. Other individuals complained that the enlarged neighborhood clubs were located so far away from their homes that it was difficult for them to attend regular meetings or participate in the reenrollment campaigns.[6]

At the time of the July convention, the American Youth for Democracy boasted a district membership of 278 youths organized into fourteen clubs and appeared to be one of Lannon's unqualified successes. But the organization had failed to funnel talented youths into the Communist Political Association and had so diluted its Communist message that it was indistinguishable from similar mainstream organizations. Worse, many of the members of the AYD and the SOS harbored strong racist sentiments. AYD's leader, Selma Wiess, confessed that the racist attitudes of her charges were so pervasive that she sometimes felt she might just as well be trying "to build a Communist club in some town in Mississippi or Georgia."[7]

By August of 1945, national and local leaders had completed the restoration of the Communist Party of the United States of America (CPUSA). Al Lannon retained the top job in District 4, but he had a new title, general secretary, adopted in honor of Joseph Stalin. The atmosphere in Maryland changed considerably. Party leaders confessed to feeling a sense of renewed spirit inspired by the excitement of once again confronting the established order. The rank and file welcomed the reestablishment of industrial units because it put them in regular contact with people who shared their experiences, interests, and general lifestyle. During its brief life, the CPA had tried but failed to organize a series of classes on Marx and Lenin. Now several classes were offered simultaneously, and dozens of Communists renewed their acquaintance with the Little Lenin Library, an inexpensive series of titles that served as basic textbooks.[8]

Along with the organizational and mood changes came profound shifts in Party policy. Following the surrender of Japan in August of 1945, the Communist Party dropped its call for an internationally engaged United States. Instead, the CPUSA loudly demanded the return of all American soldiers from overseas and vigorously opposed any interference with the emerging states in Eastern Europe or with Mao Tse-tung's Chinese Communist Party. Domestically, the Party still sought the establishment of socialism but rejected the idea that a peaceful transition was possible. During a visit to western Maryland, Lannon told a Party club in Cumberland that a socialist revolution would not be possible without the support of the Red Army, which could reach America's industrial heartland by invading Alaska and marching through Canada.[9]

Instead of the backing it had given to Roosevelt, the CPUSA viewed the Truman administration with increasing suspicion and hostility. Initially, the Party's various allies supported its criticism of the Truman administration, but subtle gaps were opening up, threatening to split the Party from its former friends. The NAACP joined the Party in its censure of Truman for failing to secure renewed funding for the Fair Employment Practices Commission (FEPC), which both organizations believed was essential to eliminating racial inequality in the postwar era. But when Dorothy Rose Blumberg and Connie Jackson accompanied an NAACP delegation to Washington to lobby for renewed FEPC funding, they were not allowed to enter congressmen's offices with the other delegates.[10]

In February of 1946, Al Lannon quietly resigned his post and departed for California. He was replaced by Philip Frankfeld, a former New England Party chief and longtime Foster supporter. Most of the individuals responsible for running the Party under Lannon remained to work for Frankfeld, but there were some changes. Whitey Goodfriend left his post in Cumberland to take up new duties in the Party organization in Cleveland. Dorothy Strange, coauthor of *A Word to Wise Women,* also relocated. Her place on the District 4 Council was taken by Mary Stalcup, the hard-working FBI informant. Shortly after Stalcup assumed her new duties, the Party began implementing the first stages of an improved security apparatus. All Party clubs were gradually divided into smaller subgroups under the control of group captains, and club membership lists were eliminated. However, central lists continued to be maintained on three by five cards for a short time. Mary Stalcup passed the FBI a stack bearing the names and addresses of 470 Communists in the Baltimore area before the practice was discontinued.[11]

Demobilization of the armed forces brought old Party members back into the state. William C. Taylor, the African American Communist who served as state chairman in the 1930s, became the head of the Communist veterans' organization after his enlistment expired. William Wood returned from Europe with a Purple Heart and lieutenant bars and went to work at the Sparrows Point steel mill. George Meyers came back from his tour of duty in the Aleutian Islands and, like Wood, went to work at Sparrows Point. Unlike Wood, Meyers openly announced his Party membership and assumed official duties as the secretary of labor for District 4.[12]

The employment of many leading cadres at Sparrows Point was not a coincidence but the result of a deliberate plan on the part of the district's leadership to colonize the steel industry. The plan, which evolved gradually over the course of a year, owed its birth to a combination of necessity and Marxist theory. By 1946, the Communists had lost most of their influence in the Baltimore maritime industries. Employee cutbacks and a concerted anti-Communist campaign had driven all but a few isolated individuals from the IUMSWA locals, and the increasingly anti-Communist attitude of Joe Curran made the Party's position in the NMU difficult. Marxist theory held that the most advanced and enlightened workers were those concentrated in large, highly organized industries. Frankfeld and Meyers, seeking a way to recoup their losses in the marine industries, naturally selected the steel mills as the major point of concentration. The Party did not give up on the waterfront, but activities there were now assigned only secondary importance, with the continuing attempt to organize electrical workers a distant third.[13]

By the fall of 1946, Frankfeld had created a militant, centralized organization ready to advance the Party agenda and do battle with American society. The Party chief had his work cut out for him because more people in Maryland were becoming openly hostile to the presence of the CPUSA. In March, barely a month after Frankfeld took up his duties, Kenneth Fooks, a candidate for the state senate from the Fifth District, announced that if elected, he would propose legislation banning Communists from the state payroll and any public office. Fooks warned against "a power grabbing socialist minority" that draped itself in the American and Maryland flags "while biding their time to unfurl the Red flag with all their despotic arrogance." These people had insinuated themselves into the Democratic Party, Fooks told his audience, and it was now time to draw the sword of truth and slash from the "ermine toga" of Maryland democracy "the red fringes of Communism."[14]

Fooks produced by far the most colorful anti-Communist rhetoric, but he was not alone in making an issue of the Red menace. In the Democratic gubernatorial primary, H. Streett Baldwin accused his opponent, incumbent governor William Preston Lane, of being surrounded by "fellow travellers, parlor pinks, and outright Communists." Theodore McKeldin, Lane's unsuccessful opponent in the general election, did not speak directly to the Communist issue, but the Republican Party ran general ads screaming out "Americanism or Communism?" Former governor Herbert O'Conor campaigned for the U.S. Senate on a platform of rooting out Communist subversion.[15]

Frankfeld countered the Party's critics by publishing the *Clarion,* a four-page monthly tabloid of Communist views directed at the citizens of Maryland and the District of Columbia. The *Clarion* published six issues, none of which appears to have survived, before it was replaced by the less expensive and less time-consuming device of running quarter-page ads in the *Baltimore Sun.* The first ad, entitled "We State Our Case, Communists Answer Critics," appeared on 16 January 1947. The ad denied the charge that the Communist Party was the agent of a foreign power, offering as proof the 15,200 Communists who had served in the armed forces and the 50,000 Party members who had advanced the Allied cause on the home front. The essay stoutly defended the Party against accusations that it sought to destroy American democracy by force and violence. It countered the charge that Communists were nothing more than troublemakers by pointing out that the same thing had been said about such outstanding Americans as Thomas Jefferson, Eugene V. Debs, and Franklin Roosevelt.[16]

Neither the *Clarion* nor the Party's ad campaign helped advance the Communist cause or reversed the growing tide of anti-Communist sentiment in Maryland. In February of 1947, Dorothy Rose Blumberg appeared before the state senate in Annapolis to speak in favor of a bill that would set the minimum wage at sixty-five cents an hour and limit the work week to forty-four hours. She began her remarks in support of the proposed legislation by announcing that she represented the Communist Party. Immediately one of the spectators, Francis Silver, a Darlington farmer, objected loudly and, when the legislators ignored him, lead a noisy march of outraged individuals out of the hearing room. Blumberg shouted after him, "Courtesy is at least part of the American way of life."[17]

Senator John Reed asked to speak in the wake of Silver's departure. Reed declared that he had carried a union card for twenty-five years and favored all labor legislation. But, he continued, "every time a good law comes up, the Communists, the CIO, and all labor cross each other up. I want to say to groups wanting labor legislation, don't send the reds here to back it up." He closed his remarks by accusing the Communist Party of ruining Maryland. Senator George Della, the chairman of the hearing, defended the right of Communists, as citizens of the state, to present their views and allowed Blumberg to speak. Afterward, members of the League of Women Voters and the American Association of University Women, who were there to speak in favor of the bill, apologized to the assembly for the Communist interruption and expressed the hope that Blumberg's presence would not endanger the bill's passage.[18]

Blumberg's difficulties in Annapolis foreshadowed the Party's experiences for the remainder of the year. In March, a conference of ten seagoing unions branded the Communists "traitors to the nation and a detriment to the solid permanency of a United States merchant marine." NMU chief Joe Curran, once a staunch Party supporter, headed the subcommittee responsible for drawing up the resolution. A few days later, the *Baltimore Sun* published an editorial by Francis R. Kent, a nationally syndicated columnist, entitled "Everybody Does It Now." Kent detailed the extensive criticism being poured on the Communist Party from all quarters, which he felt indicated an increase in the clarity of American political thought and hoped would end with the outlawing of the Communist Party.[19]

Father Ignatius Smith, dean of the School of Philosophy at Catholic University, opened the spring session of the Conference of Catholic Daughters of America at Baltimore's Southern Hotel with an anti-Communist speech. Smith called on all "liberty loving Americans" to wage an unceasing campaign against communism, an "alien enemy gnawing at the vitals of the nation." "Even in the Free State of Maryland," Smith continued, "malicious forces of communism stir up bigotry, invade the pulpit, threaten many of our labor unions with contamination, and through institutions of learning infect the student body." Two months later, at the Knights of Columbus Annual Communion Breakfast, six hundred members of the Carroll Council and Manresa Club listened as Louis Budenz, the former editor of the *Daily Worker,* now a devout convert to Catholicism, denounced his former comrades. Communists, Budenz declared, were "quislings" and "fifth columnists," each one a "potential spy" loyal only to Soviet paymasters.[20]

On 23 June 1947, Congress overrode President Truman's veto to pass the Taft-Hartley Act. The act reflected both anti-Communist sentiment and growing public discontent with the actions of organized labor. It sought to constrain the economic and political activities of unions, make it easier for companies to resist unionization, and place unions under greater federal scrutiny. A subclause struck at Communists by barring them from union office and requiring all union officials to sign an affidavit stating that they were not Party members. Initially, all of the CIO unions and many ALF affiliates refused to comply with the non-Communist affidavits. Very soon, however, resistance yielded to pragmatism, separating the Communists further from their former allies.[21]

One of the most outspoken anti-Communists in Maryland was William J. Muth, a conservative Catholic and vice president of the Baltimore City Council. The Homewood chapter of the American Veterans Committee invited Muth to address a meeting, suggesting as a topic the problem of housing for veterans. Muth agreed to speak but only if he could "fully vent his anticommunist views." Frankfeld heard of the upcoming assault and arranged to be at the back of the meeting hall during Muth's presentation. At the conclusion of the speech, Frankfeld demanded the chance to rebut the councilman on the basis that he was not only a veteran but also "a Communist and proud of it." The veterans allowed Frankfeld to speak and then passed a resolution forbidding Communists from ever again addressing an American Veterans Committee meeting. They added that as far as their organization was concerned, there was little to distinguish the Communist Party from the Ku Klux Klan.[22]

By the end of 1947, the continual assaults had severely damaged the morale of the Maryland Party. On 8 November, the thirtieth anniversary of the 1917 Bolshevik Revolution, Lee McCardell, a reporter from the *Baltimore Sun* and a prominent member of the Catholic community, went to Party headquarters at the corner of Park Avenue and Franklin Street to see if a celebration was planned. He found Herb Kransdorf and two dispirited young women minding the office. They told McCardell that for financial reasons, no commemoration of the revolution would be held. After the three Communists gave rather vague answers to questions about the Party's membership and its history in Maryland, McCardell left. McCardell's subsequent article conveyed the distinct impression that the Communist Party was in the grip of terminal illness.[23]

McCardell's impression was sorely mistaken. Instead of dying, the Maryland Communist Party was shifting its public activities and members' energy from the increasingly beleaguered and battered CPUSA to a newly formed organization, the Progressive Citizens of America (PCA). The PCA appeared nationally in December of 1946 after the merger of the National Citizens Political Action Committee and the Independent Citizens' Committee of the Arts, Sciences, and Professions. The Maryland chapters of the two organizations merged in January of 1947.[24]

Before the 1944 elections, the National Citizens Political Action Committee had been known as the CIO-PAC, the union's political pressure group, which, at least in Maryland, was run as a franchise by the Communist Political Association. As the CIO-PAC evolved into the Citizens Political Action Committee and then into the Progressive Citizens of America, most of the labor leaders dropped away. They left behind an organization inhabited by Communists, Popular Front supporters, and a broad range of individuals and groups longing for a return of New Deal–style government activism and feeling threatened by the general American shift toward conservatism.

During 1947, the Maryland PCA chapter sponsored a wide range of activities reflecting the interests of its diverse coalition. The Harvard University astronomer Harold Shapley and the writer Dorothy Parker visited Baltimore to protest HUAC's investigation of the motion-picture industry. Senator Glen Taylor came to criticize the recent loans to Greece, intended to aid the government in its fight against the Greek Communist Party, as a step toward American fascism. A PCA meeting at the Keser Torah Synagogue castigated the British for forcing the Jewish refugee ship *Exodus* back to Crete. The mystery writer and secret Party member Dashiell Hammett appeared as a "concerned citizen" to denounce the erosion of civil rights caused by anticommunism. Dr. Robert T. Kerlin, the PCA chapter head in Cumberland, launched a drive against high meat prices, and PCA activists distributed fifteen thousand "eviction notices" as part of a campaign protesting the lifting of rent controls.[25]

In October, Henry Wallace, vice president under Roosevelt, briefly secretary of commerce under Truman, and the PCA's national spokesman, paid a visit to Baltimore. Wallace stopped first at the Enon Baptist Church on Edmundson Avenue, where he told an enthusiastic crowd that the United States "shouldn't preach democracy to the Russians until we get full democracy here in the United States." At an outdoor meeting with Johns Hopkins students, Wallace cautiously endorsed Eisenhower as president. However, the former vice president made his support conditional on Eisenhower's selecting Harold Stassen as his running mate. Wallace completed his visit with a speech to eight thousand people at the Fifth Regiment Armory. There, he charged the U.S. government with preparing for war when the people wanted peace and supporting high military spending that created "misery at home and enemies abroad."[26]

At first, the Communist Party exercised only indirect influence on the PCA through officers who were fellow travelers and the activities of secret Party members. The PCA state chairman, Dr. Robert Linder, a Catonsville author of mystery stories, had no Party connections, but well-known fellow travelers, such as Dr. J. E. T. Camper, the labor lawyer I. Duke Avnet, and the District of Columbia radio personality Rheba Lewis, dominated the remaining offices. The most important Communist in the PCA, the Baltimore lawyer Harold Buchman, kept a low profile, serving mostly as a roving speaker. Buchman, who was also president of the Roosevelt Democratic Party Club, kept his Communist identity a deep secret and avoided known Party members. He maintained contact with Party leaders through regular clandestine meetings with George Meyers, the Maryland Party's secretary of labor.[27]

Not all Communists in the PCA were as discrete as Buchman, and in 1947 the organization split, both nationally and in Maryland, into the PCA and the Americans for Democratic Action (ADA). Both groups favored a return to the progressive, interventionist policies of the New Deal but differed over mem-

bership qualifications. PCA leaders, while proclaiming the group's independence would admit, if pressed that Communists were a part of its coalition.
The founders of the ADA, however, opened their doors to everyone except
card-carrying Communists and their close friends.[28]

In December, Wallace announced his intention to run for president. Hu-
bert Humphrey, the mayor of Minneapolis at that time, condemned the move,
declaring it would ensure the election of "a reactionary, isolationist, administration" and serve "the world wide interests of the Communist party." National
figures, such as the PCA's Vice Chairman Frank Kingdon, and several important organizations, such as the Amalgamated Clothing Workers of America,
promptly abandoned the PCA. In Maryland, the PCA also lost many of its
former supporters in the wake of Wallace's announcement, among them Dr.
Kerlin, the western Maryland's PCA chair, who told reporters that he could not
back a Wallace campaign because he intended to vote the Socialist ticket.[29]

The steady whittling away of the Wallace coalition increased both the
importance and the visibility of the Communist Party within the PCA. On 31
December, eighty-four Maryland labor leaders issued a joint statement favoring Wallace's candidacy. Walter McManamon, the former head of the Communist faction at IUMSWA Local 43 and now an international representative
of the Mine, Mill and Smelter Workers Union, initiated the petition. McManamon was seconded by Irv Dorvin, a Communist official and the Baltimore
port agent for the Marine Cooks and Stewards Union, who had recently arrived from the West Coast. Over half of the remaining signers were Communist Party members and fellow travelers.[30]

The Wallace for President Committee, which opened its offices in the Tow-
er Building in downtown Baltimore on 23 December, was also well salted with
Party members and supporters. Harold Buchman announced the committee's
formation and proudly reported that the office had been opened after a personal consultation with Henry Wallace in New York City. The office staff consisted of Buchman and a secretary provided from the ranks of the Communist Party. Buchman gave the press a list of forty progressives who had agreed
to serve on the committee until more permanent arrangements could be
made. Of the forty names, only eleven can be positively identified as either
Communists or fellow travelers. Significantly, only three of them—Walter
McManamon, J. E. T. Camper, and I. Duke Avnet—would have been well
known as radicals in 1947.[31]

In January of 1948, the United Auto Workers of America (UAW) publicly
refused to back Wallace's candidacy. Walter Ruether, the UAW's president,
remarked that he believed Wallace had fallen under the spell of the Communists, who "perform the most complete valet service in the world. They write

your speeches, they do your thinking . . . provide you with applause and in-flate your ego as often as necessary." Max Lerner, an editorial writer for *PM* magazine agreed with Ruether and disavowed Wallace, accusing him of com-ing to the "same conclusions as the Communists" and using the same lines of reasoning. The *Baltimore Sun* columnist C. P. Ives cited both men in his own article, which happily concluded that the final unmasking of the Wallace–Communist Party connection should put the old shibboleths of the Popular Front to rest forever.[32]

In February, the Maryland PCA met for the last time in a convention that transformed it into the first official branch of the Progressive Party on the Atlantic seaboard. Reporters attending the convention noted that blacks made up about 15 percent of the 630 delegates and that women outnumbered men. The generally youthful crowd included "educators, college students, lawyers, representatives of public housing tenants, clergymen, agents of a few labor unions, . . . and a sprinkling of persons generally considered as holding secret membership in the Communist party." James Stewart Martin, an Annapolis attorney and author who was the new state chairman, gave the closing address and repudiated charges that the Progressive Party was a Communist front. There were Communists in the party, Martin admitted, but they would follow, not lead. Martin might have moderated his statement had he known more about the new executive secretary and state director of the Progressive Party, the secret Communist Harold Buchman.[33]

Thomas O'Neill, the reporter who covered the convention, harbored deep suspicions about Buchman and pointedly commented that Buchman had once represented the Communist Party in a legal attack on Maryland election statutes. O'Neill referred to the Party's attempt to strike down the restrictive third-party ballot qualifications imposed after Dorothy Rose Blumberg's per-jury case in 1940. Communist involvement in the Progressive Party became something of an open secret once the CPUSA publicly announced its backing of Wallace. Harry Truman responded by denouncing "Wallace and his Com-munists" during his Saint Patrick's Day speech in New York City.[34]

After its founding convention, the Progressive Party nominated three can-didates to run for seats in the House of Representatives. Buchman and his corps of volunteers had no difficulty collecting the huge number of signatures required under Maryland's restrictive third-party laws, but he was concerned about the possibility of a repeat of the Dorothy Rose Blumberg case in which perjury charges were brought against signature-gathers. To forestall any prob-lems, Buchman first declared that up to one-third of the petitions' signatures were probably invalid. He then demanded permission to compare his lists with the official records held by the Board of Elections supervisors. After initial resistance and a brief court battle, the Board of Elections reluctantly grant-ed permission, and Buchman filed a foot-thick document on 16 April.[35]

Such small success did nothing to discourage the Party's opponents, and in May Councilman William Muth launched another attack on the Party. Muth introduced a city council resolution demanding a school board investi-gation to determine whether Harold Spector, a Patterson Park high school-teacher, was a member of the Communist Party. Councilman Reid criticized Muth for naming names, saying Muth had "crucified" Spector the moment his name was made public. Other councilmen thought the school board should have been consulted and implied that Muth was simply seeking publicity.[36]

The editorial staff of the *Baltimore Sun* castigated Muth for violating the rights of individuals to privacy and proper proceedings, as well as threaten-ing the public peace by promoting "needless apprehensions . . . and public hysteria." Muth responded by widening his net to include Regina Frankfeld, a Baltimore kindergarten teacher and the wife of Communist Party chief Phil-ip Frankfeld. Muth asked if anyone on the school board had been aware of Spector's 1946 discharge from employment at the Aberdeen Proving Grounds "in the interests of national security" or of the identity of Frankfeld's husband. Buchman and Camper issued a statement in the name of the Progressive Par-ty condemning Muth for bringing the Mundt-Nixon tactics of Red-baiting to Baltimore. They strongly suggested that Muth's real motive in accusing Spec-tor of communism was to attack a Henry Wallace supporter and demanded that Muth either apologize or face impeachment.[37]

Muth did not apologize, nor did the city council attempt to impeach him. Instead, the school board took up the cases against the two teachers. In mid-June, the school board announced the adoption of a new anti-Communist policy. The policy banned Communist Party members or persons holding Communist views from any position in the Baltimore school system. After proper legal procedure, all such individuals currently employed by the system would be immediately terminated. Philip Frankfeld assailed the school board ruling, which he described as an example of Red-baiting, mob hysteria, and economic crucifixion. The Party chief took particular issue with the school board's statement that Communists had "divided loyalties," insisting instead that the Communist goal of common ownership of property made them ex-ceptionally patriotic. In contrast to Frankfeld's statement that the anti-Com-munist ruling would "suppress all independent thought and expression of opinion," the Maryland Civil Liberties Committee congratulated the school board for establishing a "safe and democratic procedure."[38]

Regina Frankfeld appeared before the school board on 30 June 1948 to answer questions about her membership in the Communist Party. She freely admitted her political beliefs and did her best to calmly and rationally defend them. On the basis of her admission of membership, the board decided not to renew her contract for the next year. Harold Spector vigorously denied being a Communist and remained at Patterson Park at least through the following year.[39]

The miniature "Red scare" in the school system coincided with the passage of an anti-Communist resolution by the Maryland Bar Association at its convention in Atlantic City. The resolution condemned the Communist Party and called for action against it as a fundamental aspect of national security. However, several prominent Maryland attorneys, including William Walsh, the president of the Maryland Bar Association, objected to the severity of the resolution. Walsh agreed that communism posed a grave danger to the United States but thought that the best defense against it was to improve democracy, not adopt "any of the terrors of Communism or Socialism."[40]

Governor William Preston Lane disagreed. On 13 June, he appointed Frank B. Ober, an attorney who had backed the anti-Communist resolution, as head of a state commission to investigate the problem of subversive activities in Maryland. The Ober Commission was not directly inspired by the Maryland Bar Association's resolution but was motivated by enabling legislation passed by the state assembly in its winter session designed to "expose and expurgate subversive activities." Ober made a brief statement, saying that he hoped to have the commission organized soon and planned to begin his work by investigating the antisubversive measures enacted by other states. Ober's comments were short and mild compared with his earlier speeches that had described the Communist Party as an arm of Moscow and accused the Supreme Court "of too much attention to civil rights" in its antisedition rulings.[41]

The Communist Party issued a statement charging that the Ober Commission menaced the "liberties and freedom of every Marylander" and accusing Frank Ober of "subversion, anarchy, and despotism," as defined by the Maryland Constitution's Bill of Rights. The press release concluded by warning that because no blacks, workers, or progressives were included on the Ober Commission, the body would produce biased results. Specifically, the Party feared a "witch hunt directed against labor and the progressive movement . . . as well as the Communist party." After the heated press release, the Party paid scant attention to the Ober Commission, and the Ober Commission itself shunned publicity during the investigative phase of its work.[42]

In mid-summer, the Young Progressives held a mixed-race tennis tournament at Druid Hill Park as part of their ongoing campaign opposing segregation of city facilities. On the morning of 11 July, twenty-four players, under the supervision of the Young Progressives' leader Stanley Askin, occupied three courts along Pimlico Drive. Over five-hundred spectators watched as the participants, many of whom were Communists, began to play a series of integrated mixed-doubles matches. Park authorities, who had been informed in advance of the plan to test the segregation policy, arrived shortly afterward accompanied by Baltimore police officers and attempted to stop the games.[43]

The players refused to leave the courts, and the spectators began to call out insults and compare the police with Nazis. Finally, the officers physically carried the players off to jail and charged several with disorderly conduct. Civil authorities viewed the events at Druid Hill Park very seriously. State's Attorney J. Bernard Wells wrote to Harold Buchman, personally requesting him to refrain from staging any more interracial athletic events because of the danger of "mob violence." Buchman and Camper responded by criticizing both the arrests and the policy of segregation.[44]

The tennis court demonstration, by itself a small thing, galvanized the Communists involved, many of whom looked back on the event fondly over forty years later. In the shorter term, it inspired them to greater effort in the task of directing the work of the Progressive Party. Communists dominated the nominating process for delegates to the national Progressive Party convention, scheduled to convene in Philadelphia in late July. Surviving lists of the eighty-eight delegates, who shared sixteen votes, indicate that slightly over half of them were Party members. More important, the list of resolutions to be submitted for inclusion in the national party's platform mirrored those passed at the state Communist Party. In his keynote address to the Communist Party's 125 convention delegates, Philip Frankfeld acknowledged the strong ties between the two political groups. He praised the participants in the interracial tennis match, which would, he said, "bring credit and increased membership to the Progressive party."[45]

On 23 July, the Progressive Party delegates left Baltimore for the Philadelphia convention, traveling in a caravan of twelve autos led by a sound truck. The cars were liberally festooned with Wallace campaign signs, and the sound truck emitted ear-blasting renditions of "The Battle Hymn of the Republic," Wallace's campaign song. After arriving in Philadelphia, the Communists in the Maryland delegation linked up with their colleagues from around the country, ensuring Party control of the convention. Howard Norton, a reporter for the *Baltimore Sun,* noted that, with a single exception, every specific demand listed in the Communist Party's 13 May platform was also included in the Progressive Party's platform. The single exception concerned a statement in the *Daily Worker* reading, "Wallace has only one step to advance. He must see the illusion of his claim that the abolition of monopoly rule will usher in a system of progressive capitalism."[46]

Other Maryland journalists covering the Philadelphia convention echoed Norton's belief that the Progressive Party had become indistinguishable from the CPUSA. Richard Yardley, the *Baltimore Sun* editorial cartoonist, created a quarter-page drawing depicting a blissful Wallace perched atop the convention hall along with vice presidential candidate Glen Taylor, wearing a ten-gallon hat and providing musical accompaniment on a banjo. On the ground, hoards of masked people, under a banner reading "The Comrades," storm the building. The besieging mob is a singularly good-natured one. Yardley drew them smiling, winking, and waving American flags, while at the same time displaying Stalin buttons or hammer-and-cycle emblems. One individual lectures a small cat, Yardley's cartoon trademark, on the Party line.[47]

Yardley indulged in gentle humor, but Baltimore's premier journalist, H. L. Mencken, dipped his pen in acid before relating his impression of "Gideon's Army." Mencken began by describing the convention as a succession of dismal days of "pathological rhetoric relived only by the neat and amusing operation of the party-line steamroller" and the "large gang of picturesque characters" occupying Shibe Park. He castigated Wallace for making "a thumping ass of himself" at an early press conference and for his "bumbling and boresome" speaking style. Mencken described Taylor as "a third rate mountebank from the great open spaces . . . soak a radio clown for ten days and ten nights in the rectified juices of all the cow-state Messiahs ever heard of and you have him to the life."[48]

Mencken declared that the Communist Party dominated the convention, exercising particularly tight control over the platform committee. "The platform was drawn up by the Communists and fellow-travelers on the committee, and when it got to the floor . . . they protected it waspishly and effectively against every raid from more rational quarters." Upon reading Mencken's opinions, the Maryland delegation's steering committee—Camper, Buchman, and James Martin, the chair of Maryland's Progressive Party—drew up a resolution to censure Mencken for his "contemptible rantings." Albert Fitzgerald, the convention's chairman, refused the motion on the grounds that it would lead to a flood of similar denunciations.[49]

Even as moderate a voice as the British journalist Alistair Cooke had to admit that the convention delegates "cheered and booed in all the places where Communists would cheer and boo." He admitted that this might be "an irrelevant slur on them. But in 1948 it has to be reported." Cooke went on to describe the convention-goers in much less vitriolic terms than Mencken's, picturing them in general as young, folksy, and idealistic, "right out of a Frank Capra movie."[50]

The widespread belief that the Progressive Party was nothing more than the Communist Party writ large disturbed Party head Frankfeld, prompting him to issue a statement countering Howard Norton's *Baltimore Sun* article. Frankfeld maintained that the two parties had very dissimilar goals. The Progressive Party favored the creation of "progressive capitalism," a proposition the Communists, who advocated the establishment of a fully socialist society, knew to be an illusion. Frankfeld then undermined his own argument by praising the Progressive Party and admitting that Communists had "contributed" to the Progressive program, which would, if implemented, be of immediate benefit to the country.[51]

The Maryland delegation to Philadelphia did nothing to alter popular perceptions when it voted, forty-two to nine, against an amendment to the Progressive platform distancing the party from Soviet foreign policy. The *Labor-Herald*, the official organ of a number of Maryland labor unions, commented that Wallace and Taylor were "just like trimmings being used as a cloak by the Red brethren to do their dirty work." Martin, upon his return from Philadelphia, again denied that a minority faction controlled the party. But he did admit that the party constitution could allow a small "do-gooder" group that did not fully trust people to make decisions to exercise undo influence. Martin believed that with enthusiasm currently high, little danger existed, however. Should such a situation develop, Martin assured his listeners, he would resign as party head.[52]

After the convention, the Progressives continued their program of demonstrations and meetings, which strongly recalled the glory days of the Popular Front. Camper and Buchman championed civil rights by challenging Maryland's two senators, Millard Tydings and Herbert O'Conor, "to work collectively" to end the filibuster blocking the anti–poll tax bill. The upper northwest section of the Young Progressives, headed by the Communist William Blank, worked against militarism by collecting signatures of those opposing the draft, while the Fifteenth Ward Club hosted a lecture on the growing crises in the Middle East.[53]

In late August, the Progressive Party organized its most elaborate activity, a series of protests against high meat prices. The protests featured sign-carrying housewives, often with their children, picketing food markets and meat-processing plants while supported by a moving sound truck. Michael Clifford, one of the Progressive Party candidates for Congress, explained to reporters that the protests were intended to demonstrate the need for price controls and regulation of food-processing monopolies. Although not as dramatic as the *Emden* protest, the marching housewives showed much the same spirit.[54]

The Progressive Party could breathe life into the Popular Front, but it could not protect the Communist Party from increasingly effective attacks. During

July, all twelve members of the Party's National Committee were indicted by the Justice Department under the terms of the Smith Act, a wartime measure directed at groups plotting the overthrow of the U.S. government by force and violence. The framers of the act had pro-Nazi groups in mind, but its only use during the war was to suppress a group of Trotskyists in Minneapolis, ironically, an action the Communist Party applauded. Hard on the heels of the Smith Act arrests came the HUAC testimony of Elizabeth Bentley, the former lover of a Soviet intelligence officer. Dubbed the "blonde spy queen," Bentley gave testimony before HUAC that revealed a complex network of Soviet spies in the U.S. government. Eugene Dennis, the general secretary of the CPUSA, scoffed at Bentley's spy stories and vowed not to let any "espionage provocations" or other frame-ups interfere with the Party's fight against the trusts and monopolies.[55]

The arrest of the Party's national leaders and the snowballing spy scandals, which culminated in Whittaker Chambers's claim that the prominent Baltimorean Alger Hiss was a key Soviet agent, stirred up an enormous controversy that has taken decades to resolve. But it did little to the Maryland Communists, except considerably heighten their feelings of being at war with the established order. None of the Maryland Party members believed that Chambers's testimony was anything but an anti-Communist frame-up. The few people who could have told them differently—such as Chambers's old partner, David Carpenter, or Albert Blumberg, the former district chief— were now highly placed in the national Party organization and had no intention of enlightening anyone. Other residents of Maryland, however, took the revelations of Communist perfidy very seriously.[56]

Edwin W. Broome, the superintendent of schools in Montgomery County, approved the use of HUAC pamphlets as educational tools by the system's educators. Broome did not see the need for any special classes on communism; instead, he intended the pamphlets to be used as supplements to regular courses on civics and government. After a visit to Cumberland by Glen Taylor, Mayor Thomas B. Finan announced his belief that the Communist Party had no right to protection under the First Amendment and should be forbidden to distribute literature in public. Philip Frankfeld wrote to Finan protesting his remarks and pointing out that the CPUSA had been a legal, registered political party for twenty-nine years. Finan declined to answer Frankfeld's letter, commenting to reporters that it was "not worth replying to."[57]

In November, Maryland and the nation went to the polls and decisively rejected Henry Wallace and the Progressive Party. In a postelection statement, the Progressives accused the two major parties of blatant vote buying and hinted that some voting machines and registration books had been tampered with. The Communist Party, however, ruefully admitted in *Political Affairs,* its theoretical journal, that it had badly misjudged the mood of the country and bore much of the blame for Wallace's defeat.[58]

Maryland voters, by a vote of 230,000 to 84,000, also approved an amendment to the state constitution barring from state employment anyone advocating the overthrow of the government by force and violence. In 1947, when William McGrath, delegate from Prince George's County, first proposed the amendment, Frankfeld had approved, pointing out that the Communist Party did not advocate the overthrow of the government. Frankfeld's opinion was not widely shared. The day before the election, ads supporting the amendment appeared under the banner headline "Fight Communism! Tomorrow— Election Day! Vote Yes for Amendment 7." The only comfort the Party could take was that the amendment lacked any provisions for active enforcement.[59]

In the face of such rising hostility, the Communist Party retreated underground. Only the names of Philip Frankfeld, Party secretary Elsie Smith, and a handful of other well-known officials, such as George Meyers, were used in public. By the summer of 1948, the Party began the task of breaking its twenty or so clubs into eighty-three units of less than half a dozen members each. The breakup would eliminate the need for membership lists and restrict contact between Communists, limiting the damage government raids or public exposure of individual Party members could do to the organization.[60]

Frankfeld further tightened internal Party security by restricting knowledge of the time and location of District Committee meetings to all but a few trusted individuals. Eager to test the system, Frankfeld distributed sealed orders calling for a committee meeting, held appropriately in a basement, which dictated the exact minute each small group was to arrive. The actual practice turned into a farce because some people arrived early and others late so that a line of cars wound up circling the block looking for parking places. After everyone finally assembled, Frankfeld informed the thirty or thirty-five committee members present that because of the extraordinary times, all important decisions would henceforth be handled by the top leaders, without consulting the full District Committee.[61]

Frankfeld then required everyone to declare agreement with a recently published statement that Communists would never bear arms against the Soviet Union. Everyone affirmed agreement with the exception of Arthur Berri, who objected on the grounds that the Party was in enough hot water already. Frankfeld referred him to the "top Party leadership" for further conversation. Mary Stalcup, the FBI informant, took the oath but found the entire episode unsettling. She later commented that she believed Frankfeld had engineered the oath taking to cement group loyalty but had succeeded only in creating an atmosphere of paranoia.[62]

10

The Ober Law, the Smith Act, and HUAC

Late in 1948, the Ober Commission completed its secret deliberations and introduced its antisubversive law to the public. The bill drew heavily on the Smith Act and Truman's Loyalty Oath Act but enlarged on both measures. The proposed law required detailed loyalty oaths of all public employees, demanded rigorous efforts from schools to stamp out subversive influences, and mandated the creation of public records on all disloyal individuals and groups. Responsibility for enforcement and record keeping would rest with the attorney general's office, which would be commissioned to hire a special assistant who would actively seek out seditious elements in society.[1]

The Progressive Party had revived the agenda of the Popular Front, and the unveiling of the Ober law briefly revived the coalition itself. The Progressive Party and such remaining Communist strongholds as the United Electrical Workers local condemned the proposed law but so did the Maryland chapter of Americans for Democratic Action, the state CIO Council, the NAACP, the Civil Liberties Union, the National Lawyers Guild, and Attorney General Hall Hammond. Hammond branded the measure an attempt to create an "MBI, Maryland Bureau of Investigation" and opposed the use of the attorney general's office to enforce the law. Hammond thought that the felony of subversion should be prosecuted the same way as the felony of murder, by the state's attorneys, not the attorney general. "This special assistant is expected to set up a police state," Hammond told reporters, adding that "if you get public opinion at a high enough pitch anything can happen."[2]

Supporters of the measure, primarily from Catholic and veterans organizations, sidestepped issues of domestic civil rights and justified the bill on the grounds of a Communist threat to national security. Catholics particularly emphasized the Party's threat to America's way of life, as exemplified by Communist attacks on the church in Eastern Europe. At the final hearing on the measure in March, Frank Ober took pains to point out the bill's ultimate target, saying that "we might as well be blunt about it, we're talking about Russia." Their arguments proved persuasive. The Judiciary Committee approved the law and sent it to the legislature, where it passed both houses of the Maryland assembly with only a single dissenting vote.[3]

The lone objection came from John N. Newcomer, a Republican delegate from Washington County. Newcomer echoed Hammond's earlier criticism, saying that the law had been passed in an atmosphere of hysteria and threatened American civil liberties by placing the power of indictment in the hands of the attorney general instead of a grand jury. Newcomer's speech produced shock, then applause on the floor of the legislature. After his term expired, he never sought elective office again.[4]

Opponents hoped to block the law, scheduled to take effect 1 June 1949, by petitioning for a referendum vote. But as soon as word of the petition drive reached the legislature, supporters of the measure pushed an emergency act through the House of Delegates that allowed the Ober law to take effect immediately. Quietly backed by the Communist Party, Dr. J. E. T. Camper and H. Carrington Lancaster, a professor at Johns Hopkins University, filed a suit requesting that the court block administration of the law and find the measure unconstitutional. A few days later, Harold Buchman announced the establishment of the Citizens Committee against the Ober Law. Mary Watkins Price, one of the people Elizabeth Bentley had accused of spying, took charge of the committee's office.[5]

In the weeks after filing suit, opposition to the Ober law gained strength as additional groups, such as the Marine Cooks and Stewards Union, a group of black attorneys from Baltimore, and the Maryland chapter of the American Association of Social Workers weighed in against the antisubversive act. Not all of the renewed support came without qualifications. The black lawyers took care to distance themselves from the Communist Party, declaring that they were in sympathy with anti-Red measures and opposed the Ober law only because it was so general that it could be used to block attempts to end racial discrimination.[6]

On 15 June, Kay Lutz, the executive secretary of the Citizens Committee against the Ober Law, announced that the committee had collected enough signatures to force a referendum in the 1950 elections. Two months later, the committee's work seemed unnecessary because Judge Joseph Sherbow ruled in favor of Lancaster and Camper and declared the Ober law unconstitutional. Judge Sherbow found that the emergency legislation that had activated the law was retroactive and therefore illegal. The Ober law itself, Sherbow declared, was an unconstitutional restriction on freedom of speech and the right of due process because its extremely general language would allow an unacceptably wide range of activities to be defined as subversive.[7]

The law's opponents hailed the ruling as a great advance for democracy and civil liberties. Philip Frankfeld celebrated by distributing twenty-five thousand leaflets emblazoned with the headline "Democracy Triumphs." George Meyers called the judge's ruling a cause for "rejoicing and jubilation" and expressed the hope that the coalition that had defeated the Ober law would now turn its attention to uprooting Maryland's Jim Crow laws. John Newcomer, the lone opponent of the Ober law in the House of Delegates, expressed great satisfaction that his point of view had prevailed. Dr. Miriam E. Brailey, a Quaker employed by the Baltimore Health Department who had publicly stated that she would refuse to take a loyalty oath, said that she was "relieved and happy."[8]

Supporters of the antisubversive measure expressed varying degrees of shock at Judge Sherbow's decision, but they were pleased by Attorney General Hammond's prompt appeal of the ruling. Frank Ober declared that if the appellate court upheld Sherbow's decision, it not only would invalidate the antisubversive laws of over twenty states but also would strike a fatal blow at states' rights by denying states the ability to protect themselves. Supporters and opponents alike used the months leading up to the hearing to wage a press war against each other and to file emotionally charged briefs with the appeals court. The brief of the Citizens Committee against the Ober Law contained an appendix consisting entirely of newspaper editorials and published letters from around the country condemning the measure. The state's brief, presented by Frank Ober, included the charge of Judge Harold Medina to the jury that returned eleven guilty verdicts in the New York Smith Act trial.[9]

On 24 January 1950, the appellate court overturned Judge Sherbow's ruling that the Ober law had been illegally enacted by the 1949 emergency legislation. The court refused to rule at all on the validity of the law itself, claiming that no proper issue had been presented. However, the court did express the opinion that the law seemed well thought out and appeared to be a sincere attempt to carry out the policy established by the 1948 amendment to the Maryland Constitution prohibiting Communists in public office. The best course of action, the court recommended, was to await the results of the November referendum vote.[10]

Lawyers for the Citizens Committee against the Ober Law announced their intention to appeal the case to the Supreme Court. Attorney General Hammond, after waiting for the proper mandate to be filed, took steps to begin enforcing the law. Given Hammond's initial opposition to the Ober law, it must have been a relief to him that it appeared certain the measure's first test would be against a genuine Communist, Boyd Coleman of Cumberland, Maryland. Coleman, who had admitted his Party membership during testimony given at the New York Smith Act trials, had filed to run in the primary elections for the Cumberland City Council. Hammond told reporters that if Coleman won a place in the general election, he would be required to take the oath mandated by the Ober law. The issue never arose, however, since Coleman, who ran on a platform of civic improvements, lost the primary battle.[11]

Instead of being able to test the Ober law on a genuine Communist, Hammond was faced with the distasteful task of forcing several Quakers, whose religion forbade them from taking an oath of any kind, from their city and school district jobs. The first to lose her position was Dr. Brailey, who, true to her earlier statements, refused to go against her beliefs by taking the oath. Doris Schamleffer, a fellow Quaker, voluntarily resigned her job with the Department of Employment and Registration, and coreligionist Elizabeth Haas was fired from her position at the Enoch Pratt Library. In late March, two schoolteachers, one a Quaker and the other a member of pacifist organization, the Fellowship of Reconciliation, submitted detailed statements outlining their reasons for refusing to swear loyalty to the state of Maryland. The carefully worded statements proved to be futile since the Baltimore school board "discontinued" both teachers.[12]

The use of the Ober law against Quakers and pacifists increased opposition to the act and weakened the position of its supporters. Press coverage noted that the Quaker firings marked the first persecution in Maryland of members of the Society of Friends since 1658. The Library Staff Association condemned the Ober law and asked the electorate to reject it in November. Louis Shub, the chair of the Citizens Committee against the Ober Law, felt so encouraged that he led a delegation to Governor William Preston Lane requesting that a special session of the legislature be called to repeal the law. By early summer, it appeared that unstoppable momentum was building toward the repeal of the antisubversive measure.[13]

Then, on 25 June 1950, armored columns of North Korean troops poured across the South Korean border in an attempt to reunite the peninsula by force. Two days later, Harry Truman ordered American military units to support the Republic of Korea in cooperation with the armed forces of fourteen other United Nations member states. Barely had Maryland residents digested the fact that war had broken out between the United States and a Communist nation than the FBI announced the arrest of Julius and Ethel Rosenberg on charges of espionage. The twin events dramatically transformed Maryland public opinion, driving thousands of previously moderate citizens into the anti-Communist camp.[14]

The Communists and their Progressive Party allies denounced American involvement in the Korean War and condemned the war itself as a Wall Street–inspired act of South Korean aggression. Progressive Party gubernatorial candidate Louis Shub pledged to increase antiwar efforts and to expose the attempt of profiteers to use the war as an excuse for raising consumer prices. However, Henry Wallace, in many ways the party's reason for existing, disagreed. On 8 August, Wallace announced he could not support the Progressive Party's antiwar policies and resigned from the organization. James Stewart Martin, former cochair of the Maryland branch of the Progressive Party and one of its founding members, left the party immediately after Wallace's announcement. A week later, J. E. T. Camper, chair of the Maryland Progressive Party and previously the most loyal of fellow travelers, also announced his resignation. Camper declared that the party's war position "was just too much." "America is at war," Camper told reporters, "and that completely changes the situation as far as I am concerned . . . to me it is not my country right or wrong but my country or no country. . . . I want to live with my conscience."[15]

Shortly after Camper's statement, the Maryland attorney general rejected the filing certificates of all Progressive Party candidates for elective office on the grounds that they had not signed loyalty oaths. Harold Buchman announced he would file a law suit to challenge the ruling, and initially the party's candidates refused to sign the pledges. A few days later, fearing that the suit might not be settled before the election, four candidates signed non-Communist oaths. Two others, Shub and Thelma Gerende, a congressional candidate, pointedly declined to sign in order to test the law. In October, the Maryland court of appeals declared that Gerende, as a candidate for federal office, was not covered by the Ober law and could appear on the ballot. Candidates for state and local offices, however, fell under the Ober law's jurisdiction. The Supreme Court refused to review the case, and Shub's name remained off the ballot.[16]

While the Progressive Party struggled with the Ober law, the western Maryland city of Cumberland decided to adopt its own anti-Communist ordinance. The proposed measure banned the distribution of Communist literature within city limits and required all Communist Party members to register at city hall. George Meyers and Philip Frankfeld, joined by local Party leaders Boyd Coleman and Arthur Schusterman, attended the Cumberland City Council meeting called in early September to consider the new law. Meyers spoke to the council and a large crowd of interested citizens for a half an hour, calling the proposal "pro-fascist crap." He appealed to the various union members present by claiming that "it is impossible to pass legislation against communism without passing it against laboring groups."[17]

In response, Playford Aldridge, a member of the governing board of Textile Workers Union Local 1874, once a Communist stronghold, remarked that although no U.S. law had ever broken a union, Communists like Meyers and Schusterman had caused irreparable damage to the labor movement. "We've heard the same communist story across our union halls since we were organized," Aldridge asserted, "I regret this thing was not done twelve years ago before the egg was hatched."[18]

Schusterman reminded everyone that he had been a peaceful citizen of Cumberland for years and had never engaged in acts of sabotage or violence. Coleman declared that he had always fought for the rights of the common people and had campaigned for city council on a platform of new roads and bridges. "And new flags?" asked a member of the audience. The comment summed up the mood of the crowd. The city council unanimously passed the anti-Communist ordinance and, when Coleman and Schusterman failed to register, fined them a hundred dollars apiece. Three months later, the city of Hagerstown passed its own anti-Communist measure, and the Cumberland police commissioner proposed that regional law enforcement agencies "work together to ferret out subversive activities in the tri-state mountain industrial area."[19]

Anti-Communist rhetoric dominated the weeks leading up to the election on 7 November. The major target, however, was not the CPUSA or the Progressive Party but Millard Tydings, five-term Democratic senator. Tydings had survived Franklin Roosevelt's attempt to unseat him in his 1938 "purge" of the party, but this time the senator was no match for the Republican Party's masterful smear campaign. The height (or depth) of the assault took the form of a four-page tabloid entitled *For the Record,* which featured a photo of Earl Browder, the former Communist Party chief, whispering in Tydings's ear. Underneath, in very small print, the caption noted that the photo was a "composite." Tydings lost the election, the Progressive Party candidates received less than 5,000 votes each, and the Maryland electorate endorsed the Ober law by a 77 percent margin, 259,000 votes to 79,000 votes.[20]

In February of 1951, the national organization of the Communist Party transferred Philip Frankfeld from District 4 to Cleveland, where he relieved the former District of Columbia chief Martin Chancey as Party chairman. George Meyers, the former labor secretary and a universally popular figure in the Party, took over as District 4 chairman. Meyers provided a much-needed sense of unity and stability as the Party tried to hold together its increasingly ragged coalition and to promote its domestic and foreign policies.[21]

In April, the espionage trial of Julius and Ethel Rosenberg concluded with guilty verdicts and twin death sentences amid headlines declaring that the two Communists had betrayed the secret of the atomic bomb to the Soviet Union. In early June, the Supreme Court refused to overturn the Smith Act convictions of eleven top Party officials, exposing them to jail sentences ranging from three to five years. George Meyers denounced the Supreme Court ruling, which he compared with the infamous Dred Scott decision, as the beginning of thought control and an American police state.[22]

Top Communist leaders shared Meyers's opinion and genuinely believed that the U.S. government was preparing to destroy the CPUSA in a massive crackdown on all dissenting groups in society. In an effort to preserve Party leadership in the face of the coming storm, the National Committee ordered a number of Communists, including four of the defendants in the Smith Act trials and the former Maryland Party leader Albert Blumberg, to become "unavailable." The "unavailables" formed layers of an underground Party organization intended to allow the Party to continue functioning regardless of the extent of government oppression.[23]

No plan for a crackdown of the magnitude expected by the Communist Party existed, but events in Maryland in the summer of 1951 seemed to prove otherwise. In mid-June, over forty people received subpoenas requiring them to travel to Washington to testify before HUAC about the activities of the Communist Party in the Baltimore defense area. Long experience had taught the Party that the only defense against a government investigation was silence. The first two witnesses called to testify, Walter McManamon and Herbert Kransdorf, refused to answer any questions on the grounds of Fifth Amendment protection from self-incrimination.[24]

McManamon broke silence only to discuss his early life in Chicago and described in some detail his involvement in the 1933 murder-for-hire of his former boss. Since McManamon had been acquitted after turning state's evidence, the only result of the exchange was considerable mirth in the hearing room over the fact that one of McManamon's accomplices bore the name Jack London. Kransdorf refused to divulge any information other than his current address and could not even be induced to admit he had once lived in Baltimore.[25]

The witnesses called on the second day of testimony continued the Fifth Amendment litany begun by their predecessors. However, unlike Kransdorf, they freely answered questions about their employment, which allowed Mike Howard (formerly Mike Smith) an opportunity to put his interrogators on the defensive. When asked if he was still employed as a steel worker, Howard replied, "Up until yesterday I was." Frank Tavenner, the lawyer conducting the hearing, went on to ask Howard if he was acquainted with anyone on a numbingly long list of individuals, but Howard's remark nagged at John Wood, the committee's chair. Wood, a Democrat from Georgia, finally asked Howard what he meant by the comment. Howard replied that the press release sent out by the committee before the start of the hearings "was a clear invitation for employers to fire employees who were labeled as Communists."[26]

The complaint attracted the attention of reporters covering the hearings, and they enlarged on the brief exchange at the expense of the committee's laboriously prepared list of names. Howard's lament fired public opinion as well, and several other witnesses suggested that their appearances had endangered their livelihoods. Frustrated by the lack of progress, the committee charged Robert W. Lee, a Bethlehem Steel employee and a former Tobacco Workers organizer, with contempt of Congress for failing to answer a direct question regarding his government employment. Oscar Roberts, a self-employed Party member, also received a contempt charge for refusing to tell the committee what his name had been prior to its legal change during his naturalization.[27]

By the sixth day of testimony, press coverage had assumed a monotonous regularity, featuring headlines reading "Steelworker Keeps Silent at Probe," "Witnesses Balk at Probe on Reds," "Six Witnesses Balk at Probe," and "3 More Balk at Probe on Red Activity." The reporter Price Day felt that after hearing over fifteen witnesses, the committee had "developed little public information on the working of Communists in the city's defense plants." Some excitement occurred on 28 June when the committee called the novelty store owner William Spiegel to the stand. Spiegel testified about David Carpenter's use of his apartment in 1936 and described a meeting with Whittaker Chambers. However, Spiegel knew nothing about anything more recent than the 1930s, and the day after his testimony Tavenner announced that the hearings would be suspended until 9 July.[28]

Two days before the hearings were set to resume, reports began to circulate that a special witness was scheduled to appear who would at last provide concrete evidence of Party activities in Maryland. The witness was the former FBI informant Mary Stalcup, who now went by her married name of Markward. She had continued her double life until the onset of multiple sclerosis in 1949 forced her to resign her position as District 4 treasurer and to drop out of the Party. In late 1950, HUAC became aware that Markward had been a responsible Party official and served her with a subpoena. After consulting with the FBI, the young woman revealed her true role to HUAC investigators in closed session. Word of her confession leaked out to the Party, and she was officially expelled in February of 1951.[29]

Markward appeared before the committee the morning of 11 July, posed for several photos, and then delivered devastating testimony in a firm, precise voice. The former beautician identified nearly all of the previous witnesses as members of the Communist Party and backed up her statements by recalling personal encounters with each individual. She discussed Party labor policies, such as the shifting of energy from maritime industries to the Sparrows Point steel mills, and described the techniques used to take over the Maryland Progressive Party. Markward declared, "I don't believe the Progressive Party could have been organized without the energy and activity of various Communists in Maryland and the District of Columbia. They decided it was a desirable organization and put everything they had to see that it was organized."[30]

The committee wasted some of the force of Markward's deposition by inquiring about the Party membership of over two hundred people. Many of the individuals named were no longer in the area, and one of them—Andrew Older, an associate of the columnist Drew Pearson—was dead. Toward the end of Markward's testimony, three of the committee members asked a series of questions designed to establish that the Communist Party advocated violent overthrow of the U.S. government. Although Markward clearly believed that the CPUSA did favor the violent transformation of American society, she tried to explain the nuances of the Communist position. She told the congressional investigators that "it was the teaching of the party members that the things they want to attain can never be attained under the present form of government . . . and they did not think the government would let it [the transformation to communism] take place peacefully so violence would be necessary."[31]

Markward's appearance inspired a flood of newspaper articles, but they paid little attention to Communist activities, focusing instead on the young woman herself and the details of living an undercover life. Being a Communist, Markward told her interviewers, was a twenty-four-hours-a-day, seven-days-a-week job filled with seemingly endless meetings. To properly perform her demanding work, Markward severed ties to all but a handful of her old friends and endured a continual string of hostile rumors that circulated in her hometown of Chesterfield, Virginia.[32]

Shortly after taking her FBI assignment, she married George Markward, a master sergeant in the U.S. Army. Although she told her husband she worked for the FBI, she concealed the true nature of her employment, a task made easier by Sergeant Markward's overseas posting. In 1947, after George Markward's return to civilian life, she revealed the full extent of her activities and pressed her husband into driving her to and from Party meetings. Had she not become ill, Markward said she would have continued her work until relieved by the FBI or exposed by the Party's increasingly tight security.[33]

Eight more witnesses testified after Markward, but their sessions were anticlimactic. All eight maintained Fifth Amendment silence, and the hearings ended without further excitement on 13 July. However, federal surveillance of Maryland Party leaders increased noticeably after the conclusion of the hearings. Special agents maintained regular surveillance of Party members' homes and openly followed them about the city. In response, Meyers tightened internal security and sent several young Communists underground, including Robert W. Lee, who had appeared before HUAC, and Irving Kandel, a prominent club leader.[34]

A tense calm continued until midday on 7 August when FBI agents burst into George Meyers's Baltimore home, interrupting lunch, to arrest both Meyers and District of Columbia Party chief Roy Wood. The two men were handcuffed in front of their wives and Meyers's young children and then locked up in the city jail. Hearing of Meyers's detention, Maurice Braverman boarded a plane from New York to Baltimore, only to be placed in custody upon his arrival at Friendship Airport. Agents in New York arrested Philip Frankfeld and Dorothy Rose Blumberg, while the former Baltimore schoolteacher Regina Frankfeld was taken into custody at her home in Cleveland, Ohio. The six arrests were part of the Justice Department's Smith Act prosecution of local, "second string" Party leaders from California, Pennsylvania, and Hawaii as well as Maryland.[35]

The local publicity surrounding the jailing of the six Party leaders dwarfed that given the HUAC hearings. Headlines announced a "Red Round-up," and large photos accompanied a series of articles describing the extradition of the Frankfelds and Blumberg to Baltimore and the swift indictment of all six on charges of conspiracy to overthrow the government. A much longer series followed the legal maneuvering surrounding attempts to secure a reduction in bail. Bond for five of the indicted radicals had been set at $75,000 each, while Philip Frankfeld's was the enormous sum of $100,000. Repeated arguments eventually convinced Judge W. Calvin Chestnut to reduce the amounts. Raising money even for the smaller sums proved so difficult that Philip Frankfeld remained in jail until 6 September, while Wood and Meyers did not secure their freedom until 18 September.[36]

Upon their release, Braverman, Meyers, and Wood returned to their homes. The Frankfelds and Dorothy Rose Blumberg, prevented from leaving Baltimore by a court order, rented an apartment on the corner of Brookfield Avenue and Whitelock Street, near Druid Hill Park. The FBI, fearing that the indicted Communists might jump bail and disappear into the underground, maintained twenty-four-hour surveillance on all six people. The level of observation reached such ridiculous proportions that the *Baltimore Evening Sun* ran photos of Blumberg and the Frankfelds strolling in Druid Hill Park while being openly followed by five special agents. The photo's caption noted that five more were cruising nearby in automobiles. The three Communists complained that agents tailed them into department stores, sat next to them in movie theaters, and, on one occasion, commandeered a cab to take them home after a shopping trip on Saratoga Street.[37]

Difficulty in obtaining counsel, plus a long series of pretrial motions initiated by Philip Frankfeld, resulted in a series of postponements, pushing the case first to November, then to January of 1952, and finally to March. The stress of events leading up to the trial took a severe toll on Frankfeld's health, forcing him to spend several days in the Fort Howard Veterans Hospital during February. Frankfeld's well-being suffered further when, only days before the trial opened, he was expelled from the Communist Party for "political degeneracy," coupled with "moral degeneracy and corruption." The Party's National Committee removed Frankfeld's wife from all positions of responsibility and censured Meyers and Wood for allowing a politically dubious pamphlet written by Frankfeld to be distributed in District 4. After Frankfeld's expulsion, George Meyers announced that he would represent himself.[38]

The trial began on 11 March with an hour-and-four-minute opening statement delivered by Bernard J. Flynn, the U.S. state's attorney. Flynn declared that the prosecution would prove that the Communist Party was a revolutionary organization dedicated to the overthrow of the U.S. government and would demonstrate that the six defendants were "the local group" charged with carrying out Party instructions. Flynn made a specific point of identifying Braverman, who denied being a Party member, as a Communist official and cited several meetings and conventions attended by the defendants as proof of conspiracy. Harold Buchman promptly moved that the case against his clients be dismissed because the state had demonstrated no "specific intent to commit a crime and no power to bring about the evil." Judge Chestnut overruled the motion and, after statements from the defendants, allowed the state to call its witnesses.[39]

The first three people called—former Party members Paul Crouch, John Lautner, and William Odell Nowell—all spent considerable time discussing Communist ideology and tactics. Crouch, a Party member since the 1920s, established the revolutionary intentions of the CPUSA by reading long passages from a variety of pamphlets and books. Lautner declared that the Party not only intended to overthrow the government but was ready to carry out its plans as soon as a war or other national emergency supplied the right conditions. Nowell, a black Communist who had abandoned the Party to support the right-wing demagogue Gerald L. K. Smith, enlarged on the CPUSA's revolutionary intentions. He discussed the Party's hope (in the early 1930s) that support for an independent black republic in the South's "Blackbelt" region might spark a civil war.[40]

All three men identified Philip Frankfeld as a Communist and described personal encounters with him. Lautner knew him causally as one of many regional organizers, while Crouch had worked with Frankfeld in the New York Young Communist League drawing up plans for the infiltration of Communists into the U.S. Army. Nowell testified he had met Frankfeld in 1931 when both of them attended the Lenin School in Moscow. There, Nowell carefully noted, they had studied ideology and security techniques and had received paramilitary training.[41]

Five other witnesses, three of whom joined the Party as FBI informants, indicated they had been members of the Maryland–District of Columbia Communist Party and collectively identified all of the defendants as active Party members. As soon as each witness completed the ritual of identifying the defendants, the prosecution, with mixed results, asked them a series of questions designed to implicate the six Communists in a conspiracy to overthrow the government. Charles McRae Craig, a black maintenance supervisor for the Baltimore Housing Authority who joined the Communist Party in 1943 at the request of the FBI, testified that Party textbooks he read gave the impression that a proletarian dictatorship could be established only by force and violence. Under cross-examination, however, he freely admitted that the words *force* and *violence* were never used at Party meetings and that he had never been instructed in subversive or destructive techniques.[42]

Harry Owen Bartlett, a Garrett County timber cutter, joined the Party in 1936 but told the jury that he had become disillusioned with communism by 1940. He had planned to just drop out, but a friend put him in touch with the FBI, and he became an informant instead. Bartlett quoted Philip Frankfeld as proudly stating he "would always be a professional revolutionist" and attributed sinister overtones to an off-hand comment by George Meyers. During a 1947 meeting of the Party fraction at the Celanese Mill, Bartlett recalled, the topic of John Estes, a mill worker considered to be a reactionary, arose. After some talk of what to do, Meyers tried to move the conversation onto more profitable grounds by commenting, "After the revolution I'll take care of Estes."[43]

Mary Stalcup Markward enlarged on her HUAC testimony, recounting in detail a secret meeting that took place in Baltimore on 19 March 1949. Party members at the meeting adopted false names for emergency use and agreed to drop "comrade" as a form of address. They also decided, for security reasons, to hold large Party meetings in the most respectable hotels instead of the working-class establishments previously preferred. Small meetings of three or four Communists would henceforth be held "in automobiles or restaurants in order to make it appear that they were doing what normal American people do rather than attending a Communist meeting."[44]

Markward, whose slurred speech and nasal tone revealed the toll her illness was taking on her health, completed her testimony with an account of the proceedings of a district-level meeting held on 10 September 1949. After she described the offices held by each of the defendants at the time of the meeting, the last she ever attended, Flynn put one more question to her: "From your knowledge of, and experiences in, the Communist Party, do you believe that the Communist Party advocates the overthrow of the Government of the United States by force and violence?" In contrast to her HUAC testimony, where she tried to honestly explain Party doctrine, Markward gave a clearly well-rehearsed response: "I very definitely say that they do so teach and advocate."[45]

Harold Buchman opened the case for the defense by filing motions to strike the testimony of Crouch, Lautner, and Nowell from the record. He then moved to acquit his clients on the grounds that the prosecution had done nothing more than establish their membership in the Communist Party. Membership in the Party was not a crime, Buchman argued, and the prosecution risked involving the court in the "dangerous and sinister doctrine of guilt by association." Judge Chestnut withheld his decision regarding government testimony but firmly overruled the dismissal motion, saying that sufficient evidence existed for the case to go to the jury.[46]

In an attempt to counter the image of their clients as dangerous subversives, the defense attorneys focused on the idealism behind their decision to join the Communist Party. Buchman told the jury that Regina Frankfeld became interested in communism after a trip to Germany convinced her of the dangers of nazism. Roy Wood's attorney, James T. Wright, characterized his client as a member of an old American family. Wood, Wright declared, sought only to better the lives of his fellow workers, a task completely at odds with advocating the use of force and violence. George Meyers took the stand in his own behalf and continued the theme, asserting that he had joined the Communist Party in 1942 to "further the Roosevelt program leading toward Socialism in the United States."[47]

Meyers devoted most of his testimony to an eloquent account of his life growing up in the coal-mining town of Lonaconing, Maryland. He told of watching children picking coal slag for their families stoves and seeing John D. Rockefeller handing out dimes for charity. He talked about the danger of injuries that haunted miners and discussed the reading and thinking that eventually lead him to embrace communism. In place of Markward's images of secret meetings and basement oaths, Meyers described a Communist Party that openly broadcast its message on the radio and publicly spoke out in support of Henry Wallace in 1948. Far from advocating a forceful overthrow of the U.S. government, Meyers insisted that communism could be adopted in the United States only through the ballot. In response to Bartlett's claim that he had advocated violent revolution at union meetings, Meyers countered he had only said that given the history of industrial relations, he predicted violent resistance to change by "the minority now in power."[48]

Under cross-examination by prosecuting attorney Flynn, Meyers explained that the Communist Party sought the unification of working people with small farmers and businesspeople to oppose the rule of giant corporations, end racial discrimination, and achieve a lasting international peace. Asked if he believed the United States was an imperialistic nation, Meyers replied that it was not but that the war in Korea indicated a dangerous trend in that direction. Flynn then inquired if Meyers knew the whereabouts of Dr. Albert Blumberg (Meyers did not) and then requested the name of the person who brought Meyers into the Communist Party. Meyers refused to answer, even though the man who recruited him, Patrick Whalen, had been dead for almost ten years. Meyers feared that if he named one name, he would have to name them all, and he found the whole issue of "naming names" extremely distasteful.[49]

Herbert Aptheker, a noted Marxist historian and open Party member, followed Meyers to the stand to give expert testimony designed to counter the earlier government witnesses. Unfortunately, Aptheker tripped himself up by first claiming that the CPUSA had never advocated revolution and then, later in the day, admitting that the Party had indeed once promoted violence but had adopted new policies in the 1930s. Harold Buchman briefly interrupted Aptheker's discussion of communism with two character witnesses, who testified that Maurice Braverman had a reputation for "good order" and that they had never seen him violate the law in the courtroom. Aptheker returned to the stand and denied that the Communist Party used "Aesopian language" in its publications. The defense then unexpectedly rested its case.[50]

Buchman submitted a twenty-eight-page brief containing ninety-four points of law that he wanted included in the instructions to the jury and filed a motion requesting that Markward's testimony be stricken from the record. Judge Chestnut denied the motion, reduced Buchman's brief to three points, and instructed the jury that mere membership in the Communist Party, with knowledge of its goals and methods, constituted a crime under the Smith Act. After deliberating for two hours and fifty minutes, the jury found all six defendants guilty. Chestnut levied a thousand dollar fine on each person and sentenced them to prison terms ranging from two years, for Regina Frankfeld, to five years for her husband. All six defendants were granted bail and began immediate appeals, which were swiftly denied all the way to the Supreme Court. By the early months of 1953, all six had reported to federal correctional facilities to begin their sentences.[51]

The publicity and pressure brought against the Maryland Communist Party during the HUAC hearings and the year-and-a-half prelude to the Smith Act trial stripped the Party of all but its most dedicated members. Those remaining were subjected to extreme levels of stress. Frank Pinter, a longtime Communist, suffered a nervous breakdown from the strain and died. The others had to face community hostility and ostracism at work. The HUAC witnesses employed at Sparrows Point endured a period of "shunning," during which fellow employees refused to speak to them outside the requirements of their jobs. Despite this, the Party's steel club continued to meet. William Wood, who supervised a secret Party unit of eight, mostly black blast-furnace workers, found it possible to make small but measurable advances, which he described as "guerrilla warfare."[52]

In the same spirit of "guerrilla" tactics, the Communist Party, through a variety of front groups, took an active role in the attempt to save the Rosenbergs from execution. Sirkka Tuomi, a young actress and recent Party recruit who worked as a secretary for the Progressive Party leader Milton Bates, led the Baltimore efforts by organizing support committees, meetings, and demonstrations. As the time scheduled for the execution drew near, the Rosenbergs' supporters maintained a twenty-four-hour vigil at the White House. Tuomi brought a group down from Baltimore every evening for the midnight to morning shift. On 19 June 1953, the Baltimoreans arrived at the White House only to discover that the executions had already been carried out. Tuomi looked at the piles of placards and posters, stacked as a monument to the Rosenbergs, and broke into tears. Years later, she recalled thinking that the Rosenbergs were just "little, ordinary, Party people" and that if such a terrible thing could happen to them, it could happen to anyone.[53]

The imprisonment of the defendants in the Smith Act trials, the execution of the Rosenbergs, and end of the Korean War in July of 1953 took the edge off the anti-Communist movement, and the pressure Party members lived under began to ease. Howard Silverberg, who had appeared before HUAC, endured nearly two years of ostracism at work, had rocks thrown at his house, and was kicked out of his bowling league. In mid-1953, poor health forced him to take a leave from work and spend a lengthy period in the hospital. While recuperating, Silverberg received an unexpected but welcome visit from a fellow worker bearing a collection of money taken up at the mill to help out Silverberg and his wife. After his recovery, Silverberg returned to a completely different work atmosphere: people greeted him, asked about his health, and behaved as

though nothing had ever been wrong. All the other HUAC witnesses reported similar experiences.[54]

The relaxed public mood did not tempt the Party to ease its security measures. In 1952, Clifford Miller, a West Virginia native and former Party member employed at Sparrows Point, let several Communists know he wished to
rejoin the Party. Once Miller would have been swiftly welcomed back, but in
the cautious atmosphere of the 1950s Party leaders carefully discussed his case
and observed him for several months. Shortly before entering prison, George
Meyers visited Miller, supposedly to leave him several copies of the *Cominform
Bulletin* but in fact to give him a close look before recommending action. Finally, in September of 1953, William Wood took Miller out for a beer at a
Greenmont Avenue tavern and reenrolled him. Wood remained Miller's only
official Party contact for another year, until he was assigned to a small club of
three members, under the oversight of Aaron Ostrofsky.[55]

Since the change in atmosphere, the young "unavailables," including Irving Kandel, who assumed leadership of the Party in Meyers absence, and Robert W. Lee, returned to Baltimore. Lee's earlier disappearance had been particularly distressing to Sirkka Tuomi, who had been dating the young man. While
waiting for the Smith Act trial to begin, Regina Frankfeld took pity on Tuomi
and told her that Lee had gone into the underground in Philadelphia. Tuomi
began secretly meeting with Lee, an activity she found terribly romantic and
he found to be a great relief from the tension and monotony of underground
life.[56]

Unlike Albert Blumberg, who clandestinely organized labor groups while
in the underground, Lee had nothing to do except stay out of sight. He grew
a moustache to hide his identity and took a series of menial jobs, such as stirring pots of soup at a canning company and sorting soiled diapers at a laun-
dry service. On occasion, Lee, Kandel, and a few other "unavailables" would
risk a meeting to exchange experiences. Four of them once met in a diner, only
to discover they had all had grown mustaches, which, far from hiding their
identities, made the group stand out sharply in the clean-shaven fifties. Tuomi
and Lee married while he remained underground, but they did not announce
the news until Lee reappeared in Baltimore in 1954.[57]

After his return, Lee secured employment at Sparrows Point, and he and
Sirkka threw themselves into civil rights work. They joined the Congress of
Racial Equality (CORE) and often hosted mixed-race meetings at their home.
The presence of blacks in an all-white neighborhood distressed the neighbors,
who frequently complained to the police. On one occasion, while a Communist Party club meeting, complete with pamphlets and manifestos spread out
on the dining room table, was in progress, a police officer entered the couple's

home to report a rash of complaints. Fortunately, the policeman, who was embarrassed by the neighbors' attitudes, did not realize what kind of a meeting was being held and left after delivering his message.[58]

On 15 March 1954, HUAC investigators opened another series of Washington meetings to consider Communist activities in Baltimore. The primary targets of the HUAC investigators were the former Baltimore clergymen John Hutchinson and Joseph Nowak. Nowak, who had left the ministry, sadly confessed to his activities with the Communists in Baltimore, but Hutchinson denied ever having had any contact with the Party. Earl Reno, the former head of the Baltimore Party who had turned against communism after the ouster of Earl Browder, also testified fully about his Party activities, evidencing a mixture of pride and regret on the witness stand. Mary Himoff, who had moved to New York City, appeared before the committee as well but refused to acknowledge Reno and pled the Fifth Amendment to all questions. The hearings lacked any sting and had no discernible impact on the Party's situation in Baltimore. A month later, the televised Army-McCarthy hearings destroyed Senator Joseph McCarthy's reputation and led to his eventual humiliation and censure by the U.S. Senate. The Party's long nightmare seemed to be ending.[59]

In 1954, FBI agents arrested Albert Blumberg in New York City on charges of violating the Smith Act. Quickly extradited to Philadelphia, Blumberg was indicted in October, which began a lengthy legal process that brought his case to trial in February of 1956. Blumberg's trial followed the pattern of other Smith Act cases, even featuring appearances by several of the same prosecution witnesses, but it lacked the intensity and assurance of the previous cases. John Lautner recapped his discussion of Party goals and methods, while Mary Stalcup Markward, now visibly ill from her chronic disease, endured three grueling days on the stand. Defense lawyers succeeded in subpoenaing Markward's highly secret and previously unobtainable original FBI reports. Attorney Michael Von Moschzisker used the reports in cross-examination to demonstrate that although Markward had testified that Party members spoke of the need for violent revolution, her reports of the meetings she attended contained no such language. Markward protested that Party leaders had "implied" the need for violence and that security precautions had often prevented her from taking down exact words.[60]

The most damaging testimony came not from Markward but from two FBI informants in the Philadelphia Communist Party. The two men testified that while "unavailable," Blumberg had been in charge of steel organizing on the East Coast. They told a compelling tale of clandestine meetings in attics and remote rural locations, complete with elaborate safeguards and secret names.

Blumberg, one witness related, always went by the name "Paul" or "Doc." Asked how he could be sure of "Paul's" identity, the informant, Herman Thomas, a Philadelphia grocer, replied that he had seen Blumberg at several Party conventions before he entered the underground. The jury deliberated for three and a half hours before returning a guilty verdict.[61]

At eight o'clock on the morning of 24 March 1956, George Meyers walked through the gates of the Petersburg, Virginia, federal penitentiary as a free man. Reporters greeted Meyers at the prison entrance, asking him what he thought of the recent Soviet condemnations of Joseph Stalin. Meyers replied that he had been somewhat out of touch lately but still had "great admiration for Stalin as a leader." He then got into a car with his wife, daughter, and three-year-old son and left for Baltimore. After a brief but bruising factional fight with Irving Kandel, Meyers resumed his duties as head of District 4, just in time to oversee a disastrous split in the national Party.[62]

At the Twentieth Congress of the Communist Party of the Soviet Union (CPSU), General Secretary Nikita Khrushchev shocked the assembled delegates with a speech denouncing the crimes of his predecessor, Joseph Stalin. Khrushchev read his speech to a closed session of the congress, but details quickly leaked out. Portions of the speech appeared in the United States in March, and the entire text of his disclosures was published in June by both the U.S. State Department and the *Daily Worker*.[63]

The contents of the speech rocked the entire Communist world and caused the CPUSA to split into a hard-line faction, led by William Foster, and a reformist faction, led by the *Daily Worker* editor, John Gates. Gates, supported in Maryland by Irving Kandel and Harold Buchman, advocated a thorough overhaul of the Party. In September, Gates mustered enough support on the National Committee to pass a Party program that dropped the Party's advocacy of Soviet-style communism in favor of militant New Deal liberalism. Foster admitted Stalin may have made mistakes but believed these were far outweighed by his achievements, and he resisted Gates's reforms. George Meyers backed Foster and welcomed the confrontation, commenting to sympathetic union leaders, "The Party is going through a real crisis, and frankly speaking, I think it was long overdue."[64]

The Soviets, appalled by the direction some of the international parties had taken after the Khrushchev's speech, praised Foster in the pages of *Pravda*. Gates and his faction, which held a majority on the National Committee, refused to listen to Moscow's criticism and increased their distance from the Soviet Union by loudly voicing support of the coup in Hungary that toppled the Stalinist regime in Budapest. The crisis point came in November when Khrushchev sent the Red Army into Budapest to prevent Hungary from withdrawing from the Warsaw Pact. Hard-line Hungarian Party members deposed Imir Nagy and executed him and a number of his supporters. Party chair Eugene Dennis, formerly neutral in the Gates-Foster battle, threw his support behind Foster, calling the Soviet intervention "anti-fascist and pro-peace." A special Party convention met in February of 1957, which, on the surface, seemed to find a compromise between the factions but in fact marked the victory of the Foster group.[65]

The triumph of the hard-liners began a process of disintegration in the Party as Gates's supporters, both nationally and in Maryland, fell away from the CPUSA in increasing numbers. Among anti-Communists, the Party's support of Soviet actions in Hungary confirmed their beliefs about the true nature of American communism and inspired a renewed assault against their much weakened enemy. On 1 May 1957, spokesmen for HUAC and the Maryland Subversive Activities Unit announced that over thirty witnesses had been subpoenaed to testify in a series of public hearings regarding Communist activities in Baltimore. The substance of the planned hearings, an investigation of Communist activities in local industry, differed little from the 1951 HUAC investigation. The style, however, would be very different. The 1951 hearings had lost much of their intended effect by being held in Washington and stretched out over three weeks. The new hearings would last only three days, would be held in Baltimore, and would broadcast live on television. To ensure an appreciative "studio" audience, HUAC investigators invited the members of "patriotic and civic" organizations to attend in large numbers.[66]

The hearings opened at ten in the morning on Tuesday, 7 May, in the main federal courtroom on the fifth floor of the Post Office Building on the corner of Fayette and Calvert streets. The clerk of court called Clifford Miller, the West Virginian who had rejoined the Party in 1953, as the first witness. Miller's lawyer, Harold Buchman, had not arrived, but Miller took the stand anyway and shocked everyone present by revealing himself to be an informant for both the FBI and Maryland's Ober Commission. Miller spent most of the day on the stand discussing the ideological struggles that lead to his brief but genuine Party membership in the late 1940s. He provided a dramatic account of his decision to rejoin the Party as an informant after being contacted by FBI agents in 1952. The bespectacled young man recited a list of the names of everyone he had ever known as a Party member and described the heavy security and atmosphere of paranoia that had hung over the Party in the early and mid-fifties.[67]

Miller, unlike Mary Stalcup, did not come across in either his testimony or later newspaper interviews as an attractive personality. Instead, he suffered from a lack of self-esteem brought about by false pride in his intellectual accomplishments combined with a deep sense of frustration that life had never given him the success and recognition he felt he deserved. Miller joined the Party in the 1940s because it appealed to his sense of intellectual superiority, and, when approached by the FBI in 1952, he relished the thought of becoming a spy. Unfortunately for Miller, although he had met dozens of Communists in open Party meetings during his first period of membership, tight Party security allowed him to add only three names to his original list after two years as an FBI informant. In 1955, the FBI told Miller to stop submitting reports. Miller, however, had become so fond of his secret life that instead of quietly dropping out of the Party, he offered his services to the Ober Commission. After two-and-a-half largely unproductive years, Miller was handed over to Richard Arens, HUAC's chief investigator, who asked him to testify publicly. Miller still did not want to give up being a spy and initially tried to remain undercover, but he gave in once he realized there was no alternative.[68]

Irving Kandel followed Miller to the stand, constantly rocked back and forth in his chair, and only reluctantly yielded such small pieces of information as his address and educational background. Audience members gasped in shock when Herbert Nickol identified himself as a teacher at a boys' school. One man stood up and shouted, "Stand up like a red blooded American and deny you're a member of the Communist party." Irving Spector and Abraham Kotelchuk also drew boos and hisses when the two men admitted they had been employed at the Aberdeen Proving Grounds until the army revoked their security clearances.[69]

Sirkka Tuomi Lee wore a stylish dress with matching hat and gloves and played to the cameras. She gamely tried to use the witness stand as a podium to speak out against the McCarran Act and to urge Marylanders to participate in civic organizations. She also took the Fifth Amendment sixteen times, which deprived her testimony of much of its strength. Irene Barkaga, a Party member and FBI informant, followed Lee to the witness stand. She provided some comic relief by revealing that as the only Communist employed at the Bendix Corporation, she had to spy on herself. Barkaga, whose Party contact was Sirkka Lee, had been "put on ice" for security reasons in 1953 and had very little else to report.[70]

George Meyers, described by reporters as "clumping" to the witness stand, denounced the hearings as a violation of his constitutional rights and angrily denied he had ever been part of a conspiracy. Harold Buchman accused the committee of unconstitutionally usurping powers reserved to the judicial branch of government and of grossly overstepping its legitimate investigative powers. Both men were right, but it did them little good.[71]

The 1957 HUAC hearings devastated the Maryland Communist Party. The day after the hearings ended, Bethlehem Steel fired all six of the men who appeared before the committee. Within a week, five more witnesses lost their jobs, while others were publicly threatened or had their homes vandalized. Party leaders realized that the FBI would never have given up all of its informants and began an obsessive hunt for the remaining spies. Levi Williamson, one of the fired steelworkers, personally appealed to Bethlehem Steel and was given back his job. The action convinced most Communists that the innocent man was a stool pigeon, and he was expelled from the Party. Irving Kandel and his supporters, especially those who had opposed Meyers after his return from prison, dropped out of the Party one by one. Subjected to almost unbearable social pressure, riven internally by factionalism, and consumed by paranoia, the Maryland Communist Party, in the words of William Wood, "tore at itself in frustration" and nearly perished.[72]

Epilogue

Factionalism and paranoia gripped the Maryland Party for at least two years after the 1957 HUAC hearings, reducing the Party to just seventy members (forty-five in Baltimore and twenty-five in Washington) by 1959. By the early 1960s, after virtually all of Irving Kandel's faction had dropped out, the suspicions and fears dissipated, and the remaining members became a tightly knit, self-supporting group. George Meyers, Roy Wood, and Joseph Henderson, one of the fired Bethlehem Steel employees, started an awning company, which kept them and several other Communists gainfully employed. Howard Silverberg's wife, Jeanette, arranged regular get-togethers and visited troubled members, which contributed tremendously to the Party's psychological well-being. Some Party members, such as William and Corine Wood, recharged themselves by traveling behind the Iron Curtain. While visiting Poland, the Woods lost their luggage, which contained their birth control, and they brought a daughter as well as restored spirits back from Eastern Europe.[1]

In 1959, Gus Hall, the newly elected leader of the national CPUSA, visited Baltimore and outlined a plan to divide the Party into "circles." The outer circle would consist of mass organizations, such as the NAACP, labor unions, and social groups like the Elks Lodge or the Moose. Party members belonging to any of these organizations would work to advance Communist goals but keep their membership secret. The inner circles would consist of groups allowing greater degrees of openness. The center circle would be the Party itself. Hall hoped this new configuration would give Party members more flexibility and revive Party activity. But the Maryland Party did not have the energy to do much more than meet and distribute the *Daily Worker*.[2]

In 1961, George Meyers, who was rising in national Party ranks, accompanied Henry Winston and a delegation of Communist Party leaders to the Soviet Union to attend the Twenty-second Party Congress. Meyers made several speeches in the USSR and was invited to a private dinner with Nikita Khrushchev. The Soviet leader spoke about the crimes of the Stalin era and discussed current problems facing the Soviet Union, such as the poor state of the nation's housing. He admitted that many of the apartment blocks in Moscow would have to be torn down in less than thirty years but defended rapid construction as the only way to solve the country's severe housing shortage.[3]

Meyers returned to the States very impressed with Soviet accomplishments, although he admitted years later that some aspects of Russian life bothered him. The exclusive use of abacuses in shops seemed archaic in a country leading the space race, and he found the sight of Lenin's corpse on public display very unsettling. Meyers kept these reactions to himself, however, partly out of respect for Russian traditions but primarily because he believed that any criticism of the Soviet Union only provided ammunition for reactionaries and damaged the progress of socialism.[4]

In the summer of 1963, the *Baltimore News-Post* ran a series of articles about Floyd Rogers, another FBI informant in the Maryland Party. The Rogers articles bore a strong similarity to the Clifford Miller series six years earlier. They recounted Rogers's early membership in the American Youth Congress, a Communist front group advocating civil rights, which eventually earned him a poor security rating; his subsequent recruitment by the FBI; and tantalizing stories of secret Party activities. However, the tone of the articles differed greatly. The Clifford Miller series projected an air of deadly earnestness, even to the point of trying to mask some of Miller's less attractive personality traits. The Floyd Rogers articles exhibited an amused air of tolerant nostalgia, rather like essays on bootleggers in the 1920s.[5]

The Party's slow healing and the fading of anticommunism inspired Meyers, Henderson, and Robert W. Lee to take part in a national initiative to open a chain of Party-owned bookshops. A fund-raising letter, circulated in August of 1963, announced that the New Era Book Shop would be stocked with over sixteen hundred books on such diverse subjects as "peace, civil liberties, trade unionism, the struggle to abolish colonialism, socialism, [and] Marxism-Leninism." Meyers and his cofounders, a group that included Madalyn Murray, later famous as the atheist activist Madalyn Murray O'Hair, hoped the bookstore would serve as an intellectual center for Baltimore's left-leaning population.[6]

The store brought the Maryland Party back into contact with former District 4 head Philip Frankfeld. Although expelled from the Party before his Smith Act trial, Frankfeld had remained dedicated to Communist principles and was readmitted in the late 1950s. After regaining his Party membership, Frankfeld opened World Books, a New York–based company that contracted as a sales and distribution agent for International Books, Progress Publishers, and English translations of Chinese works. Frankfeld's firm supplied books to a wide range of American outlets but specialized in stocking Party–owned bookshops.[7]

The New Era Book Shop opened its doors on 15 September 1963, with the boast that "either we have it, or we can get it for you." Lee, who had been getting by on odd jobs, managed the store and, after a slow start, built up a clientele and moved the shop to its permanent home at 408 Park Avenue. In February 1967, the store, possibly as an unintended consequence of its celebration of black history week, attracted the attention of Philip Jenkins and Xavier Edwards. Jenkins was a deeply disturbed self-proclaimed Nazi and anti-Communist, while the twenty-six-year-old Edwards led the Interstate Knights of the Ku Klux Klan, an ultraviolent offshoot of the older United Klans. Edwards and Jenkins announced that one of their joint goals was to shut down the New Era Book Shop within one month. A few days later, hooded Klansmen picketed the shop, and a series of violent incidents began. Over the next four weeks, the New Era Book Stop had a brick thrown through its window, Lee's car was splashed with red paint, a firebomb was set off in the shop doorway, and Lee was physically assaulted.[8]

The book store's insurance company canceled its policy, and in March Lee's landlord gave him thirty days to vacate the premises. Edwards chortled on local television that now that the campaign against the New Era Book Shop had been won, he would turn his attention to Baltimore's Jewish-owned businesses. Lee, however, refused to concede defeat and launched a vigorous letter-writing campaign that gained nationwide attention and forced Baltimore's Mayor Theodore McKeldin to intercede in the struggle. McKeldin ordered the chief of police to post a round-the-clock watch on the New Era Book Shop, convinced the store's landlord to reconsider his eviction notice, and pressured Maryland's insurance board to reinstate the New Era Book Shop's policy. In the meantime, Jenkins was extradited to Massachusetts to face outstanding felony charges, and Edwards was forced by "police pressure" to resign his post as Interstate Klan leader. Ironically, left-wing and student groups picketed the New Era Book Shop, accusing the Communists of being pro-establishment for accepting police protection. The incident symbolized a profound shift in Maryland popular opinion. Anticommunism, once a serious mainstream issue, was now seen as the ideology of violent extremists, while the Communists themselves had become moderates compared with the student and counterculture movements of the day.[9]

From 1968 to Lee's death from cancer in 1971, the New Era Book Shop provided a forum for promoting Communist policies and a link to the student and radical movements. Several individuals who visited the book shop and engaged Lee in long discussions joined the Communist Party, giving it badly needed new blood. One of the new members, Margaret Baldridge, a twenty-eight-year-old high school teacher from Delaware, became an active and highly effective Communist. She agitated against the war in Vietnam and helped found the Baltimore Committee to Free Angela Davis, as well as a local branch of the National Alliance against Racist and Political Repression. In 1974, Baldridge ran for a seat in the Maryland House of Delegates as a candidate of the Young Workers Liberation League (YWLL) on a platform supporting school integration, union-only labor for state jobs, increases in mass transit service, and price rollbacks to 1971 levels.[10]

In the fall of 1974, the *Baltimore Sun* interviewed Tim Wheeler, a second-generation Communist whose parents had taken refuge on the West Coast during the McCarthy era. Only recently arrived in Baltimore, Wheeler was the Washington correspondent for the *Daily World,* the replacement for the defunct *Daily Worker.* Wheeler extolled recent Party growth, which had brought membership up to twenty thousand people nationally, a number he arrived at by dividing the circulation figures of the *Daily World* in half. The Party journalist emphasized the democratic nature of the changes the Party sought to bring to the United States and praised the socialist system of the USSR, which had "a higher standard of living for the masses of people" than the United States did. Wheeler characterized recent Soviet defectors as unprincipled opportunists and expressed deep regret that Chinese Communist leaders had abandoned Marxism and set the struggle for socialism in China back by decades. The article's title, "How Does a Real, Live, American Communist Think?" gave the impression that Wheeler represented a rare but completely normal aspect of American life.[11]

Throughout the remainder of the 1970s and into the 1980s, the Maryland Communist Party engaged more openly in political and social activities. Communist union members began introducing political resolutions at union meetings and working for a Communist presence at labor rallies in Washington, D.C. However, vivid memories of the 1950s in the minds of veteran Party members prevented the Party from acting in its own name until the campaign against the Supreme Court nomination of Robert Bork. Joe Henderson, the chair of the Maryland Party, and Margaret Baldridge, the executive secretary, participated openly in the Baltimore campaign as representatives of the Communist Party. They helped collect the "Bork barrels" full of postcards protesting the Supreme Court nomination and personally transported the barrels to Washington.[12]

In February of 1988, a young Baltimore resident died tragically while playing Russian roulette. A coalition of groups announced the organization of a series of public forums entitled "Youth Speak Out against the Senseless Use of Guns." Members of the Baltimore Young Communist League decided to participate and, along with Baldridge, attended an early planning session. When the chair of the meeting asked all the participants to identify themselves by name and organization, the YCLers, who had no living memories of the McCarthy era, gave their real names and announced their membership in the league. Baldridge had not foreseen the situation and recalled holding her breath and thinking, "Well this is it." But the committee chair simply continued around the room, and the Baltimore YCL worked with the group until the end of the campaign. The forums, held in local churches, also promoted Maryland's Proposition 3, a gun control measure, which passed in the face of intense opposition from the National Rifle Association.

That same year, the Party sponsored the first in a series of banquets designed to raise funds for the *People's Daily World,* yet another incarnation of the Party's official paper, and commemorate its own history. The inaugural banquet, held at St. John's Methodist Church on St. Paul Street, honored George Meyers, now a member of the National Committee, as one of labor's unsung heroes. The second gala event, held at the steelworkers' union hall in 1989, featured former Berkeley mayor Gus Newport, who had long been sympathetic to the Party. Subsequent dinners honored longtime Communists Joe Henderson and Jake Green as well as a trio of non-Communist women activists and organizers. In late 1989, Morgan State University hosted a celebration of the Communist Party's seventy years in Maryland. The event, captured on video, combined songs, vintage photos, and reminiscences by veteran Party members with a narrative highlighting Party history from its founding to its support of the Pittston, West Virginia, coal miners' strike. By the early 1990s, the Maryland Party had reestablished itself as an advocate of political activism and had gained respect as the repository of a grand tradition of historical radicalism.

The Maryland Party's greatest challenge in the 1990s came not from anti-Communist critics but from the collapse of communism in Eastern Europe and the Soviet Union. Initially, the Party enthusiastically supported the reforms of Mikhail Gorbachev because they eased cold war tensions and seemed to repudiate conservative claims of the impossibility of democratic reforms in the Soviet Union. Tim Wheeler made a point of repeating to interested individuals that it did not matter how far Gorbachev pushed his reforms since, according to Marxism, once a society adopted socialism it was impossible to return to earlier forms of social relations. Even the dramatic collapse of the Communist regimes in Eastern Europe in 1989 failed to shake Wheeler's optimism.

On 4 March 1990, the representatives of seven left-wing organizations—

the CPUSA, Communist Labor Party, Democratic Socialists of America, Front Line Political Association, New Democratic Movement, Socialist Action, and Workers World Party—held a conference at St. John's Methodist Church to consider the changes in Eastern Europe. Reactions ranged from angry denunciations of American subversion and Gorbachev's abandonment of the region to cautious optimism that the passing of the old Stalinist regimes would open the door to genuine socialist development. Wheeler, speaking for the Communist Party, declared that capitalist propaganda to the contrary, communism was not dead. In fact, he continued, because of widespread support for Gorbachev's arms control initiatives, the opportunity existed to create a new world order modeled on the Soviet leader's ideals. Capitalism, Wheeler pointed out, sought to conceal the existence of a viable alternative by trumpeting the death of communism, a situation that could be changed by proper mass work by left-wing organizations. Little more than a year later, the outlawing of the Communist Party of the Soviet Union convinced Wheeler of Gorbachev's utter perfidy and generated a national split in the ranks of the CPUSA.[13]

The split, which took place at the Party's twenty-fifth convention in December of 1991, divided the Party into two groups. The reformist social democratic faction left the Party en masse to form the Committees of Correspondence, a name borrowed from the history of the American Revolution. A hard-line group that backed the aging leader Gus Hall remained in possession of the Party's name and resources. In California and New York, major centers of Party strength, the CPUSA divided virtually in half, with the younger members leaving the Party. Membership loss in Maryland followed the same pattern; although relatively few individuals dropped out, those who did came from among the younger, more recent recruits. Margaret Baldridge, who had initially supported the need for new Party leadership, remained a Hall loyalist but shortly after the convention resigned from her post as executive secretary.

In the spring of 1994, financial problems and poor management forced the Party to close the New Era Book Shop and sell the building, which had also housed Party headquarters. Despite the setback, George Meyers wrote to the author in September of the same year saying, "I want you to know that our Party is growing—in some places by leaps and bounds." At the time of his writing, national membership in the CPUSA was estimated to be one to two thousand. In Maryland, the Party numbered less than a hundred, with many members in their seventies and eighties. Meyers's letter demonstrated the kind of optimism and resolve that had brought the Party through tough times in the past. Previously, however, the Party had had the Soviet Union and the Communist nations of Eastern Europe as a source of legitimacy and support. Now, the Soviets are gone, their ideology discredited, and their old empire ravaged by pollution, poverty, corruption, and ethnic hatred. The Communist Party of Maryland is also finished as a significant political force and, like the Soviet Union, leaves behind an ambiguous legacy.[14]

The Communist Party of Maryland must be respected for raising tough, pointed questions and challenging the assumptions of mainstream society. It was one of the earliest advocates of civil rights for blacks, it consistently questioned the enormous gap between rich and poor, and it always urged reforms to improve the lot of working Americans. Such idealistic goals brought the Party such talented leaders as Earl Reno, Patrick Whalen, Al Lannon, Albert Blumberg, and Dorothy Rose Blumberg, the best and the brightest that the United States had to offer.

But the Party's commendable goals were ultimately dictated not by domestic American conditions but by the needs of Soviet politics and foreign policy, causing constant shifts in strategy and tactics. The most egregious example of such switches took place in the years before World War II, when the Party went from fighting fascism in Spain, to advocating noninterventionism in Europe, and back to focusing on antifascism, all in perfect step with Stalin's complex dance with Hitler. The Party's devotion to the USSR is understandable in the light of its unshakable belief in Moscow's role as the leading light of world revolution. But the Party's collective faith required deliberate acts of blindness on the part of its members. Gilbert Green's appallingly tortured justification for the winter war against Finland and Benjamin Field's breezy dismissal of the Moscow show trials are simply the more painful examples.

Worse, the ideals that Maryland's Communists fought for were corrupted by the fundamental errors of Marxism/Leninism, an ideology that reduces history to a series of inevitable stages and portrays highly complicated social situations as phases of a black-and-white struggle between oppressors and oppressed. At the core of Marxism/Leninism is the profound belief that a professional enlightened vanguard knows what is best for everyone. This belief enabled Stalin to construct a horrifying personal dictatorship and allowed American Communists to dismiss any opposition to their programs as false consciousness, class treason, or opportunism.

As a consequence, the Maryland Party sowed confusion and divisiveness in the ranks of both friends and opponents alike. Maryland's Senator John Reed, a labor supporter, begged the CIO and the Communist Party to stop crossing each other up, and Party control of the Progressive Citizens of America divided American liberals in the face of resurgent conservatism. Progressive-minded conservatives, such as Father Cronin, found Communist ideology so abhorrent that they distorted their own views by allying themselves with unsavory elements on the basis of anticommunism alone. The Party can not be blamed for the excesses of its opponents, but its presence in society was so divisive that it ultimately did more harm than good.

Notes

Introduction

1. Nelson, *Workers on the Waterfront,* 100.

2. Quoted in Personal and Confidential FBI Report to the Director of the FBI, 29 January 1944, Maryland Manuscripts 4008, Maryland Room, McKeldin Library, University of Maryland, College Park, Maryland (hereafter Maryland Manuscripts).

Chapter 1: Bolsheviks in Baltimore

1. Quoted in Salvatore, *Eugene V. Debs,* 291.

2. For a good brief description of the factionalism surrounding the birth of the American Communist movement, see Klehr and Haynes, *The American Communist Movement,* 15–26.

3. William Doyas, Report, 5 January 1920, including a copy of Party minutes by Dr. Louis Hendin, Bureau of Investigation File 379607, Microfilm File M1085, National Archives, Washington, D.C. (hereafter NA).

4. William M. Doyas, Report on Radical Activities in the Baltimore District, 28 February 1920, File 275205, NA; H. W. Hess, Report on IWW in Baltimore, 22 August 1917, District 2 Reports, in *U.S. Military Intelligence Reports.*

5. Sergeant Lynn D. Copeland, Corps of Intelligence Police, to Major Henry G. Pratt, Military Intelligence Division, Confidential Memo, 2 December 1919, in *U.S. Military Intelligence Reports.*

6. Johnson served as master of ceremonies for Benjamin Gitlow, the Party's second in command, during Gitlow's 1926 visit to Baltimore. "Gitlow at Open Forum," *Baltimore Sun,* 27 December 1926.

7. William Doyas, Report, 22 May 1920, File 275205, NA; Brugger, *Maryland,* 385–95; Dozer, *Portrait of the Free State,* 516–25; *The Sun Almanac for 1921,* 104.

8. Brugger, *Maryland,* 418–24; *The Sun Almanac for 1920,* 55.

9. Walsh and Fox, *Maryland,* 551–56.

10. Ibid., 506; Dozer, *Portrait of a Free State,* 4–5.

11. Brugger, *Maryland,* 432–33; Dozer, *Portrait of a Free State,* 507.

12. *The Sun Almanac for 1913,* 71–109.

13. Ibid., 98, 108; Brugger, *Maryland,* 434.

14. Powers, *Secrecy and Power,* 42–46.

15. C. E. Ruthenberg to L. Hendin, 22 September 1919, File 379607, NA; Party minutes, 26 September 1919 and week of 10 December 1919, in William Doyas, Report, 5 January 1920, File 379607, NA.

16. Undated sessions of the Baltimore Central Committee, in William Doyas, Report, 5 January 1920 and 2 January 1920, File 379607, NA.

17. C. E. Ruthenberg to L. Hendin, 30 September 1919, File 383256, NA.

18. The description of the meeting is based on a transcription of Party minutes, in William Doyas, Report, 5 January 1920, and in William Doyas, Report re Communist Party Radicals, 10 November 1919, File 379607, NA.

19. William Doyas, Report re Morris Isaac Berezin, 7 November 1919, File 331764, NA.

20. William Doyas to Frank Burke, 20 November 1919 and 20 December 1920, File 379607, NA; William Doyas, Report re Louis Hendin, 14 November 1919, File 383256, NA.

21. Henry Stein, Report, 14 November 1919, File 383256, NA; Powers, *Secrecy and Power,* 69–71.

22. Murray, *Red Scare,* 191–93; Party minutes, in William Doyas, Report, 5 January 1920, File 379607, NA.

23. William Doyas, Report, 5 January 1920, File 379607, NA.

24. Ibid.; William Doyas, Report, 2 January 1920, File 379607, NA.

25. William Doyas, Report, 21 January 1920, including attached list of names and addresses of individuals to be arrested, File 379607, NA; "Twenty-three Reds Taken in Baltimore Round-Up," 3 January 1920, *Baltimore News.*

26. "Twenty-three Reds Taken in Baltimore Round-Up," *Baltimore News,* 3 January 1920; "Over 4,500 Seized in Raids on Alleged Reds; 31 Arrested in Baltimore; 7 Released," *Baltimore Evening Sun,* 3 January 1920; "Four Colored 'Reds' Caught in US Net," *Afro-American,* 16 January 1920.

27. William Doyas, Report, 21 January 1920, including sample of testimony for each subject, File 379607, NA.

28. "Twenty-three Reds Taken in Baltimore Round-Up," *Baltimore News,* 3 January 1920; "Raids in Baltimore a Complete Success, Federal Agents Say," *Baltimore Evening Sun,* 3 January 1920; Julius Ohsis, interview, 2 January 1920, File 385964, NA; Katie Ohsis, interview, 2 January 1920, File 385963, NA.

29. Vasily Trimlove, interview, 3 January 1920, File 385804, NA.

30. Bertha Zimmermann, interview, 3 January 1920, File 391151, NA.

31. Ibid.

32. David Zimmermann, interview, 3 January 1920, File 46773, NA.

33. John Kufel, interview, 12 December 1919, File 382919, NA; "Twenty-three Reds Taken in Round-Up," *Baltimore News,* 3 January 1920.

34. Ibid.

35. William Doyas, Report re Thomas Truss, 18 May 1920, File 382986, NA.

36. William Doyas, Report re Embry Niles, 18 May 1920, and William Doyas, Report re Thomas Truss, 18 May 1920, File 382986, NA.

37. U.S. Military Attache, Copenhagen, Report, 7 January 1920, File 383073, NA.

38. Ibid.

39. William Doyas, Report, 28 January 1920, File 383073, NA.

40. K. C. Parrish, Report, 13 January 1920, File 3832565, NA.

41. "But Four Held as Radicals," *Baltimore Sun,* 12 February 1920.

42. Ibid.

43. L. Hendin to Comrade Bentzevitch, 18 February 1920, and William Doyas, Report, 26 February 1920, File 383256, NA.

44. The description of the ball is based on Confidential Informants, Report, 3 February 1920, and William Doyas, Report re Communist Party, 18 May 1920, File 379607, NA; Sergeant Lynn D. Copeland, Report re Workers Defense Union of Baltimore and New York, 2 December 1919, in *U.S. Military Intelligence Reports.*

45. William Doyas, Report, 1 June 1920, File 383256, NA; Minutes of the [New York] City Executive Committee Meeting, 10 January 1934, Earl Browder Papers, microfilm edition, University of Maryland, College Park, Md.

46. Notice of Deportation re David and Bertha Zimmermann, 9 April 1920, File 46733, NA; Murray, *Red Scare,* 246–49; Powers, *Secrecy and Power,* 114–22.

47. William Doyas, Report, 2 June 1920, 26 June 1920, and 17 August 1920, File 379607, NA; William Doyas, Report re Distribution of *The Communist,* 22 September 1920, File 368782, NA.

Chapter 2: The Lovestonite Expulsion

1. "New Party Planning Revolution in U.S.," 25 December 1921, "Moscow International Endorses Workers Party," 18 July 1922, and "Gompers Throws down Glove to Reds," 18 April 1923, *Baltimore Sun.*

2. District 3 Organizer to Comrade Miller re adoption of H. Cooper as pseudonym, 19 September 1922, 12; H. Cooper to Comrade Miller, 13 October 1922, 19; Comrade Jones to Comrade Miller, 30 October 1922, 32; District 3 Organizer to G. Lewis, 4 January 1922, 1, all in File 515-1-104, Russian Center for the Preservation and Study of Documents of Recent History, Moscow, Russian Federation (hereafter RTzKhIDNI).

3. G. Lewis to District 3 Organizer, 16 January 1922, 3; J. Miller to District 3 Organizer re lack of effort in recruiting Italians, 17 October 1922, 23; Headquarters to District 3, October [date illegible] 1922, 28, all in File 515-1-104, RTzKhIDNI.

4. National Office to Baltimore District Organizer, October 22, 1924, 11, File 515-1-317, RTzKhIDNI. Information on the Maryland careers of Jakira, Bail, and Ben-

jamin can be found throughout the following files: 515-1-104, 317, 750, 552, 654, 659, 1027, and 1028, KTzKhIDNI. For additional material on Benjamin, see Klehr, *The Heyday of American Communism.*

5. Irving Solinsky to Alfred Wagenknecht, October 24, 1924, 14; Solinsky to Wagenknecht, telegram, October 25, 1924, 17; Abram Jakira to Wagenknecht, 31 October 1924, 21, all in File 515-1-317, RTzKhIDNI.

6. Irving Solinsky to Earl Browder, 26 January 1925, 1 (quote), File 515-1-493; Solinsky to Browder, 17 February 1925, 3, File 515-1-493; Executive Secretary to Chatty [Nicholas Ciattei], 15 July 1925, 52, File 515-1-491; Alex Bail to Charles Ruthenberg, 16 October 1925, File 515-1-492; Summary of Branch Reports for District, 1924, 25–28, File 515-1-380; Acting Secretary to Irving Solinsky, 30 February 1925, 49, File 515-1-491; Executive Secretary to N. Chatty, 15 July 1925, 52, File 515-1-491; A. Bail, Report to Jay Lovestone on Reorganization of the Baltimore Party, 1 February 1926, 10–12, File 515-1-750, all in RTzKhIDNI.

7. Statement of the City Central Committee of Baltimore in regards to the Action Taken by the Jewish Branch at Abramovich Meeting, n.d., 33, File 515-1-551, RTzKhIDNI.

8. Executive Secretary to Irving Solinsky, 5 June 1925, 48, File 515-1-491; Solinsky to Browder, 12 March 1925, 5, File 515-1-493; Thomas N. Owerking to Comrades, 9 April 1925, 7, File 515-1-493; N. Chatty to Earl Browder, 22 April 1925, 8, File 515-1-493; A. Litvakoff, Report on the Baltimore Situation, 21 July 1925, 17, File 515-1-552, all in RTzKhIDNI.

9. The discussion of the team's assessment of the Party in Baltimore is based on A. Bail, Report to Jay Lovestone on Reorganization of the Baltimore Party, 1 February 1926, 10–12 (quote on 10), File 515-1-750, RTzKhIDNI.

10. Change of Addresses of Secretaries during Month of July, 1924, 21, File 515-1-380; Executive Secretary to A. Jakira, 5 May 1925, 3, File 515-1-491; Executive Secretary to A. Jakira, 24 December 1924, 39, File 515-1-317; A. Jakira to Comrade Ruthenberg, 29 December 1924, 41, File 515-1-317; Alex Bail to Charles Ruthenberg, 15 April 1926, 36, File 515-1-657; Norman Tallentire to Charles Ruthenberg, 28 June 1926, 76, File 515-1-654, all in RTzKhIDNI.

11. Barbara Danilova Suvarova to "America, Baltimore—to the Communist Party," 20 August 1926, 3–5, translated by Dasha Lotareva, File 515-1-1027, RTzKhIDNI.

12. Alex Bail, Report on the Reorganization of the Baltimore Party, 10–12; Norman Tallentire to Jay Lovestone, 3 February 1926, 15, both in File 515-1-750, RTzKhIDNI.

13. Ellen Zetron to Charles Ruthenberg, 11 November 1925, 17, File 515-1-493; Memorandum Adopted Unanimously, August 24, 1927, by the City Executive Committee, Local Baltimore, 68, File 515-1-1142, both in RTzKhIDNI.

14. "Gitlow at Open Forum," 27 December 1926, and "New York Communists Deny Secret Activities," 21 December 1923, *Baltimore Sun.*

15. Charles Ruthenberg to N. Chatty, 7 October 1926, 23, File 515-1-659, RTzKhIDNI.

16. District 3 Executive Committee, Minutes, 7 April 1926, 25, File 515-1-874; Alex Bail to Charles Ruthenberg, 15 April 1926, 34–35, File 515-1-657; Charles Ruthenberg to Norman Tallentire and David Howatt, 26 April 1926, 36, File 515-1-656, all in RTzKhIDNI.

17. Alex Bail to Jay Lovestone, 12 February 1926, 31, File 515-1-750, RTzKhIDNI.

18. Alex Bail to Benjamin Gitlow (who forwarded the letter to Lovestone), 15 February 1926, 37, File 515-1-750, RTzKhIDNI.

19. Alex Bail reacted to news of Ruthenberg's death by sending a letter to Jay Lovestone that began "This is a horrible calamity . . . ," 3 March 1927, 45, File 515-1-1027, RTzKhIDNI.

20. Report of the Majority of the Credentials Committee, District Convention, District 3, 21 August 1927, 42, File 515-1-1142, RTzKhIDNI.

21. Memorandum Adopted Unanimously, August 24, 1927, by the City Executive Committee, Local Baltimore, 68, File 515-1-1142, RTzKhIDNI.

22. Jay Lovestone to Alex Bail, 21 September 1927, 28, File 515-1-1028; Alex Bail to Jay Lovestone, 2 October 1927, 33, File 515-1-1028, both in RTzKhIDNI.

23. "Predicts Next War as Civil Conflict," *Baltimore Sun,* 21 November 1927.

24. Pat Devine to Org Department, 27 December 1927, 80, File 515-1-1142; *Sparrow's Point Worker,* May 1928, 11–13, File 515-1-1396, both in RTzKhIDNI.

25. "Revolution and Civil War Held Radical Inspiration," *Baltimore Sun,* 5 July 1928.

26. John Pepper, "America and the Tactics of the Communist International," *Communist,* April 1928, 219–27.

27. Baltimore Central Committee, Minutes, 23 April 1929, 14–16, File 515-1-1745, RTzKhIDNI; "Communist Party Holds Meeting in City May First," *Baltimore Sun,* 28 April 1929.

28. [Baltimore] Central Committee, Minutes, 3 May 1929, 19, File 515-1-1745, RTzKhIDNI.

29. Ibid., 8 May 1929, 23–28.

30. Klehr, *The Heyday of American Communism,* 38.

31. Ibid., 28–31; "Open Air Meeting Held Here but Heat Prevents Parade," *Baltimore Sun,* 7 July 1929.

32. "Communists Held for Curb Meeting," *Baltimore Sun,* 30 July 1929.

33. Jon O'Ren, "Down the Spillway," *Baltimore Sun,* 31 July 1929.

34. "Says Banks Caused Radicals Arrest," 31 July 1929, and "Captain Mooney and Communists," 1 August 1929, *Baltimore Sun.*

35. "Captain Mooney and Communists," 1 August 1929, "Two Hundred Attend Anti-War Demonstration in City," 2 August 1929, "Communists Hold Meeting," 6 August 1929, "Communists Hold Meeting," 8 August 1929, and "Framing in Strike Is Charged," 23 August 1929, *Baltimore Sun.*

36. Communist Party of U.S.A. Baltimore Section, City Committee Minutes, 15 September 1929, 42–43, File 515-1-1745, RTzKhIDNI.

37. Ibid.

38. Ibid., 42.

39. "Workers Funeral Held for Cobbler," *Baltimore Sun,* 1 March 1936.

40. Communist Party of U.S.A. Baltimore Section, City Committee Minutes, 15 September 1929, 42–43, File 515-1-1745, RTzKhIDNI.

41. "Girl Communist Tells of Strike," *Baltimore Sun,* 28 September 1929.

42. "Communist Party Worker to Speak Here Tonight," 20 October 1929, and "Anti-Communists Routed by Police," 14 October 1929, *Baltimore Sun.*

43. [Baltimore] Central Committee, Minutes, 8 May 1929, 27, File 5151-1-1745, RTzKhIDNI; "Election Returns for 1936," in State of Maryland, *Maryland Manual,* 309; Joseph Nowak, testimony, in U.S. Congress, *Investigation of Communist Activities in the Baltimore Area* (1954), 4141.

44. [Baltimore] Central Committee, Minutes, 8 May 1929, 27, File 5151-1-1745, RTzKhIDNI; "Two Hundred Celebrate Czar's Downfall," *Baltimore Sun,* 9 November 1929.

Chapter 3: The Third Period

1. Argersinger, *Toward a New Deal in Baltimore,* 22–23; Brugger, *Maryland,* 494–95; Walsh and Fox, *Maryland,* 730–31.

2. Brugger, *Maryland,* 495 (quotes); "Communist Party Here Plans Demonstration," *Baltimore Sun,* 27 February 1930.

3. "Four Communists Arrested at Jobless Rally," *Baltimore Sun,* 2 March 1930.

4. "Trusting to Clubs," *Baltimore Sun,* 1 March 1930,

5. "Jobless Rally Set for Thursday Noon," 4 March 1930, and "Communists Plan Parade Minus Permit," 5 March 1930, *Baltimore Sun.*

6. The official Party report submitted the day after the parade claimed 500 marchers, 1,000 "followers," and 5,000 spectators. The description of the demonstration is based on the Report on March Sixth Demonstration, District 3, 7 March 1930, 62, File 515-1-1953, RTzKhIDNI; "Nine Hundred Policemen Assigned to Handle Parade," 6 March 1930, and "Baltimore Parade Quiet as Nine Hundred Policemen Watch," 7 March 1930, *Baltimore Sun;* "City's Jobless in Orderly Parade" and "Turnipseeds Plentiful, But George Can't Be Found," *Baltimore Evening Sun,* 6 March 1930.

7. "As the Communists Marched up Biddle Street," *Afro-American,* 15 March 1930; "Baltimore Parade Quiet as Nine Hundred Policemen Watch," *Baltimore Sun,* 7 March 1930; Gerald W. Johnson, "The Red Menace Comes to Baltimore," *New Republic,* 26 March 1930, 150.

8. "Riots Mark Observance of Unemployment Day in Both Hemispheres," "Radical Killed by Berlin Police," "Communists Turn New York Demonstration into Disorder," and "Police Suppress Capital Disorder with Tear Gas" (quote), *Baltimore Sun,* 7 March 1930; "Single Tear Gas Bomb Ends Fuss at White House," *Baltimore Evening Sun,* 6 March 1930.

9. "Three Hundred New Members Join Communist Group Here," 8 March 1930, and "Four Communists Arrested a Jobless Rally," 2 March 1930, *Baltimore Sun;* Report on March Sixth Demonstration, District 3, 7 March 1930, 63 (quote), File 515-1-1953, RTzKhIDNI.

10. "Radicals Scorn May Day Permit," 6 April 1930, "Parade Planned by Communists," 29 April 1930 (quote), and "Radicals to March by Daylight Time," 1 May 1930, *Baltimore Sun.*

11. "450 Policemen Guard Radical Meeting," 2 May 1930, and Jon O'Ren, "Down the Spillway," 2 May 1930 (quote), *Baltimore Sun.*

12. "Communist Coffers Succumb to Bills of Capitalists," 24 June 1930, and "Light Still Shines upon Communists," 25 June 1930, *Baltimore Sun.*

13. "Samuel Parker for Governor as Communist," *Afro-American,* 5 July 1930.

14. "Negro Longshoreman Picked for Governor by Communists," *Baltimore Sun,* 30 June 1930.

15. Ibid.

16. "$1,080 to Place Candidates on Ticket? Radicals Just Grin," *Baltimore Sun,* 1 July 1930,

17. "Two Candidates of Radicals Out," 2 July 1930 (quote), and "Names of Nineteen Candidates to Be Placed on Ballots," 10 October 1930, *Baltimore Sun.*

18. "Communist Leaders Open New Party Headquarters," 13 October 1930, "Communists Granted Permit for Tag Day Saturday," 13 October 1930, "Communists Sell Tags for Missionary Drive Fund," 19 October 1930, "Israel Amter to Address Communists' Rally Today," 23 October 1930, and "Radicals Greet Party Organizer," 24 October 1930, *Baltimore Sun.*

19. E. Gardos, Report on the Election Campaign, 8 November 1930, 76–80 (quote on 80), File 515-1-1953, RTzKhIDNI.

20. "What They Will Learn," *Baltimore Evening Sun,* 6 March 1930.

21. George G. Henry, chief inspector of Baltimore police, to Hamilton Fish, 20 November 1930, Box 148, Folder 2, J. B. Matthews Papers, Special Collections, Perkins Library, Duke University, Durham, N.C. (hereafter Matthews Papers); "Baltimore Woman at Radical Probe," *Baltimore Sun,* 26 November 1930.

22. Mrs. Ruben Ross Holloway, testimony, in U.S. Congress, *Investigation of Un-American Activities* (1930), 167, 168.

23. Ibid., 168.

24. "Baltimore Woman at Radical Probe," *Baltimore Sun,* 26 November 1930.

25. Richmond, *A Long View from the Left,* 109.

26. "Speaker Predicts War with Soviets," *Baltimore Sun,* 22 December 1930.

27. "Radicals Fined for Breaking Up Soup Line," *Baltimore Sun,* 11 December 1930.

28. Klehr, *The Heyday of American Communism,* 50–54.

29. "Landlord Asks Negro for Rent, Gets Communist Tracts Instead," *Baltimore Sun,* 21 January 1931.

30. "Moving Men and Irate Radicals Play Checkers with Furniture," 24 January 1931, "Police and Radicals Again Play Games with Furniture," 26 February 1931, and "Arrested for Attempt to Block Eviction," 11 September 1931, *Baltimore Sun.*

31. "League Plans Hunger March," 15 January 1931, and "Idle Communist Crusaders Camp," 1 April 1931, *Baltimore Sun.*

32. "Delegates Clash with Communists," *Baltimore Sun,* 2 April 1931.

33. Ibid.

34. Elizabeth Painter, interview with author, 5 November 1989; "Hunger March Gets Kid-Glove Treatment Here," 6 December 1931, and "Marchers Enjoy Communist Food," 9 December 1931, *Baltimore Sun;* "450 Black, 1,050 White Hunger Marchers Going," *Afro-American,* 5 December 1931; "Police Ready for Hunger Army," 4 December 1931, "Red Columns Here Tonight," 6 December 1931, and "Hunger Army Leaves Today," 8 December 1931, *Washington Post.*

35. Klehr, *The Heyday of American Communism,* 62.

36. Richmond, *A Long View from the Left,* 123.

37. "ILD Attorney Continues Fight," 14 November 1931, *Afro-American;* "Farmer Testifies Lee Made Threat against Davis over Pay for a Day," *Baltimore Sun,* 19 January 1932.

38. Memorandum, "Equal Protection of the Law and Fair Trials in Maryland," 155–56.

39. Ibid., 157.

40. "Plan Duel Lee Mass Meeting Here Friday," *Afro-American,* 14 November 1931.

41. "State Militia to Curb Eastern Shore Mob at Cambridge," 21 November 1931, and "Sho' Mob Active as Ades Seeks Venue Change," 28 November 1931, *Afro-American.*

42. "Sho' Mob Active as Ades Seeks Venue Change," 28 November 1931, and "Eyewitness to Lynching Tells How Mob Acted," 12 December 1931, *Afro-American.*

43. This account is based on "Eyewitness to Lynching Tells How Mob Acted" and "Lynchers in Salisbury Had Right of Way," *Afro-American,* 12 December 1931.

44. "Eyewitness to Lynching Tells How Mob Acted," "Lynchers in Salisbury Had Right of Way," and "Salisbury Times Condones Lynching," *Afro-American,* 12 December 1931; "A Statement," *Salisbury Times,* 6 December 1931 (first quote); "Salisbury Mayor Rounds up Leaders," *Afro-American,* 12 December 1931 (second quote).

45. "Governor Ritchie Promises Sweeping Investigation" and "Ritchie Orders Mob Members Arrest; Lee Trial Deferred," *Baltimore Sun,* 6 December 1931; "Lee Trial Set in Towson Next Week," *Afro-American,* 9 January 1932.

46. "Colored Jurors May Serve in Lee Case," *Afro-American,* 16 January 1932; "Farmer Testifies," *Baltimore Sun,* 19 January 1932 (quote).

47. "Farmer Testifies," *Baltimore Sun,* 19 January 1932.

48. "First Day of Trial Found Lee a Mile from Murder Scene," "Ades Accuses Ocean City Chief Cop of Framing Defendant Lee," "Lee Found Guilty," and "Mistrial Asked, Court Says, 'No,'" 23 January 1932, *Afro-American.*

49. Memorandum, "Equal Protection of the Law and Fair Trials in Maryland," 160 (quote); Judge Morris Soper, *In the Matter of Bernard Ades,* U.S. District Court for the District of Maryland, Petition Docket, Number 978.

50. "State Keeps Three Negroes off Jury for Lee Trial," *Baltimore Sun,* 27 September 1932; "Negro Woman Takes Stand in Ades Case," *Baltimore Evening Sun,* 1 March 1932; McGuinn, "Equal Protection of the Law and Fair Trials in Maryland," 160–61.

51. "Defenders of Lee Meet with Defeat," *Baltimore Sun,* 19 May 1932; McGuinn,

"Equal Protection of the Law and Fair Trials in Maryland," 163–64; "The By-Products of the Lee Case," *Afro-American,* 23 January 1932.

52. "G.O.P. to Sponsor Negro Meetings," *Baltimore Sun,* 27 November 1933.

53. Editorial Column, *Afro-American,* 4 March 1932; McGuinn, "Equal Protection of the Law and Fair Trials in Maryland," 156.

Chapter 4: The Communist Party and the New Deal

1. Klehr, *The Heyday of American Communism,* 77–78.

2. John W. Schilling, Report, 13 November 1932, in *U.S. Military Intelligence Reports* (quote); Paul Cline to the Language Commission, 9 February 1933, RTzKhIDNI.

3. "Hunger Army Scouts Renew Demands on City of Cumberland," 3 December 1932, and "Hunger Army Swished through City by Police," 4 December 1932, *Cumberland Evening Times.*

4. Minutes of Committee Meeting for Final Arrangements for National Hunger March, held November 18, 1932; Joint Committee for National Hunger March, Statement of Cash Receipts and Disbursements for Period, 13 November 1932 to 10 December 1932, Third Corp Area, both in *U.S. Military Intelligence Reports.*

5. "Armory Rings with Red Songs of Marchers," *Baltimore Sun,* 4 December 1932; Carl Winter, interview with author, 19 June 1989.

6. "Hunger Army Scouts Renew Demands on City of Cumberland," *Cumberland Evening Times,* 3 December 1932.

7. "Hunger Army Swished through City by Police," *Cumberland Evening Times,* 4 December 1932.

8. Ibid.; "Cumberland Guns Avert Crises," *Washington Post,* 4 December 1932.

9. "1,700 Invaders Face Guns in Winchester," and "Writ to Free Marchers from Police Net Sought," *Washington Post,* 5 December 1932.

10. "Marchers to Parade and Go," 6 December 1932, and "Marchers on Way Home Given Food in Baltimore," 7 December 1932, *Washington Post.*

11. "Marchers May Return Here Late Tonight," *Cumberland Evening Times,* 7 December 1932; "Complaint Made in Marcher Exodus," *Washington Post,* 9 December 1932.

12. "Mixed Dance Leads to Riot," *Baltimore Sun,* 9 January 1933.

13. Ibid.

14. "Mooney Hall Mixed Color Dance Blocked," 22 January 1933, and "Bar Mooney Hall to Labor Defense," 23 January 1933, *Baltimore Sun.*

15. "Order to Stop Communists Rally Dropped," *Baltimore Sun,* 26 January 1933.

16. "Communists Are People," *Baltimore Evening Sun,* 26 January 1934 (first quote); "Mixed Color Dance Held by Communists in Condemned Hall," *Baltimore Sun,* 29 January 1933 (second quote).

17. Mable Pierce to Earl Browder, 28 April 1933, 121, File 515-1-3220; A. J. Rinis to Comrade Weiner, 17 March 1933, 37–39, both in RTzKhIDNI.

18. Alex Bail to Jay Lovestone, 26 September 1927, 31, File 515-1-1028; A. J. Rinis

to Comrade Weiner, 17 March 1933, 37–39 (quote on 38), File 515-1-3220, both in RTzKhIDNI.

19. Paul Cline to William Wiener, 12 April 1933, 50, File 515-1-3220, RTzKhIDNI.

20. Baltimore Secretariat to District 3, 25 January 1933, 18; Paul Cline to William Wiener, 12 April 1933, 50–52, both in File 515-1-3220, RTzKhIDNI.

21. W. W. to Baltimore Section District 3, 30 March 1933, 41; H. K. Shore to Comrade Hochberger, 16 March 1933, 42–45; Section Committee, Baltimore Section, to Central Committee CPUSA, 53–54 (Cline's response), all in File 515-1-3220, RTzKhIDNI.

22. Paul Cline to Central Committee Organization Department, 11 May 1933, 70; Paul Cline to Comrade Weiner, 11 May 1933, 71, both in File 515-1-3220, RTzKhIDNI.

23. Quoted in Klehr, *The Heyday of American Communism,* 95 (Amter quote), 94 (Browder quote).

24. Labor's Public Works Plan for Baltimore, 28–29, File 515-1-3219, RTzKhIDNI.

25. Ibid., 29–30.

26. Paul Cline to Central Committee, Org Department, 30 June 1933, 126; Paul Cline to Central Committee, Org Department, 14 July 1933, 137, both in File 515-1-3220, RTzKhIDNI.

27. H. Baxter to R. B. Hudson, 23 November 1933, 188–89, File 515-1-3220, RTzKhIDNI.

28. Jack Roth to J. Peters, December 1933, 231–33, File 515-1-3220, RTzKhIDNI.

29. Klehr, *The Heyday of American Communism,* 160–61; Rudy Baker, Short Report on the Work of the Secret Apparatus of the US Communist Party, File 495-74-472, RTzKhIDNI.

30. J. Peters to AWM [Mills], 21 March 1933, 22, File 515-1-3150, RTzKhIDNI.

31. H. Williams to J. Peters, 25 April 1934, 45, File 515-1-3536.

32. Despite the coincidence of names, Carpenter should not be confused with Baltimore Party founder David Zimmermann. Background on Carpenter was drawn from his college records at the University of Virginia, entries in the *Baltimore City Directory,* and the following sources: Henry Julian Wadleigh, "Why I Spied for the Communists," *New York Post Home News,* 12 July 1949 (quote describing Carpenter's physical appearance); Tanenhaus, *Whittaker Chambers,* 106 (FBI quote); and Chambers, *Witness,* 384.

33. Jack Roth to J. Peters, December 1933, 233, File 515-1-3220, RTzKhIDNI.

34. Andrew and Gordievsky, *KGB,* 229–30; Chambers, *Witness,* 369–70; Rudy Baker, Short Report on the Work of the Secret Apparatus of the US Communist Party, File 495-74-472, RTzKhIDNI.

35. Jack Roth to J. Peters, December 1933, 231, File 515-1-3220, RTzKhIDNI.

36. Richmond, *A Long View from the Left,* 103–4.

37. G. P., "The Shop Nucleus at Sparrows Point," *Party Organizer,* March 1934, 28–29.

38. Klehr, *The Heyday of American Communism,* 105–6.

39. S. [David] Howatt, "The Work of the Baltimore Section," *Party Organizer,* April 1934, 19; Klehr, *The Heyday of American Communism,* 94–96; Lt. Colonel J. C. Pegram, "Communist Activities in Baltimore," Third Corps Area, 23 January 1934, in *U.S. Military Intelligence Reports.*

40. Lt. Colonel J. C. Pegram, "Communist Activities in Baltimore," Third Corps Area, 23 January 1934, and "Two Month Plan of Work," December 1933, Third Corps Area, both in *U.S. Military Intelligence Reports;* S. [David] Howatt, "The Work of the Baltimore Section," *Party Organizer,* April 1934, 19.

41. Comrade Manuilsky and American Comrades, interview, 31 August 1930, 1–16, File 495-37-73; Minutes of the National Convention of the Marine Workers League, New York City, 26–27 April 1930, 2–10, File 515-1-2179, both in RTzKhIDNI.

42. Lt. Colonel J. C. Pegram to Assistant Chief of Staff, G-2, 27 June 1932, Lt. Colonel J. C. Pegram, "Estimate of Subversive Situation," 14 July 1932 (quote), and Bartholomew Bratton, Report to W. H. Moran, Third Corps Area, 26 October 1932, all in *U.S. Military Intelligence Reports;* "Police Battle Agitators, Two Are Injured," *Baltimore Sun,* 27 June 1932; "Officer, Speaker, Taken to Hospital," *Baltimore News-Post,* 27 June 1932.

43. William C. McCuiston, testimony, in U.S. Congress, *Investigation of Un-American Activities and Propaganda* (1940), 6640.

44. Richmond, *A Long View from the Left,* 168–73; Nelson, *Workers on the Waterfront,* 96–97.

45. "Baltimore out for Real Relief," *Dog House News,* 2 January 1934, 1, and "Surprises Luck in Office Quiz," *Dog House News,* 8 February 1934, 8, File 515-1-3688, RTzKhIDNI; William C. McCuiston, testimony, in U.S. Congress, *Investigation of Un-American Activities and Propaganda* (1940), 6626; Zeidman and Hallengren, "The Baltimore Soviet," 167.

46. "Seamen Getting Aid Here Deny Communist Control," *Baltimore Sun,* 3 March 1934; Zeidman and Hallengren, "The Baltimore Soviet," 167–8; William C. McCuiston, testimony, in U.S. Congress, *Investigation of Un-American Activities and Propaganda* (1940), 6626–27; "Support the Baltimore Fight," *Dog House News,* 13 February 1934, 12, File 515-1-3688, RTzKhIDNI.

47. "Labor Official Says Communists Control Seamen's Relief Funds," 2 March 1934, and "Deny Communist Control," 3 March 1934, *Baltimore Sun.*

48. Zeidman and Hallengren, "The Baltimore Soviet," 169 (quote); Nelson, *Workers on the Waterfront,* 99–100; "Baltimore in Arms Again," *Dog House News,* 21 March 1934, 28, and "Baltimore Back in Control," *Dog House News,* 16 May 1934, 33, File 515-1-3688, RTzKhIDNI.

49. Nelson, *Workers on the Waterfront,* 98; William C. McCuiston, testimony, in U.S. Congress, *Investigation of Un-American Activities and Propaganda* (1940), 6631.

50. M. Zeibel to Comrade Brown, 12 July 1934, 120–22 (quotes on 122), File 515-1-3536, RTzKhIDNI.

51. H. Williams to J. Peters, 13 July 1934, 132; J. Gaal to F. Brown, 18 August 1934, 158; and J. Gaal, Report on Situation in Baltimore Section, 7 September 1934, 178, all in 515-1-3536, RTzKhIDNI.

52. J. Gaal, Report on Situation in Baltimore Section, 7 September 1934, 178, 515-1-3536, RTzKhIDNI.

53. Ibid., 178–80.

54. Klehr, *The Heyday of American Communism*, 108–9; J. Gaal, Report on Situation in Baltimore Section, 7 September 1934, 178–80, File 515-1-3536, RTzKhIDNI.

55. Nelson, *Workers on the Waterfront*, 135–36; Klehr, *The Heyday of American Communism*, 127–28.

56. "Lessons of the San Francisco General Strike," 22 August 1934, 6–10 (all quotes on 6), File 515-1-3400, RTzKhIDNI.

57. Jack Stachel to J. Gaal, 2 February 1935, 12; J. Gaal to F. Brown and Central Committee Organization Commission, 20 February 1935, 15, both in File 515-1-3822, RTzKhIDNI.

58. Richard McAlister to Editor, *Daily Worker*, n.d., 228, File 515-1-3220, RTzKhIDNI.

59. Editorial Department to Max Bedacht, 31 December 1933, 226, File 515-1-3220; Editorial Department to Richard McAlister, 31 December 1933, 227, File 515-1-3220; J. Gaal to F. Brown, 14 January 1935, 22, File 515-1-3763; Org Commission to J. Gaal, 24 January 1935, 23, File 515-1-3763, all in RTzKhIDNI.

60. Edward S. Lewis, executive secretary, Baltimore Urban League, to Earl Browder, 18 April 1935, 137, File 515-1-3750, RTzKhIDNI; Earl Reno, testimony, in U.S. Congress, *Investigation of Communist Activities in the Baltimore Area* (1954), 4083.

Chapter 5: "Let's Make Baltimore a Union Town"
1. "The Communist International, from the Sixth to the Seventh Congress—1928–1935," October 1935, and "The Seventh World Congress of the Communist International and the Tasks of Our Party," December 1935, *Communist;* Klehr, *The Heyday of American Communism*, 167–70.

2. Hudson to L. Philips, 26 April 1935, 43; Earl Dixon to Org Committee, Attention Comrade Brown, 29 April 1935, 44–45; Earl Dixon to Comrade Brown, 16 May 1935, 60–62, all in File 515-1-3822, RTzKhIDNI.

3. AWM (Mills) to Org Commission, 27 April 1934, 4, File 515-1-3536; AWM to Org Department, 15 June 1934, 8, File 515-1-3536; E. Dixon to Comrade Brown, 16 May 1935, 60–62, File 515-1-3822, all in RTzKhIDNI. (Org Commission, Org Committee, and Org Department are used interchangeably in the documents; they all refer to the same unit.)

4. E. Dixon to Comrade Brown, 16 May 1935, 60–62; E. Dixon to Jack Stachel, 1 June 1935, 70–71, both in File 515-1-3822, RTzKhIDNI.

5. E. Dixon to Jack Stachel, 1 June 1935, 70–71, File 515-1-3822, RTzKhIDNI.

6. Jack Stachel to Comrade Dixon, 4 June 1935, 72, File 515-1-3822, RTzKhIDNI.

7. Undated fragment, 138–40, File 515-1-3822, RTzKhIDNI.

8. E. Dixon to Jack Stachel, 16 May 1935, 63–64, File 515-1-3822, RTzKhIDNI.

9. Naison, *Communists in Harlem during the Depression,* 155–56; Leonard Patterson, testimony, in U.S. Congress, *Investigation of Communist Activities in the Baltimore Area* (1954), 4124, 4126; E. Dixon to Org Committee, Attention Comrade Brown, 29 April 1935, 44–45, File 515-1-3822; E. Dixon to Comrade Brown, 16 May 1935, 60–62, File 515-1-3822, RTzKhIDNI.

10. Leonard Patterson, testimony, in U.S. Congress, *Investigation of Communist Activities in the Baltimore Area* (1954), 4122–24; Earl Reno, testimony, ibid., 4094–95.

11. Joseph S. Nowak, testimony, ibid., 4135.

12. Ibid., 4139.

13. Ibid., 4135, 4141–42.

14. Ibid., 4142–43; Leonard Patterson, testimony, ibid., 4126–27.

15. Earl Reno, testimony, ibid., 4089, 4093.

16. Earl Dixon to Comrade Brown, 18 October 1935, 104–5, File 515-1-3822, RTzKhIDNI.

17. Earl Reno, testimony, in U.S. Congress, *Investigation of Communist Activities in the Baltimore Area* (1954), 4093.

18. Ibid., 4093–94; Joseph S. Nowak, testimony, ibid., 4143–47.

19. Mary Himoff to Central Committee Agitprop Department, 23 July 1935, 85; Mary Himoff to F. Brown, 23 October 1935, 106, both in File 515-1-3822, RTzKhIDNI.

20. Mary Himoff to Central Committee Agitprop Department, 23 July 1935, 85, File 515-1-3822; Mary Himoff to Pat Toohey, 16 March 1936, 114–15, File 515-1-3977, both in RTzKhIDNI.

21. Mary Himoff to Pat Toohey, 16 March 1936, 114–15, File 515-1-3977, RTzKhIDNI.

22. Quoted in Pat Toohey to Comrade Brown, 3 April 1936, 62, 515-1-4009, RTzKhIDNI.

23. Ibid.; Mary Himoff to Pat Toohey, 16 March 1936, 114–15, File 515-1-3977; Mary Himoff, open letter, 1 April 1936, 137, File 515-1-3977, all in RTzKhIDNI.

24. Chambers, *Witness,* 385; Wadleigh, "Why I Spied for the Communists," *New York Post Home News,* 2 July 1949, 3, 36.

25. William Spiegel, testimony, in U.S. Congress, *Hearings relating to Communist Activities in the Defense Area of Baltimore* (1951), 1046, 1050.

26. Earl Dixon to Jack Stachel, 11 May 1936, 79–80, File 515-1-4009, RTzKhIDNI; Argersinger, *Toward a New Deal in Baltimore,* 158–62.

27. Report of the State Convention of the Maryland State Federation of Labor, 2 June 1936, 51–52, File 515-1-3979, RTzKhIDNI.

28. Ibid., 53–54.

29. Ibid., 55.

30. Argersinger, *Toward a New Deal in Baltimore,* 161.

31. Earl Reno, testimony, in U.S. Congress, *Investigation of Communist Activities in the Baltimore Area* (1954), 4084; Reutter, *Sparrows Point,* 311–12.

32. Sirkka Lee Holm, interview with author, 15 November 1989; Reutter, *Sparrows Point,* 252, 311, 265 (Smith quote).

33. Earl Dixon to Jack Stachel, 7 June 1935, 74; Earl Dixon to J. W. Johnson, 7 June 1935, 73; Earl Dixon to Tony Minerich, 7 June 1935, 75, all in File 515-1-3822, RTzKhIDNI.

34. Earl Reno, testimony, in U.S. Congress, *Investigation of Communist Activities in the Baltimore Area* (1954), 4086, 4110–11.

35. Ibid., 4086; Fee, "George Meyers: Labor Leader," 192.

36. Rubin, *The Log of Rubin the Sailor,* 183, 187; Nelson, *Workers on the Waterfront,* 214–16; Goldberg, *The Maritime Story,* 152–54.

37. Jon O'Ren, "Down the Spillway," *Baltimore Sun,* 5 April 1934 and 27 March 1936.

38. Ibid., 26 June 1936.

39. "Browder Speaks to Crowd of 1,600," *Baltimore Sun,* 19 October 1936.

40. Louis J. O'Donnell, "What's This?" 20 October 1936, "Says Communists Were Not Spied On," 22 October 1936, "Hoover Seeks Fake G-Men Evidence Here," 23 October 1936, "Customs Unit Upholds Aide's Rally Activity," 28 October 1936, and "Phantom of the Opera, or the Mystery of the Missing G-Man" (Richard Yardley cartoon), 28 October 1936, *Baltimore Sun.*

41. Goldberg, *The Maritime Story,* 155–57.

42. Avnet, "Pat Whalen," 249–50.

43. Rubin, *The Log of Rubin the Sailor,* 160.

44. Zeidman and Hallengren, "The Fall/Winter Strike of 1936," 169–70; Avnet, "Pat Whalen," 251.

45. The account of the strike is based on Zeidman and Hallengren, "Speeding up Broadway," 170–71; Zeidman and Hallengren, "The Midnight March of the Baltimore Brigade," 172; and Argersinger, *Toward a New Deal in Baltimore,* 166–68.

46. Earl Dixon, Report, 84–88, File 495-38-84, RTzKhIDNI.

47. Earl Dixon, "Baltimore Sets the Pace for Party Recruiting," *Party Organizer,* December 1936, 7; Earl Reno, testimony, in U.S. Congress, *Investigation of Communist Activities in the Baltimore Area* (1954), 4096.

Chapter 6: The Popular Front

1. Committee to Defend Albert Blumber, *Thinking Forbidden Thoughts,* Box 112, Folder 10, Matthews Papers; Albert Blumberg, testimony, in U.S. Congress, *Investigation of Un-American Propaganda Activities in the United States* (1944), 7512–13; Lt. Colonel J. C. Pegram, "Communist Activities in Baltimore," Third Corps Area, 23 January 1934, in *U.S. Military Intelligence Reports.*

2. "Elections Held by Ships' Crews to Pick Union," 21 January 1937, and "Sea Union Protests Cut in WPA Fund," 31 January 1939 (Whalen quote), *Baltimore News-Post;* Avnet, "Pat Whalen," 254; Minutes of the District Buro Meeting, District 34, 5 August 1937, 104–6, File 495-14-50, RTzKhIDNI (Benjamin quote); Conversation with George Meyers, 25 October 1989 (Meyers quote).

3. Federal Bureau of Investigation, General Intelligence Memorandum re Communist Activities, Baltimore, Md., 2 December 1941, Maryland Manuscripts.

4. Minutes of the District Buro Meeting, District 34, 29 July 1937 and 3 February 1938, File 495-14-50, RTzKhIDNI.

5. Minutes of the District Buro Meeting, District 34, 13 January 1938, 27 January 1938, and 16 July 1938, File 495-14-50, RTzKhIDNI.

6. Minutes of the District Buro Meeting, District 34, 16 July 1937, 95–100, File 495-14-50, RTzKhIDNI; Albert Blumberg, testimony, in U.S. Congress, *Investigation of Un-American Propaganda Activities in the United States* (1944), 7507, 7513; Executive Committee, Legislative District 4, Reports, Box 148, Folder 1, Matthews Papers; "Workers School Offers Nineteen Courses for $2 Each," *Baltimore Evening Sun*, 28 February 1938.

7. Minutes of the District Buro Meeting, District 34, 12 August 1937, File 495-14-50, RTzKhIDNI.

8. Earl Reno, testimony, in U.S. Congress, *Investigation of Communist Activities in the Baltimore Area* (1954), 4109; "How Carl Bradley Earned His Three Bars," *Volunteer for Liberty: Organ of the International Brigades*, 4 October 1937, 4–5.

9. Quoted in Spalding, *The Premier See*, 353.

10. Minutes of the District 34 Committee, 11 September 1937, File 495-14-50, RTzKhIDNI.

11. Ibid.

12. Chambers, *Witness*, 421–23.

13. Ibid., 35–37 (quote on 35), 42; Andrew and Gordievsky, *KGB*, 231; Rudy Baker, Short Report on the Work of the Secret Apparatus of the US Communist Party, File 495-74-472, RTzKhIDNI.

14. "Communists Are Certified," 3 September 1938, and "Text of Editorial President Read as 'Own Statement,'" 17 August 1938, *Baltimore Sun*.

15. District 34, Minutes of the State Committee Meeting, 16 July 1938, File 495-14-50, RTzKhIDNI; "Communist's Stand Defied by Tydings," 14 August 1938 (quote), and "Communists Endorse Candidacy of Lewis," 4 September 1938, *Baltimore Sun*.

16. "A Playground at Last," and "May Day and Elections," *Good Neighbor,* issued by the Twenty-sixth Ward branch of the Communist Party of Maryland, William Andrews, editor, April 1939; "It's Happening Here," "The White Paper and Palestine," and "For a Free Junior College," *Your Neighbor,* issued by the Druid Hill branch of the Communist Party of Baltimore, Carl Breen, editor, June–July, 1939, all in Box 148, Folder 1, Matthews Papers.

17. "By Way of Introduction," *Your Neighbor,* June–July, 1939 (first quote); "What Is the Communist Party," *Good Neighbor,* April 1939 (second quote), both in Box 148, Folder 1, Matthews Papers.

18. "By Way of Introduction," *Fourth District News,* November 1938; "What Is Communism?" *Liberty Bell,* August 1939, both in Box 148, Folder 1, Matthews Papers.

19. *Vote Communist* (election pamphlet, published by authority of William C. Taylor, chairman of the Campaign Committee), April 1939, Box 148, Folder 2, Matthews Papers.

20. Klehr, *The Heyday of American Communism,* 388; "Hear Roy Powers and I. Samuelson Speak on the Soviet-German Non-Aggression Pact" (flyer), 26 August 1939, and "Do You Know What the Soviet Non-Aggression Pact with Germany Means" (flyer), 1 September 1939, Box 148, Folder 2, Matthews Papers.

21. "Communists Will Speak at Five Meetings Here," 11 September 1939, and "Russia No Friend of Reich, Communist Secretary Says," 12 September 1939, *Baltimore Sun.*

22. Klehr, *The Heyday of American Communism,* 390.

23. "Calls European War Bandits' Fight for Loot," *Baltimore Sun,* 2 October 1939.

24. Klehr, *The Heyday of American Communism,* 396–97.

25. "The Truth about Finland," *Champion,* January 1940, Box 148, Folder 1, Matthews Papers.

26. "Communist Calls Finland Gangster," *Baltimore Sun,* 15 January 1940.

27. "The Truth about Father Coughlin and Anti-Semitism" (flyer) and "Attention East Baltimore" (flyer), Box 148, Folder 2, Matthews Papers; "Communist Flag Hangs at JHU; Swastikas Banned at Peace Rally," *Baltimore Sun,* 28 April 1938.

28. "Fray Produces Names of C.I.O. Leaders He Terms Communists," 14 August 1938, "Dies Probers to Scan Labor Department," 17 August 1938, and "Says Reds Use Civic Leaders as Stooges," 18 August 1938 (quote), *Baltimore Sun.*

29. "Two Persons Ordered to Appear in Capital Today for Questioning," *Baltimore Sun,* 29 March 1940.

30. "Maryland Secretary of Party Summoned," *Baltimore Evening Sun,* 29 March 1940.

31. "Two Persons Ordered to Appear in Capital Today for Questioning," *Baltimore Sun,* 29 March 1940.

32. Lt. Colonel J. C. Pegram, "Communist Activities in Baltimore," Third Corps Area, 23 January 1934, in *U.S. Military Intelligence Reports.*

33. Mary Roberts, interview with author, 10 January 1990, Baltimore.

34. "Blumberg Maintains Party Line of Silence," *Baltimore Sun,* 30 March 1940.

35. Albert Blumberg, testimony, in U.S. Congress, *Investigation of Un-American Propaganda Activities in the United States* (1944), 7519–20.

36. "Dies and K.K.K. Acts Linked in Probe Demand," 12 April 1940, "Maryland W.P.A. to Oust Nazis, Reds, by July," 23 June 1940, and "Affidavits Show No Reds in State WPA," 6 July 1940, *Baltimore Sun;* "Hopkins Bars Blumberg; He Talks in Park," 11 April 1940, and "Asks Another Probe of City's Communists," 19 June 1940, *Baltimore Evening Sun.*

37. "Five Red Leaders Indicted by Jury," *Baltimore Sun,* 4 May 1940. All of the records referred to in transcripts of the Dies Committee hearings, plus a number that go unmentioned, are now a part of the Matthews Papers at Duke University.

38. "Loses Opening Round in Fight on Extradition," *Baltimore Sun,* 5 June 1940.

39. "Fraud Evidence Found by Dies Group against Baltimore Communists," *Baltimore Sun,* 29 August 1940.

40. "Red Petition Signers to Be Questioned," 31 August 1940, and "Grand Jury Presents Six in Red Probe," 19 September 1940, *Baltimore Sun.*

41. "Communists Assail Probe of Petitions," *Baltimore Sun,* 3 September 1940.

42. C. P. Ives, "Mr. Dies and the Epistle to the Marylanders," *Baltimore Sun,* 2 September 1940.

43. "Says State CIO Condemned Reds," *Baltimore Sun,* 16 December 1940.

44. James Atkins to Philip Van Gelder, 1 June 1938, Box 68, William Sinclar to Philip Van Gelder, 13 June 1939, Box 68, and Carl Bradley to Philip Van Gelder, 10 January 1941, Box 73, IUMSWA Records, Maryland Room, McKeldin Library, University of Maryland, College Park, Md. (hereafter IUMSWA).

45. "Two Men Here Are Expelled by CIO as Reds," *Baltimore Sun,* 2 April 1941.

46. Ibid.

47. "CIO Union Drops Two on Red Charges," *Baltimore News-Post,* 21 April 1941; "Two Men Expelled Here as Reds," *Baltimore Sun,* 22 April 1941; Philip Van Gelder to Carl Bradley, 20 April 1941, Philip Van Gelder to Edward Dorland, 20 April 1941, Philip Van Gelder to Charles George, 20 April 1941, Charles George to James Drury, telegram, 22 April 1941, and Charles George to Frank J. Bender, 6 May 1931, Box 73, IUMSWA.

48. "The Whole Truth about Local 31, IUMSWA" (undated flyer), Charles George to James Drury, telegram, 22 April 1941, Joseph Curran to John Green, 25 April 1941, and Charles George to Frank J. Bender, 6 May 1941, Box 73, IUMSWA; "Two Workers Fired by Order of Navy," 15 May 1941, and "CIO Reinstatement Refused Two City Men," 26 September 1941, *Baltimore Sun;* "Marine Union Here First to Purge Reds," *Baltimore News-Post,* 12 June 1941.

49. George J. Hiltner, "City Teacher Says Blumberg Cited Need for 'Force, Blood,'" and "Blumberg's Defense Due," Box 66, Folder 21, Matthews Papers.

50. "Counsel for Reds Consider Appeal," *Baltimore Sun,* 13 February 1941.

51. "Mrs. Blumberg Found Guilty on Six Counts," 9 October 1940, "Communists Will Get New Perjury Trials," 2 February 1941, "Mrs. Blumberg Loses Motion for New Trial," 7 December 1941, and "$1,943 Fines Paid by Three Communists," 22 February 1941, *Baltimore Sun.*

52. "House Rushes Bill on Minor Parties," 18 March 1941, "Communists to Appear on State Ballot," 12 October 1940, "Aid Bill Scorned by Red Speaker," 3 February 1941, and "Reds Join Women in Jury Bill Fight," 25 January 1941, *Baltimore Sun;* "Judge Explains Court Order on Communists," *Baltimore Evening Sun,* 12 October 1940.

53. "House Rushes Bill on Minor Parties," 18 March 1941, "Petition Measure Debated in House," 20 March 1941, and "Group Opens Fight on Election Bill," 25 May 1941, *Baltimore Sun.*

Chapter 7: Club Convoy and the Great Patriotic War

1. "State Communists Ask Aid for Hitler's Enemies," *Baltimore Sun,* 1 July 1992.

2. FBI, General Intelligence Memorandum, 2 December 1941, Maryland Manuscripts; "CIO Reinstatement Refused Two City Men," *Baltimore Sun,* 26 September 1941.

3. FBI, General Intelligence Memorandum, 2 December 1941, Maryland Manuscripts; "Communist Denounces Labor Policy of Lewis," *Baltimore Sun,* 24 November 1941 (quote).

4. "Communists Give Pledge of Devoted Loyalty," *Baltimore Sun,* 8 December 1941 (quote); "Maritime Group to Register for Civil Defense," *Baltimore News-Post,* 21 December 1941.

5. J. Edgar Hoover, on authority from Franklin Roosevelt, began surveillance of the CPUSA in 1936; it was not until 1941, however, that an agent of the General Intelligence Branch began to make regular reports on the Party's activities in Maryland. The first report appears to have been General Intelligence Memorandum on the Ramifications of the Communist Party—State of Maryland, 14 March 1941, Baltimore Field Division, Maryland Manuscripts.

6. FBI, General Intelligence Memorandum, 14 March 1941, 2 January 1942, and 3 August 1942, Maryland Manuscripts.

7. George Meyers, interview with author, 1993.

8. FBI, General Intelligence Memorandum, 4 April 1942 and 4 April 1943, Maryland Manuscripts.

9. FBI, General Intelligence Report, 4 April 1942, 4 February 1943, 4 September 1942, and 3 October 1942, Maryland Manuscripts.

10. "Named by Communists," *Baltimore Sun,* 18 November 1942; FBI, General Intelligence Report, 4 April 1942 and 4 March 1943, Maryland Manuscripts.

11. "Flag for Communist Seamen Is Dedicated," *Baltimore Sun,* 12 December 1942.

12. William Wood, interview with author, 23 May 1990; FBI, General Intelligence Memorandum, 4 February 1942, Maryland Manuscripts; "Peace with Hitler Is Called Treason," *Baltimore Sun,* 11 November 1942.

13. FBI, General Intelligence Report, 2 January 1942, 4 March 1942, 3 August 1942, and 3 October 1942, Maryland Manuscripts.

14. "Peace with Hitler Is Called Treason," *Baltimore Sun,* 11 November 1942; FBI, General Intelligence Report, 3 August 1942 and 4 November 1942, Maryland Manuscripts.

15. "Union Asks for War with Finland," 21 July 1942, and "Ship-Builders Pledge to Speed Up," 5 August 1942, *Baltimore News-Post;* FBI, General Intelligence Report, 4 June 1942 and 3 October 1942, Maryland Manuscripts; Lawrence Graiver to the IUMSWA National Offices, 26 July 1943, Box 91, IUMSWA.

16. FBI, General Intelligence Report, 4 September 1942, Maryland Manuscripts.

17. Ibid., 4 December 1942 and 4 February 1943.

18. Ibid., 4 December 1942 and 4 March 1943.

19. Ibid., 4 April 1943.

20. Jake Green, presentation at the Communist Party of Maryland's seventieth anniversary celebration, 2 December 1989, Morgan State University, Baltimore; Avnet, "Pat Whalen," 253 (quote).

21. FBI, General Intelligence Memorandum, 4 February 1942 and 4 March 1942, Maryland Manuscripts.

22. Ibid., 4 February 1943 and 4 April 1943.

23. Fee, "Dr. John E. T. Camper: Civil Rights Activist," 75–76.

24. FBI, General Intelligence Memorandum, 4 March 1943, Maryland Manuscripts.

25. "School of Social Action," Cronin Correspondence, Joseph Nelligan Collection, Archives of the Archdiocese, Baltimore, Maryland (hereafter Nelligan Collection); Father John Francis Cronin, interview by the Reverend Thomas E. Blantz, 17 March 1978, 2, John Francis Cronin Papers, University of Notre Dame Archives, South Bend, Ind. (hereafter Cronin Papers). Spalding, *The Premier See,* 361.

26. Cronin, interview by Blantz, 15–16; *The Church Speaks out for Unions* (pamphlet), Box 91, IUMSWA.

27. *The Church Speaks out for Unions,* Box 91, IUMSWA; Cronin, interview by Blantz, 16; John Francis Cronin to Chancellor Joseph Nelligan, 20 October 1939, Nelligan Collection.

28. Reutter, *Sparrows Point,* 305; Freeman and Rosswurm, "The Education of an Anti-Communist," 202; John Green, telegram of congratulations, 18 October 1942, and General Executive Board, Local 43, Report, October 1942, Box 91, IUMSWA.

29. FBI, General Intelligence Memorandum, 3 October 1942 and 4 November 1942, Maryland Manuscripts.

30. General Executive Board, "Rank and File Program," August 1942, Box 91, IUMSWA; FBI, General Intelligence Memorandum, 3 October 1942 and 4 November 1942, Maryland Manuscripts.

31. General Executive Board, "Americans Drive Out the Invaders," August 1942, Box 91, IUMSWA; FBI, General Intelligence Memorandum, 3 October 1942 and 4 November 1942, Maryland Manuscripts.

32. Tabulation of Election Results, 10 July 1942, and Charles Hansen to Philip Van Gelder, 11 July 1942, Box 91, IUMSWA.

33. John F. Cronin, Confidential Report of Communist Activities at Bethlehem-Fairfield Yard, week of 16 November 1942, and Affidavit "A" in Expulsion Hearing for Shriner et al., Camden, N.J., 10 February 1943, Box 91, IUMSWA.

34. John Cronin, Confidential Report of Communist Activities at Bethlehem-Fairfield Yard, week of 16 November 1942, and John Pinter, statement in the Expulsion Hearing for Shriner et al., Camden, N.J., 10 February, 1943, Box 91, IUMSWA.

35. George Shriner, transcript of statement to John Green, 20 November 1942, and Father Cronin to John Green, 20 November 1942, Box 91, IUMSWA.

36. Spalding, *The Premier See,* 376–77.

37. Father Cronin to John Green, 20 November 1942, George Shriner, transcript of statement to John Green, 20 November 1942, and Philip Bowman, statement, 20 November 1942, Box 91, IUMSWA.

38. Joseph Poe and J. L. Stallings statements, 20 November 1942, Box 91, IUMSWA.

39. Ibid.

40. John Green to Parios Fleezanis, 21 November 1942 (unsent), Box 91, IUMSWA.

41. George Shriner et al., letter and petition to General Executive Board, 25 November 1942, and Charges against Officers of Local 43, n.d. (received after 27 November 1942), Box 91, IUMSWA.

42. Father Cronin to Lucian Koch, enclosed in Koch to Philip Van Gelder, 30 November 1942, Box 91, IUMSWA.

43. "Statement of Philip Van Gelder," undated flyer, *Fairfield Yardbird,* Box 91, IUMSWA.

44. Report of the Special Committee of the G.E.B. Appointed to Investigate and Make Findings on Certain Charges of Communism amongst the Membership in Baltimore, Maryland, 571 (quote), Box 91, IUMSWA; "Union Group Clears Five," *Baltimore News-Post,* 30 December 1942.

45. "Charges against the Officers of Local 43" (petition), 16 December 1942, Box 91, IUMSWA.

46. John Cronin to John Green, 19 December 1942, Box 91, IUMSWA.

47. Copies of Cronin's "Keep This Secret" memos all found their way into the hands of union officials at Camden. John Cronin to John Green, 17 January 1943, and Parios Fleezanis to Philip Van Gelder, 8 January 1943 and 18 January 1943, Box 91, IUMSWA.

48. John Cronin to John Green, 28 January 1943, Box 91, IUMSWA.

49. "Let's Look at the Record" (flyer), and John Francis Cronin to Joseph Nelligan, 1 February 1943, Nelligan Collection.

50. Joint Response to Charges Submitted by David Cooper and Fifteen Members of Local 43, enclosed in an unsigned letter to John Green, 29 January 1943, and Expulsion Hearings for Shriner et al., Camden, N.J., 10 February 1943, Box 91, IUMSWA.

51. FBI, General Intelligence Memorandum, 4 December 1942, Maryland Manuscripts.

52. "Dr. Blumberg Is Agent of Communists," *Baltimore Evening Sun,* 29 May 1943; "United War Effort Aim of Moscow," *Baltimore Sun,* 23 May 1943.

Chapter 8: The Communist Political Association

1. Sobolev et al., *Outline History of the Communist International,* 513; Werth, *Russia at War,* 671–72 (Stalin quote).

2. "United War Effort Aim of Moscow," "Text of Red Resolution to Dissolve Comintern," and "Unaffected Browder Says," *Baltimore Sun,* 23 May 1943; FBI, General Intelligence Memorandum, 3 June 1943, Maryland Manuscripts.

3. "His Job Near End, Reaction of Dies," 23 May 1943, and C. P. Ives, "Moscow Gives Mr. Browder the Brush Off," 31 May 1943, *Baltimore Sun.*

4. FBI, General Intelligence Memorandum, 3 June 1943, Maryland Manuscripts.

5. Ibid., 4 August 1943.

6. Ibid.

7. FBI, Quarterly Intelligence Summary, 15 November 1943, Maryland Manuscripts.

8. FBI, General Intelligence Memorandum, 29 January 1944, Maryland Manuscripts.

9. John Cronin to John Green, 29 September 1943, Box 92, IUMSWA.

10. Ibid.

11. Ibid.

12. "We The Undersigned Shop Stewards" (petition), 22 November 1943 (quote); Bernard Jaffe to John Green, 16 December 1943, Bernard Jaffe to Philip Van Gelder, 17 December 1943, and Report on the Situation in Local 43, 20 March 1944, Box 92, IUMSWA.

13. John Cronin, "Dear Friend" (general mailing to supporters), December 1943, and Chuck Kaswan to Philip Van Gelder, 25 January 1944, Box 92, IUMSWA.

14. Lyman Covert to Philip Van Gelder, 27 January 1944, Box 92, IUMSWA.

15. Report on the Situation in Local 43, 20 March 1944, Box 92, IUMSWA; "Charges Union 'Machine' of Communists," *Baltimore News-Post,* 22 March 1944; Walter McManamon to Melvin Hodgkinson, management representative, 29 March 1944, Bernard Levinson, "On Public Relations and Publicity," 14 April 1944, and Charles A. Leone, letter, 11 January 1945, Box 92, IUMSWA.

16. John F. Cronin, "The Menace of Communism," 7 April 1944 (first and second quotes), and John F. Cronin, "Communists Are Active in Baltimore Shipyards and Munitions Factories," 14 April 1944 (third quote), *Catholic Review.*

17. "Smear Charge Laid to Priest by CIO Leader," *Baltimore Sun,* 15 April 1944.

18. "Priest Points to Communist Official Here," ibid., 17 April 1944.

19. U.S. Congress, *Investigation of Un-American Propaganda Activities in the United States* (1944), 10351–87.

20. Father John Francis Cronin, interview by the Reverend Thomas E. Blantz, March 17, 1978, and "Problem of American Communism in 1945," Cronin Papers; Morris, *American Catholic,* 246–47.

21. Personal and Confidential Report to the Director of the FBI, 29 January 1944, Maryland Manuscripts.

22. John F. Cronin, "Communist Influences on Youth," *Catholic Review,* 28 April 1944.

23. Personal and Confidential Report to the Director of the FBI, 29 January 1944 (Weiss quote) and 29 April 1944 (Lannon's activities), Maryland Manuscripts.

24. "MD. Red Party Is Dissolved," *Baltimore Sun,* 4 June 1944.

25. FBI, General Intelligence Memorandum, 4 August 1944, Maryland Manuscripts.

26. Mary Stalcup Markward, testimony, in U.S. Congress, *Hearings related to Communist Activities in the Defense Area of Baltimore* (1951), 740–43.

27. Ibid.

28. Ibid.

29. FBI, General Intelligence Memorandum, 4 August 1944, Maryland Manuscripts.

30. "Mayor Will Talk and Go," *Baltimore News-Post,* 27 May 1944; FBI, General Intelligence Memorandum, 4 August 1944, Maryland Manuscripts.

31. FBI, General Intelligence Survey, 3 October 1944, Maryland Manuscripts.

32. Ibid., 3 November 1944 (included Elizabeth Searle and Dorothy R. Strange, *A Word to Wise Women: What Is the World Coming To?*), Maryland Manuscripts.

33. FBI, General Intelligence Report, 3 October 1944, Maryland Manuscripts.

34. Ibid.

35. Ibid., 3 November 1944.

36. Ibid., 4 December 1944.

37. Ibid.; Isserman, *Which Side Were You On?* 212.

38. FBI, General Intelligence Report, 4 December 1944, Maryland Manuscripts.

39. Ibid., 4 November 1944.

40. "Third Union Quits CIO Council," *Baltimore News-Post,* 9 January 1945.

41. FBI, General Intelligence Survey, 4 December 1944, Maryland Manuscripts.

42. Ibid., January 1945, Maryland Manuscripts.

43. Eugene Gordon, "Did Maryland Frame Negro Youths?" *Daily Worker,* 6 May 1945; FBI, General Intelligence Survey, May 1945, Maryland Manuscripts.

44. Report of Charles Leone, regional director, to Ross D. Blood, secretary-treasurer, 3 February 1945, and Charles Leone to Walter McManamon, 26 March 1945, Box 92, IUMSWA.

45. FBI, General Intelligence Survey, April and May 1945, Maryland Manuscripts.

46. John Green to Charles Mesko, letter suspending local's autonomy, 12 April 1945, and "National Fiddles While Local 43 Burns," Box 92, IUMSWA.

47. Report of Joe DeKleva to Ross D. Blood on the situation in Local 24, 14 May 1945, Box 63, IUMSWA; FBI, General Intelligence Survey, February and March 1945, Maryland Manuscripts.

48. FBI, General Intelligence Survey, March 1945 and May 1945 (quote), Maryland Manuscripts.

49. Ibid., February 1945 and May 1945 (quote).

50. Ibid., April 1945.

51. Ibid., June 1945.

52. "Three Congressmen Shun Gathering," 10 March 1945, and "Senator Chavez Fails to Appear," 12 March 1945, *Baltimore Sun;* FBI, General Intelligence Survey, March 1945, Maryland Manuscripts.

53. FBI, General Intelligence Survey, February and March 1945, Maryland Manuscripts.

54. Ibid., April 1945.

55. Ibid., January, February, March, and June 1945.

56. Browder, *America's Decisive Battle;* FBI, General Intelligence Survey, March and April 1945, Maryland Manuscripts.

Chapter 9: "Wallace and His Communists"

1. Isserman, *Which Side Were You On?* 216–21; "Communists Plan Revival," *Baltimore Sun,* 25 May 1945 (quote).

2. FBI, General Intelligence Survey, June 1945, Maryland Manuscripts.

3. Ibid.

4. Letter to the Editor, *Daily Worker,* 19 June 1945.

5. FBI, General Intelligence Survey, July 1945, Maryland Manuscripts.

6. Ibid.

7. Ibid.

8. Mary Stalcup Markward, testimony, in U.S. Congress, *Hearings relating to Communist Activities in the Defense Area of Baltimore* (1951), 745–48.

9. Lannon, *Second String Red,* 108.

10. FBI, General Intelligence Report, June 1945, Maryland Manuscripts; Mary Stalcup Markward, testimony, in U.S. Congress, *Hearings relating to Communist Activities in the Defense Area of Baltimore* (1951), 748.

11. Communist Party of Maryland Membership List, Box 148, Folder 1, Matthews Papers; Mary Stalcup Markward, testimony, in U.S. Congress, *Hearings relating to Communist Activities in the Defense Area of Baltimore* (1951), 759.

12. Mary Stalcup Markward, testimony, in U.S. Congress, *Hearings relating to Communist Activities in the Defense Area of Baltimore* 19 June–13 July 1951; George Meyers, interview with author, 1993; William Wood, interview with author, 23 May 1990.

13. Information about Party reorganization is all taken from various places in Markward's testimony, in U.S. Congress, *Hearings relating to Communist Activities in the Defense Area of Baltimore* 19 June–13 July 1951.

14. "Fooks Urges Ban on Communists," *Baltimore Sun,* 2 March 1946.

15. Quoted in Callcott, *Maryland and America,* 117.

16. "Communists Map Campaign," 15 January 1947, and "We State Our Case: Communists Answer Critics," 16 January 1947, *Baltimore Sun.*

17. Helen Delich, "Communist Ends Assembly Hearing," *Baltimore Sun,* 13 February 1947.

18. Ibid.

19. "Ship Unions Urge Communist Ban," 16 March 1947 (quote), and Francis R. Kent, "Everybody Does It Now," 21 March 1947, *Baltimore Sun.*

20. "Communism Warning Is Given, Spring Meeting Opened Here by Catholic Daughters," 26 April 1947, and "Communists Tactics Cited, Budenz Says Aim Is to Split Catholic Laity, Hierarchy," 2 June 1947, *Baltimore Sun.*

21. Zieger, *The CIO,* 246–47.

22. "Homewood AVC Hits Communism," *Baltimore Sun,* 11 September 1947.

23. "Two Meetings Hear *Daily Worker* Editor," 3 November 1947, "Communists in U.S. Decide against Joining Cominform," 3 November 1947, and Lee McCardell, "Bolshevik Anniversary Fails to Arouse City's Communists," 8 November 1947, *Baltimore Sun.*

24. "State PCA Sets Lyric Meeting," *Baltimore Sun,* 1 February 1947.

25. "PCA Meeting Makes Protest," 18 September 1947, "Fascism Peril Taylor Warns," 24 March 1947, "Registry of Youth for Voting Urged," 26 July 1947 (Hammett quote), "Lower Meat Price Drive Opens Today," 1 October 1947, and "15,000 Will Get 'Eviction Notice,'" 20 February 1947 (eviction quote), *Baltimore Sun.*

26. "Wallace Charges U.S. Military Outlay Makes Enemies Abroad" and "Civil Liberties to Be Discussed," *Baltimore Sun,* 16 October 1947.

27. "Progressives Name Officers," 19 May 1947, "Progressive Citizens to Meet," 6 July 1947, and "Attack Made on U.S. Policy," 11 December 1947, *Baltimore Sun.* While preparing for the Communist Party's seventieth anniversary, I asked George Meyers whether Harold Buchman had been a Communist Party member. Meyers responded, "Of course he was. He reported to me." Conversation with George Meyers, October 25, 1989.

28. "Top Echelon of PCA Splits on Independent Wallace Boom," *Baltimore Sun,* 18 December 1947.

29. Ibid. (quotes); "PCA Head Resigns over Wallace Stand," *Baltimore Sun,* 3 January 1948.

30. "Wallace Backed by Eighty-four Unionists," *Baltimore Sun,* 16 October 1947.

31. "Wallace for President Unit Sets Up Headquarters Here," *Baltimore Sun,* 24 December 1947.

32. Ruether and Lerner quoted in C. P. Ives, "Mr. Wallace Is a Part of a Healthy Trend," *Baltimore Sun,* 5 January 1948.

33. Thomas O'Neill, "State Party Organized to Back Wallace," *Baltimore Sun,* 16 February 1948.

34. "'Wallace and His Communists,'" 18 March 1948, *Baltimore Sun.*

35. "Petition List for Wallace Found Faulty," 7 April 1948, "Want Access to Voting List," 8 April 1948, "Court to Get Vote Petition," 9 April 1948, "Judge Rules Progressives May See Books," 14 April 1948, and "Progressives File Petition for Wallace," 17 April 1948, *Baltimore Sun.*

36. "Muth Seeks Teacher Probe," *Baltimore Sun,* 21 May 1948.

37. "Councilman Muth Offers a Silly Resolution," 22 May 1948 (first quote), "Mr. Muth Evades the Point," 23 May 1948, "Muth Says Teacher Is Wife of High Communist Official," 23 May 1948 (second quote), and "Muth Censure Move Denied," 2 June 1948, *Baltimore Sun.*

38. "Communist Ban Decided by Schools," 19 June 1948, "Rule Assailed by Frankfeld," 20 June 1948, and "School Officials Lauded for Stand," 23 June 1948, *Baltimore Sun.*

39. "Mrs. Frankfeld Report Released," 3 September 1948, and "No Plans Made to Replace Spector as School Teacher," 6 September 1948, *Baltimore Sun.*

40. George J. Hiltner, "Communists Draw Fire of Lawyers," *Baltimore Sun,* 27 June 1948.

41. "Lane Names Commission," *Baltimore Sun,* 1 July 1948.

42. "Communist Party Scores Ober Unit," *Baltimore Sun,* 3 July 1948.

43. "Basketball Games Wait for Park Board Hearing," 7 January 1948, and "Police Stop Interracial Tennis and Arrest Twenty-four," 12 July 1948, *Baltimore Sun.*

44. Howard Silverberg, interview with author, 6 November 1989; "Buchman Asks for Action," *Baltimore Sun,* 18 July 1948; "Segregated Sports," 12 July 1948, and "Racial Tennis Group to Face Grand Jury," 12 July 1948, *Baltimore Evening Sun.*

45. "Wallace Session Delegates Named," 11 July 1948, "Progressives Offer Planks," 12 July 1948, "Communists Convene Here," 18 July 1948, and "Communists Name Officers," 19 July 1948 (quote), *Baltimore Sun.*

46. Bradford Jacobs, "Maryland Delegation," 24 July 1948, and Howard Norton, "Marxist Line Followed by Third Party," 26 July 1948 (quote), *Baltimore Sun.*

47. "Shut the Door, They're Coming in the Window" (Yardley cartoon), *Baltimore Sun,* 24 July 1948.

48. H. L. Mencken, "Mencken Tastes the Cake: Finds Several Raisins in Paranoiac Confection," *Baltimore Sun,* 26 July 1948.

49. Ibid.; "So Mencken Goes Uncensored," *Baltimore Sun,* 26 July 1948,

50. Alistair Cooke, "A British View: Emergence of 'No, But' Party," *Baltimore Sun,* 26 July 1948.

51. "Platform's Unity Denied," *Baltimore Sun,* 27 July 1948.

52. Bradford Jacobs, "Marylanders Split, 42 to 9," 26 July 1948, "Labor Papers Snub Wallace," 3 August 1948 (quote), and "Would Quit if Minority Ruled New Party, State Head Says," 31 July 1948, *Baltimore Sun.*

53. "Progressive Leaders Urge Anti-Poll Tax Law," 1 August 1948, "Dr. Shane to Address Progressives Tonight," 10 August 1948, and "Political Unit against Draft," 16 August 1948, *Baltimore Sun.*

54. "Housewives Protest Meat Prices," 18 August 1948, and "Price Rally Ends as Police Rule on Truck," 20 August 1948, *Baltimore Sun.*

55. "Progressive Party Lauded by W. Z. Foster" and "Budenz Warns of Peril in Communist U.S. Aides," *Baltimore Sun,* 3 August 1948.

56. "Two Baltimore Men Named in Spy Probe," 4 August 1948, "Hiss Brothers Deny Charges," 4 August 1948, "Spy Probers Will Hear New Mystery Witness," 6 August 1948, "Text of Denial by Donald Hiss," 14 August 1948, "Farm Called New Hiss Link to Chambers," 28 August 1948, and "Probers Seek Data on Carroll Farm," 28 August 1948, *Baltimore Sun.*

57. "Communist Party Ban to Be Sought," 24 July 1950, and "Cumberland Bill Hits Communists," 6 September 1950, *Baltimore News-Post;* "Anti-Communist Teaching Planned," 13 August 1948, "Communists Want Public Hearing," 19 October 1948, and "Communists' Note Ignored," 28 September 1948 (quote), *Baltimore Sun.*

58. "Unfairness at Polls Charged by Progressives, Dixiecrats," *Baltimore Sun,* 3 November 1948; Callcott, *Maryland and America,* 122; National Committee,

CPUSA, "Resolutions on the Situation Growing out of the Presidential Election," *Political Affairs,* July 1953.

59. "Six Amendments Are Approved," *Baltimore Sun,* 4 November 1948; Callcott, *Maryland and America,* 123; "Fight Communism! Tomorrow—Election Day! Vote Yes for Amendment 7," *Baltimore Sun,* 1 November 1948.

60. "Communists Name Officers," *Baltimore Sun,* 19 July 1948; "Communist Phones Silent," *Baltimore News-Post,* 14 June 1949; Mary Stalcup Markward, testimony, in U.S. Congress, *Hearings relating to Communist Activities in the Defense Area of Baltimore* (1951), 759.

61. Mary Stalcup Markward, testimony, in U.S. Congress, *Hearings relating to Communist Activities in the Defense Area of Baltimore* (1951), 759–61.

62. Ibid.

Chapter 10: The Ober Law, the Smith Act, and HUAC

1. Callcott, *Maryland and America,* 123.

2. "Fiery Hearing Held on Law to Ban Reds," 11 February 1949, and "Modification Urged in Md. Subversive Bill," 4 March 1949 (quotes), *Washington Post.*

3. "Modifications Urged in Md. Subversive Bill," *Washington Post,* 4 March 1949.

4. Callcott, *Maryland and America,* 123; "Ober Bill Foes Hail Opinion of Sherbow," 15 August 1949, Box 148, Folder 4, Matthews Papers.

5. "Ten File Suit on Ober Law," "Citizens Suit Challenges Ober Law," and "Ober Law Foes Engage Miss Price as Secretary," Box 148, Folder 4, Matthews Papers.

6. "Negro Attorneys Hit Ober Law," "Social Worker Group Opposes Ober Law," and "Hears Council on Ober Law," Box 148, Folder 4, Matthews Papers.

7. "Vote Is Forced on Ober Law" and "Subversive Act Held Invalid after Test," Box 148, Folder 4, Matthews Papers.

8. "Decision Pleases Also Displeases" (Meyers quote) and "Ober Foes Hail Opinion of Sherbow" (Brailey quote), Box 148, Folder 4, Matthews Papers.

9. "Ober's Brief in Sherbow Ruling Filed" and "Seldom Offered Devices Seen in Ober Case," Box 148, Folder 4, Matthew Papers.

10. T. Denton Miller, "Rule on Validity Is Declined on Lack of Issue," *Baltimore Evening Sun,* 24 January 1950.

11. "Primary May Lead to Ober Law Test," Box 148, Folder 4, Matthews Papers.

12. "Dr. Brailey Must Go Now Office Rules" and "Two Teachers Out, Refused Loyalty Oath," Box 148, Folder 4, Matthews Papers.

13. John Goodspeed, "Ober Act Marks First Big Tilt with Quakers since 1658"; "Library Group Attacks Ober Law Dismissal"; "Shryock Doubtful of Loyalty Oaths"; and "Citizens Ask Lane Act for Ober Repeal," all in Box 148, Folder 4, Matthews Papers.

14. Callcott, *Maryland and America,* 128–29.

15. "Peace Appeal Being Pressed," "Progressives Name Ticket," "Wallace Quits Progressives," "Martin to Quit Progressives," and "Dr. Camper Quits Progressives," Box 463, Folder 2, Matthews Papers.

16. "Three Progressives Filings Rejected," "Ober Affidavit Signed by Four, Two Progressives to Test Law," and "Shub Again Seeks High Court Ruling," Box 463, Folder 2, Matthews Papers.

17. "Reds in City Must Register," *Cumberland News,* 6 September 1950.

18. Ibid.

19. Ibid. (quotes); "Cumberland Area Forms Group to Ferret Out Communists," 30 September 1950, and "Communist Bill Ordered Drawn," 7 December 1950, *Baltimore Sun.*

20. Callcott, *Maryland and America,* 124–26.

21. Martha Richards, interview with author, 10 January 1990; Elizabeth Painter, interview with author, 5 November 1989; "Communist Chief Here Transferred," *Baltimore Evening Sun,* 19 February 1951.

22. George Meyers and Roy Wood, open letter circulated as a flyer, 8 June 1951, Box 148, Folder 5, Matthews Papers.

23. Klehr and Haynes, *The American Communist Movement,* 136–37.

24. "House Probe of Reds in City Is Set," 15 June 1951, and Robert W. Ruth, "Defy Probe Queries on Communists," 20 June 1951, *Baltimore Sun.*

25. Walter McManamon, testimony, in U.S. Congress, *Hearings relating to Communist Activities in the Defense Area of Baltimore* (1951), 957–58; Herbert Kransdorf, testimony, ibid., 790.

26. Robert W. Ruth, "Probers Get No Clues on Subversives," *Baltimore Sun,* 21 June 1951; Mike Howard, testimony, in U.S. Congress, *Hearings relating to Communist Activities in the Defense Area of Baltimore* (1951), 806–7.

27. "Contempt Action Urged against Two from City," Box 148, Folder 3, Matthews Papers.

28. "Steelworker Keeps Silent at Probe"; Price Day, "Witnesses Balk at Probe on Reds" (quote); "Six Witnesses Balk at Probe"; "Three More Balk at Probe on Red Activity"; Price Day, "Probers Uncover 'Black Box' Clue"; and "Defense Area Probe for Red Cells Delayed until July 9," all in Box 184, Folder 3, Matthews Papers.

29. "Woman Spied on Washington Reds for Seven Years for FBI," Box 148, Folder 3, Matthews Papers; Mary Stalcup Markward, testimony, in U.S. Congress, *Hearings relating to Communist Activities in the Defense Area of Baltimore* (1951), 740–41.

30. Price Day, "City's Industrial Firms Called Communist Goals," *Baltimore Sun,* 12 July 1951; Mary Stalcup Markward, testimony, in U.S. Congress, *Hearings relating to Communist Activities in the Defense Area of Baltimore* (1951), 748 (quote).

31. Mary Stalcup Markward, testimony, in U.S. Congress, *Hearings relating to Communist Activities in the Defense Area of Baltimore* (1951), 777.

32. Coit Hendley Jr., "Home Town Learns of Girl's Role as Agent for FBI in Red Ranks," Box 148, Folder 3, Matthews Papers.

33. Ibid.

34. George Meyers, interview with author, 1993.

35. Ibid.; "Braverman, Two Others to Get Hearings," *Baltimore Evening Sun,* 9 August 1951.

36. "Braverman, Two Others to Get Hearings," *Baltimore Evening Sun,* 9 August 1951; "Frankfelds on Way Here for Hearing," "Bail Reduced for Six Held in Conspiracy," "Two Communist Women Freed on Lower Bail," "Bail Is Posted on Frankfeld," "Two Accused Communists Freed on Bail," and "Officials Puzzled about Red Bail," Box 148, Folder 5, Matthews Papers.

37. "FBI Keeps 24-Hour Watch on Three Indicted Communists," 17 September 1951, and "FBI Silent about Close Checking on Reds Here," 18 September 1951, *Baltimore Evening Sun.*

38. "Frankfeld Seeks Delay In Hearing" and "Prison 'Too Good' for Reds, Member of Jail Board Says," Box 148, Folder 5, Matthews Papers; "Philip Frankfeld Patient at Veterans Hospital," 29 February 1952, and "Red Party Ousts Frankfeld Penalizes Wife, Three Others," 7 March 1952 (quotes), *Baltimore Evening Sun.* Frankfeld's expulsion appears connected with rumors that the Party leader was a sexual predator; nothing concrete is known about his "political degeneracy."

39. "Prosecutor Pins Red Label on Braverman," Box 148, Folder 5, Matthews Papers.

40. "U.S. Jury Hears Ex-Red at Plot Trial Here," "Widespread Plot Charged to Reds," "Frankfeld Red Leader Plot Jury Told," and "Says Reds Plan Revolt in Crisis," Box 148, Folder 5, Matthews Papers.

41. "Instructed at Moscow with Frankfeld Witness Says" and "Frankfeld Took War Lessons Court Told," Box 148, Folder 5, Matthews Papers.

42. "Ex-Red Tells of Plans for U.S. Revolt" and "Knew Six in Plot Trial as Reds, Witness Says," Box 148, Folder 5, Matthews Papers.

43. "Revolution Label Given Frankfeld," Box 148, Folder 5, Matthews Papers.

44. "Va. Housewife Testifies on Six Years' Work as FBI Undercover Agent," *Baltimore News-Post,* 19 March 1952.

45. "Mrs. Markward Says Braverman Headed Secret Red Units," Box 148, Folder 5, Matthews Papers.

46. "U.S. Rests Red Plot Case; Defense Opens Monday" and "Defense Pleas Heard in Trial of State Reds," Box 148, Folder 5, Matthews Papers.

47. "Didn't Advocate Force Meyers Tells Jury" and "Says Reds Backed Wallace in 1948 Vote," Box 148, Folder 5, Matthews Papers.

48. "Ex-Communist Takes Stand Here," "Says Reds Backed Wallace in 1948 Vote," and "Didn't Advocate Force Meyers Tells Jury" (quote), Box 148, Folder 5, Matthews Papers.

49. "Meyers Reluctant to Give Name of Former Red Leader," "Meyers Refuses Again to Name Other Reds," and "Meyers Ruled in Contempt of Court," Box 148, Folder 5, Matthews Papers.

50. "Defense Submits Expert at Red Plot Trial," "Defense in Red Plot Trial Nearing End, Counsel Reveals," and "Two Witnesses Testify for Braverman," Box 148, Folder 5, Matthews Papers.

51. "Eliminate Spy's Data, Plot Trial Defense Asks," "Jury Deliberates Two Hours and Fifty Minutes, Finds Second String Group Guilty Here," "Six in Red Plot Get Jail Here," "Six Convicted in Red Plot Free in Bail," and "Conviction of Six Backed by Tribunal," Box 148, Folder 5, Matthews Papers.

52. Sirkka Lee Holm, interview with author, 15 November 1989; Martha Richards, interview with author, 10 January 1990; William Wood, interview with author, 23 May 1990.

53. Sirkka Lee Holm, interview with author, 15 November 1989.

54. Howard Silverberg, interview with author, 6 November 1989.

55. Clifford Miller, testimony, in U.S. Congress, *Investigation of Communist Activities in the Baltimore, Maryland, Area* (1957), 910–13; William Wood, interview with author, 23 May 1990.

56. Sirkka Lee Holm, interview with author, 15 November 1989.

57. Ibid.

58. Ibid.

59. U.S. Congress, *Investigation of Communist Activities in the Baltimore Area* (1954), 4056–4161.

60. George J. Hiltner, "Red Teaching Told at Trial," 9 February 1956, and "Revolution Plan Is Told," 20 February 1956, *Baltimore Sun.*

61. George J. Hiltner, "Blumberg Trial Hears Data on Secret Meetings of Reds," 21 February 1956, and "Dr. Blumberg Is Convicted on Smith Act," 7 March 1956, *Baltimore Sun.*

62. "Meyers, Ex-Red Official Freed after Thirty-eight Months," Box 148, Folder 5, Matthews Papers; William Wood, interview with author, 23 May 1990.

63. Klehr and Haynes, *The American Communist Movement,* 142–43.

64. U.S. Congress, *Investigation of Communist Activities in the Baltimore, Maryland, Area* (1957), 979.

65. Klehr and Haynes, *The American Communist Movement,* 144–45.

66. "Four More Called in Baltimore Probe" and "Red Probe Here to Be Telecast," Box 148, Folder 3, Matthews Papers.

67. Richard K. Tucker and William F. Pyne, "Miller's Break with Reds Was Intellectual Decision," *Baltimore Evening Sun,* 17 May 1957.

68. Ibid.

69. Charles G. Whiteford, "Three Called Red Leaders in Local Area," *Baltimore Sun,* 9 May 1957.

70. Ibid.

71. "Unfriendly Witnesses Total Twenty-two as House Unit Ends Its Hearings Here," *Baltimore Sun,* 10 May 1957.

72. "Bethlehem to Fire Six," 10 May 1957, "Brick Thrown into Home of One," 10 May 1957, and "Legal Group Plans Another Action on Buchman," 11 May 1957, Box 148, Folder 3, Matthews Papers; William Wood, interview with author, 23 May 1990.

Epilogue

1. FBI, Internal Security Report on Communist Party, United States of America, District of Maryland and Washington, D.C., Baltimore Division, 10 January 1966, in possession of author; William Wood, interview with author, 23 May 1990.

2. FBI, Report, 2 October 1959, in possession of author; Bill Burnett, "Rogers Says

Commies in State Waste Talents on Talk, Talk, Talk," *Baltimore News-Post,* 25 July 1963.

3. George Meyers, interview with author, 4 August 1995.

4. Ibid.

5. Bill Burnett, "Patriot to FBI Looks Back on Black Despair," 22 July 1963; Bill Burnett, "A Little Work Offered by FBI Lasts Ten Years," 23 July 1963; Bill Burnett, "Rogers Gets Full Training in Red Political Tricks," 24 July 1963; and Bill Burnett, "Rogers Says Commies in State Waste Talents on Talk, Talk, Talk," 25 July 1963, *Baltimore News-Post.*

6. New Era Book Shop Inc., Joseph P. Henderson, president, Robert W. Lee, secretary, Herman Heyn, vice president, and Madalyn Murray, res. agent, letter, 18 August 1962, Box 431, Folder 4, Matthews Papers; Sirkka Lee Holm, interview with author, 15 November 1989.

7. Philip Frankfeld, testimony, in U.S. Congress, *Hearing before the Committee on Un-American Activities* (1962), 1742–50.

8. Sirkka Lee Holm, interview with author, 15 November 1989.

9. Newspaper clipping file owned by Margaret Baldridge.

10. Jeffries Baldridge Campaign Committee, open letter to the people of Baltimore, fall 1974, in possession of author.

11. Randi Henderson, "How Does a Real, Live, American Communist Think?" *Baltimore Sun,* 30 December 1974; Klehr and Haynes, *The American Communist Movement,* 173.

12. This and the following paragraphs are based on information found in the Maryland Communist Party records held by Margaret Baldridge, executive secretary of the Maryland Communist Party.

13. The comments of Wheeler and others are from notes taken at the conference by the author.

14. George Meyers to Vernon L. Pedersen, 13 September 1994, in author's possession.

Selected Bibliography

Primary Sources

Curley, Michael J. Collection. Archives of the Archdiocese of Baltimore, Catholic Center, 320 Cathedral Street, Baltimore, Md.

Bureau of Investigation. Investigative Case Files of the Bureau of Investigation, 1908–1922, Reference Number M1085. National Archives, Washington, D.C.

Browder, Earl. Papers. Emory University, Atlanta, Georgia. Microfilm edition, University of Maryland, College Park, Md.

CIO Labor Relations Board of Baltimore. Records. Maryland Room, Enoch Pratt Library, Baltimore, Md.

Cronin, John Francis. Papers. University of Notre Dame Archives, South Bend, Ind.

Federal Bureau of Investigation. Investigation of Communist Activities in Maryland. Maryland Manuscripts 4008, Maryland Room, McKeldin Library, University of Maryland, College Park, Md.

Fond 495. Comintern Files. Russian Center for the Preservation and Study of Documents of Recent History, Moscow, Russia.

Fond 515. Archives of the CPUSA. Russian Center for the Preservation and Study of Documents of Recent History, Moscow, Russia.

Fond 534. Profintern Files. Russian Center for the Preservation and Study of Documents of Recent History, Moscow, Russia.

General Correspondence and Chancery Records. Archives of the Archdiocese of Baltimore, Catholic Center, 320 Cathedral Street, Baltimore, Md.

Industrial Union of Marine and Shipbuilding Workers of America (IUMSWA). Records. Maryland Room, McKeldin Library, University of Maryland, College Park, Md.

Matthews, J. B. Papers. Special Collections, Perkins Library, Duke University, Durham, N.C.

Nelligan, Joseph. Collection. Archives of the Archdiocese of Baltimore, Catholic Center, 320 Cathedral Street, Baltimore, Md.

Oral History Interviews. Neighborhood Heritage Project, Baltimore Regional Institutional Studies Center. Special Collections, Langsdale Library, University of Baltimore, Baltimore, Md.

Political Thought and Social Commentary. Pamphlet collection of Communist, Socialist, and Fascist material. Special Collections, Albin O. Kuhn Library, University of Maryland, Baltimore County, Md.

U.S. Congress. House of Representatives. Committee Investigating Un-American Activities (Fish Committee). *Investigation of Un-American Activities.* 71st Cong., 2d sess. Washington, D.C.: Government Printing Office, 1930.

U.S. Congress. House of Representatives. Committee on Un-American Activities. *Hearings relating to Communist Activities in the Defense Area of Baltimore, Parts 1–3.* 82d Cong., 1st sess. Washington, D.C.: Government Printing Office, 1951.

U.S. Congress. House of Representatives. Committee on Un-American Activities. *Investigation of Communist Activities in the Baltimore Area, Parts 1–3.* 83d Cong., 2d sess. Washington, D.C.: Government Printing Office, 1954.

U.S. Congress. House of Representatives. Committee on Un-American Activities. *Investigation of Communist Activities in the Baltimore, Maryland, Area, Parts 1–2.* 85th Cong., 1st sess. Washington, D.C.: Government Printing Office, 1957.

U.S. Congress. House of Representatives. Special Committee on Un-American Activities. *Investigation of Un-American Activities and Propaganda.* 76th Cong., 2d sess. Washington, D.C.: Government Printing Office, 1940.

U.S. Congress. House of Representatives. Special Committee on Un-American Activities. *Investigation of Un-American Propaganda Activities in the United States.* Washington, D.C.: Government Printing Office, 1962.

U.S. Congress. House of Representatives. Special Committee on Un-American Activities. *Investigation of Un-American Propaganda Activities in the United States, Parts 1–2.* 78th Cong., 2d sess. Washington, D.C.: Government Printing Office, 1944.

U.S. Military Intelligence Reports: Surveillance of Radicals in the United States, 1917–1941. Washington, D.C.: University Publications of America, 1986. Microfilm.

Newspapers and Periodicals

Afro-American (Baltimore), 1919–36.

Baltimore Evening Sun, 1919–57.

Baltimore News-Post, 1919–32.

Baltimore Sun, 1919–48.

Communist (New York), 1919–48.

Cumberland Evening Times (Maryland), 1932–63.

Daily Worker (New York), 1919–48.

Party Organizer (New York), 1928–36.

Interviews with Author

Holm, Sirkka Lee. Francestown, New Hampshire, 15 November 1989.

Meyers, George. Baltimore, Maryland, 1993, 4 August 1995.

Painter, Elizabeth. Baltimore, Maryland, 5 November 1989.

Richards, Martha. Baltimore, Maryland, 10 January 1990.

Roberts, Mary. Baltimore Maryland, 10 January 1990.

Silverberg, Howard. Baltimore, Maryland, 6 November 1989.

Winter, Carl. Baltimore, Maryland, 19 June 1989.

Wood, William. Baltimore, Maryland, 23 May 1990.

Memoirs

Ameringer, Oscar. *If You Don't Weaken: The Autobiography of Oscar Ameringer.* New York: Henry Holt, 1940.

Bentley, Elizabeth. *Out of Bondage: The Story of Elizabeth Bentley.* New York: Devin-Adair, 1951.

Chambers, Whittaker. *Witness.* 1952. Reprint, Washington, D.C.: Regnery Gateway, 1959.

Dennis, Eugene. *Ideas They Cannot Jail.* New York: International, 1950.

Dennis, Peggy. *The Autobiography of an American Communist: A Personal View of a Political Life, 1925–1975.* Westport, Conn.: Creative Arts, 1977.

Flynn, Elizabeth Gurley. *I Speak My Own Piece.* New York: Masses and Mainstream, 1955.

Foster, William Z. *Pages from a Worker's Life.* New York: International, 1939.

Gold, Ben. *Memoirs.* New York: William Howard, n.d.

Green, Gil. *Cold War Fugitive: A Personal Story of the McCarthy Years by Gil Green.* New York: International, 1984.

Lannon, Albert Vetere. *Second String Red: The Life of Al Lannon, American Communist.* Lanham, Md.: Lexington Books, 1999.

Lattimore, Owen. *Ordeal by Slander.* Boston: Little, Brown, 1950.

Lightfoot, Claude M. *Chicago Slums to World Politics: Autobiography of Claude M. Lightfoot.* Edited by Timothy V. Johnson. New York: New Outlook, 1985.

Mitford, Jessica. *A Fine Old Conflict.* 1977. Reprint, New York: Vintage Books, 1978.

Rice, Charles Owen. "Confessions of an Anti-Communist." *Labor History* 30 (Summer 1989).

Richmond, Al. *A Long View from the Left: Memoirs of an American Revolutionary.* Boston: Houghton Mifflin, 1973.

Rubin, Charles. *The Log of Rubin the Sailor.* New York: International, 1973.

General Secondary Sources

Abbott, Philip. *The Exemplary Presidency: Franklin D. Roosevelt and the American Political Tradition.* Amherst: University of Massachusetts Press, 1990.

Adler, Les K. *The Red Image: American Attitudes toward Communism in the Cold War Era.* New York: Garland, 1991.

Adler, Leslie K., and Thomas G. Paterson. "Red Fascism: The Merger of Nazi Germany and Soviet Russia in the American Image of Totalitarianism, 1930's–1950's." *American Historical Review* 75 (April 1970).

Alexander, Robert J. *The Right Opposition: The Lovestoneites and the International Communist Opposition of the 1930's.* Westport, Conn.: Greenwood, 1981.

Andrew, Christopher, and Oleg A. Gordievsky, *K.G.B.: The Inside Story of Its Operations from Lenin to Gorbachev.* New York: Harper Collins, 1990.

Argersinger, Jo Ann E. *Toward a New Deal in Baltimore: People and Government in the Great Depression.* Chapel Hill: University of North Carolina Press, 1988.

Avnet, I. Duke. "Pat Whalen." *Phylon* 12 (September 1951): 249–54.

Bart, Philip, Theodore Bassett, William W. Weinstone, and Arthur Zipser, eds. *Highlights of a Fighting History: Sixty Years of the Communist Party, USA.* New York, International, 1979.

Bauman, John F., and Thomas H. Goode. *In the Eye of the Great Depression: New Deal Reporters and the Agony of the American People.* DeKalb: Northern Illinois University Press, 1988.

Baxandall, Rosalyn. "Women in the Communist Party." Paper presented at the "Seventy Years of U.S. Communism, 1919–1989" Conference, City University of New York, November 1989.

———. *Words on Fire: The Life and Writing of Elizabeth Gurley Flynn.* New Brunswick, N.J.: Rutgers University Press, 1987.

Brinkley, Alan. *Voices of Protest: Huey Long, Father Coughlin, and the Great Depression.* 1982. Reprint, New York: Vintage Books, 1983.

Broué, Pierre. "Biographie: George Mink." *Cahiers Leon Trotsky* [France] (July–September 1979).

Browder, Earl. *America's Decisive Battle.* New York: New Century, 1945.

Brugger, Robert J. *Maryland: A Middle Temperament, 1634–1980.* Baltimore: Johns Hopkins University Press, 1988.

Buckley, William F., Jr. "The End of Whittaker Chambers." *Esquire,* September 1962.

———, ed. *Odyssey of a Friend: Whittaker Chambers' Letters to William F. Buckley, Jr., 1954–1961.* New York: Putnam, 1969.

Callcott, George H. *Maryland and America, 1940 to 1980.* Baltimore: Johns Hopkins University Press, 1985.

Carr, E. H. *Twilight of the Comintern, 1930–1935.* New York: Pantheon, 1982.

Caute, David. *The Fellow Travelers: Intellectual Friends of Communism.* New Haven, Conn.: Yale University Press, 1988.

Cooke, Alistair. *Generation on Trial: U.S.A. v. Alger Hiss.* New York: Alfred A. Knopf, 1950.

Cowley, Malcolm. "Echos from Moscow: 1937–1938." *Southern Review* 20 (January 1984).

Dilling, Elizabeth. *The Red Network: A "Who's Who" and Handbook of Radicalism for Patriots.* Chicago: By the author, 1934.

Donner, Frank. *Protectors of Privilege: Red Squads and Police Repression in Urban America.* Berkeley: University of California Press, 1990.

Dozer, Donald Marquand. *Portrait of the Free State: A History of Maryland.* Cambridge, Md.: Tidewater, 1976.

Draper, Theodore. *American Communism and Soviet Russia.* New York: Vintage Books, 1986.

———. *The Roots of American Communism.* New York: Viking, 1957.

Dubofsky, Melvyn. *We Shall Be All: A History of the Industrial Workers of the World.* New York: Quadrangle/New York Times, 1969.

Dyson, Lowell K. *Red Harvest: The Communist Party and American Farmers.* Lincoln: University of Nebraska Press, 1982.

Elbaum, Max. "Upheaval in the CPUSA: Death and Rebirth?" *CrossRoads* (January 1992).

Falk, Candace. *Love, Anarchy, and Emma Goldman.* New York: Holt, Rinehart and Winston, 1984.

Fee, Elizabeth. "Dr. John E. T. Camper: Civil Rights Activist." In *The Baltimore Book: New Views of Local History,* edited by Elizabeth Fee, Linda Shopes, and Linda Zeidman. Philadelphia: Temple University Press, 1991.

———. "George Meyers: Labor Leader." In *The Baltimore Book: New Views of Local History,* edited by Elizabeth Fee, Linda Shopes, and Linda Zeidman. Philadelphia: Temple University Press, 1991.

Folsom, Franklin. *Impatient Armies of the Poor: The Story of Collective Action of the Unemployed, 1808–1942.* Niwot: University Press of Colorado, 1991.

Fox, William Lloyd. "Social-Cultural Developments from the Civil War to 1920." In *Maryland: A History, 1632–1974,* by Richard Walsh and William Lloyd Fox. Baltimore: Maryland Historical Society, 1974.

Freeman, Joshua, and Steve Rosswurm. "The Education of an Anti-Communist." *Labor History* 33 (Spring 1992).

Fried, Richard M. *Nightmare in Red: The McCarthy Era in Perspective.* New York: Oxford University Press, 1990.

Gentry, Curt. *J. Edgar Hoover: The Man and the Secrets.* New York: W. W. Norton, 1991.

Goldberg, Joseph P. *The Maritime Story: A Study in Labor-Management Relations.* Cambridge, Mass.: Harvard University Press, 1958.

Gordon, Max. "The Communists and the Drive to Organize Steel, 1936." *Labor History* 23 (Spring 1982).

Gornick, Vivian. *The Romance of American Communism.* New York: Basic Books, 1977.

Hallengren, Eric C. "In Baltimore Town the Boys Are Rough: The Role of Baltimore Seamen in the National Maritime Strike of 1936–1937." Unpublished paper, June 1978.

Haynes, John Earl. *Dubious Alliance: The Making of Minnesota's DFL Party.* Minneapolis: University of Minneapolis Press, 1984.

Haynes, John Earl, and Harvey Klehr. *Venona: Decoding Soviet Espionage in America*. New Haven, Conn.: Yale University Press, 1999.

Hoover, J. Edgar. *Masters of Deceit: The Story of Communism in America and How to Fight It*. New York: Holt, 1958.

———. *A Study of Communism*. New York: Holt, Rinehart and Winston, 1962.

Isserman, Maurice. *Which Side Were You On?: The American Communist Party and the Second World War*. Middletown, Conn.: Wesleyan University Press, 1982.

Jaffe, Philip J. *The Rise and Fall of American Communism*. New York: Horizon, 1975.

Jeansonne, Glen. "Women Anti-Communists in the Age of FDR." Paper presented at the annual meeting of the Organization of American Historians, City University of New York, October 1990.

Johanningsmeier, Edward P. *Forging American Communism: The Life of William Z. Foster*. Princeton, N.J.: Princeton University Press, 1994.

Josephson, Matthew. "Scenes of the Nineteen Thirties: A Soiree with Whittaker Chambers." *Southern Review* 3 (1967).

Kampelman, Max M. *The Communist Party vs. the C.I.O.: A Study in Power Politics*. New York: Frederick A. Praeger, 1957.

Keeran, Roger. *The Communist Party and the Auto Workers Union*. Bloomington: Indiana University Press, 1980.

Kelley, Robin D. G. *Hammer and Hoe: Alabama Communists during the Great Depression*. Chapel Hill: University of North Carolina Press, 1990.

Kimeldorf, Howard. *Reds or Rackets? The Making of Radical and Conservative Unions on the Waterfront*. Berkeley: University of California Press, 1989.

Klehr, Harvey. *Communist Cadre*. Stanford, Calif.: Hoover Institution Press, 1978.

———. *The Heyday of American Communism: The Depression Decade*. New York: Basic Books, 1984.

Klehr, Harvey, and John Earl Haynes. *The American Communist Movement: Storming Heaven Itself*. New York: Twayne, 1992.

———. "The End: The CPUSA Expires." *New Republic,* March 23, 1992.

Klehr, Harvey, John Earl Haynes, and Kyrill M. Anderson. *The Soviet World of American Communism*. New Haven, Conn.: Yale University Press, 1998.

Klehr, Harvey, John Earl Haynes, and Fridrikh Firsov. *The Secret World of American Communism*. New Haven, Conn.: Yale University Press, 1995.

Kraditor, Aileen S. *"Jimmy Higgens": The Mental World of the Rank-and-File Communist, 1930–1958*. Westport, Conn.: Greenwood, 1988.

Leab, Daniel J. "'United We Eat': The Creation and Organization of the Unemployed Councils in 1930." *Labor History* 8 (Fall 1967).

Lewy, Guenter. *The Cause That Failed: Communism in American Political Life*. New York: Oxford University Press, 1990.

Lichtenstein, Nelson. *Labor's War at Home: The CIO in World War II*. Cambridge and New York: Cambridge University Press, 1982.

Lyons, Eugene. *The Red Decade: The Classic Work on Communism in America during the Thirties.* New York: Arlington House, 1971.

MacDougall, Curtis D. *Gideon's Army.* New York: Marzani and Munzell, 1965.

Margulies, Sylvia R. *The Pilgrimage to Russia: The Soviet Union and the Treatment of Foreigners, 1924–1937.* Madison: University of Wisconsin Press, 1968.

McGuinn, Henry J. "Equal Protection of the Law and Fair Trials in Maryland." *Journal of Negro History* 24 (1940).

Morgan, Ted. *A Covert Life: Jay Lovestone, Communist, Anti-Communist, and Spymaster.* New York: Random House, 1999.

Morris, Charles R. *American Catholic: The Saints and Sinners Who Built America's Most Powerful Church.* New York: Times Books, 1997.

Murray Robert K. *Red Scare: A Study in National Hysteria, 1919–1920.* 1955. Reprint, New York: McGraw-Hill, 1964.

Naison, Mark. *Communists in Harlem during the Depression.* Urbana: University of Illinois Press, 1983.

Nash, Michael. "Schism on the Left: The Anti-Communism of V. F. Calverton and His *Modern Quarterly.*" *Science and Society* 45 (1981–82).

National Committee, CPUSA. "Resolutions on the Situation Growing out of the Presidential Election." *Political Affairs* 42 (July 1963).

Nelson, Bruce. *Workers on the Waterfront: Seamen, Longshoremen, and Unionism in the 1930s.* Urbana: University of Illinois Press, 1988.

O'Reilly, Kenneth. *Hoover and the Un-Americans: The FBI, HUAC, and the Red Menace.* Philadelphia: Temple University Press, 1983.

Ottanelli, Fraser M. *The Communist Party of the United States from the Depression to World War II.* New Brunswick, N.J.: Rutgers University Press, 1991.

Peterson, Frank Ross. "Harry S. Truman and His Critics: The 1948 Progressives and the Origins of the Cold War." In *Essays on Radicalism in Contemporary America,* edited by Jerome L. Rodnitzky, Frank Ross Peterson, Kenneth R. Philip, and John A. Garraty. Austin: University of Texas Press, 1972.

Powers, Richard Gid. *Not without Honor: The History of American Anticommunism.* New York: Free Press, 1995.

———. *Secrecy and Power: The Life of J. Edgar Hoover.* New York: Free Press, 1987.

Prendergast, William. "Maryland: The Ober Anti-Communist Law." In *The States and Subversion,* edited by Walter Gellhorn. Ithaca, N.Y.: Cornell University Press, 1952.

Record, Wilson. *The Negro and the Communist Party.* Chapel Hill: University of North Carolina Press, 1951.

Reutter, Mark. *Sparrows Point: Making Steel.* New York: Summit Books, 1988.

Rosenzweig, Roy. "Radicals and the Jobless: The Musteites and the Unemployed Leagues, 1932–1936." *Labor History* 16 (Winter 1975).

Salvatore, Nick. *Eugene V. Debs: Citizen and Socialist.* Urbana: University of Illinois Press, 1982.

Schmidt, Karl M. *Henry Wallace: Quixotic Crusade, 1948.* Syracuse, N.Y.: Syracuse University Press, 1960.

Sobolev, A. I., et al. *Outline History of the Communist International.* Translated by Bernard Isaacs. Moscow: Progress, 1971.

Spalding, Thomas W. *The Premier See: A History of the Archdiocese of Baltimore, 1789–1989.* Baltimore: Johns Hopkins University Press, 1989.

State of Maryland. *Maryland Manual.* Baltimore: Sun Publications, 1912–48.

Sun Almanac. Baltimore: A. S. Abell, 1913, 1920, 1921.

Tanenhaus, Sam. *Whittaker Chambers: A Biography.* New York: Random House, 1997.

Theoharis, Athan G., ed. *Beyond the Hiss Case: The FBI, Congress, and the Cold War.* Philadelphia: Temple University Press, 1982.

Theoharis, Athan G., and John Stuart Cox. *The Boss: J. Edgar Hoover and the Great American Inquisition.* Philadelphia: Temple University Press, 1988.

Ulam, Adam B. *The Communists: The Story of Power and Lost Illusions: 1948–1991.* New York: Charles Scribner's Sons, 1992.

Walsh, Richard, and William Lloyd Fox. *Maryland: A History, 1632–1974.* Baltimore: Maryland Historical Society, 1974.

Walton, Richard J. *Henry Wallace, Harry Truman, and the Cold War.* New York: Viking, 1976.

Waters, W. W. *B.E.F.: The Whole Story of the Bonus Army.* New York: Arno and New York Times, 1969.

Weinstein, Allen. *Perjury: The Hiss-Chambers Case.* New York: Alfred A. Knopf, 1978.

Weinstein, Allen, and Alexander Vassiliev. *The Haunted Wood: Soviet Espionage in America—The Stalin Era.* New York: Random House, 1999.

Weiss, Nancy J. *Farewell to the Party of Lincoln: Black Politics in the Age of FDR.* Princeton, N.J.: Princeton University Press, 1983.

Werth, Alexander, *Russia at War, 1941–1945.* 1964. Reprint, New York: Carroll and Graf, 1984.

Work Projects Administration. *Maryland: A Guide to the Old Line State.* New York: Oxford University Press, 1940.

Zeidman, Linda, and Eric Hallengren. "The Baltimore Soviet." In *The Baltimore Book: New Views of Local History,* edited by Elizabeth Fee, Linda Shopes, and Linda Zeidman. Philadelphia: Temple University Press, 1991.

———. "The Fall/Winter Strike of 1936." In *The Baltimore Book: New Views of Local History,* edited by Elizabeth Fee, Linda Shopes, and Linda Zeidman. Philadelphia: Temple University Press, 1991.

———. "The Midnight March of the Baltimore Brigade." In *The Baltimore Book: New Views of Local History,* edited by Elizabeth Fee, Linda Shopes, and Linda Zeidman. Philadelphia: Temple University Press, 1991.

———. "Radicalism on the Waterfront." In *The Baltimore Book: New Views of Local History,* edited by Elizabeth Fee, Linda Shopes, and Linda Zeidman. Philadelphia: Temple University Press, 1991.

———. "Speeding up Broadway." In *The Baltimore Book: New Views of Local History,* edited by Elizabeth Fee, Linda Shopes, and Linda Zeidman. Philadelphia: Temple University Press, 1991.

Zieger, Robert H. *The CIO, 1935–1955.* Chapel Hill: University of North Carolina Press, 1995.

Zeligs, Meyer A. *Friendship and Fratricide: An Analysis of Whittaker Chambers and Alger Hiss.* New York: Viking, 1967.

Index

AA. *See* Amalgamated Association of Iron, Steel, and Tin Workers
Aberdeen Proving Grounds, 86
Abraham Lincoln Battalion, 102-3
Abramovich, Raphael, 32-33
activities. *See* espionage networks; *specific groups*
ADA. *See* Americans for Democratic Action
Ades, Bernard: as defense attorney in murder case, 57-61; election platform of, 78; as gubernatorial candidate, 61-62; interracial dances and, 67
AFL. *See* American Federation of Labor
African Americans. *See* blacks
African Blood Brotherhood, 44
Afro-American (newspaper), 61, 86, 95, 122
Agitprop Committee, 41, 45, 83-84, 100
Alabama Communist Party, 2, 5
Albert, Sheridan, 136
Aldridge, Playford, 171
Alexander, Charles, 49
Allen, A. J., 122
Alpert, Leo, 108-9, 110-11, 114
Amalgamated Association of Iron, Steel, and Tin Workers (AA), 84-85, 93
Amalgamated Clothing Workers of America, 88, 92, 101, 152
American Association of Social Workers, 167
American Association of University Women, 153

American Council of Bishops, 136
American Federation of Labor (AFL): alliances of, 36, 37; Cline's alternative New Deal and, 70; conventions of, 9, 91-92; fractions in, 68, 71, 79, 80, 84-85, 100, 102; leadership of, 31; Taft-Hartley Act and, 154; takeover attempt in Fairfield Yards, 134-35; TUEL's work with, 42
American League against War and Fascism, 79, 87, 88, 102
American League for Peace and Democracy, 102
American Negro Labor Congress, 44
American Revolution, 114, 192
Americans for Democratic Action (ADA), 156-57, 166
American Soviet Friendship Committee, 140
American Veterans Committee, 154-55
American Youth Congress, 188
American Youth for Democracy (AYD): emergence of, 137; public acceptance of, 146-47; racism in, 150; recruitment for, 12, 140; SOS clubs of, 137, 142, 150. *See also* Young Communist League
America's Decisive Battle (Browder), 147
Amter, Israel, 52, 68, 70
anarchists: crackdown on, 18, 20-21
anarcho-communism: concept of, 15
Anchorage Hotel (Baltimore), 76-77, 97
Anderson, Sherwood, 63

Vernon L. Pedersen received his Ph.D. from Georgetown University in 1993. He has taught at Shepherd College, West Virginia, and currently teaches American and Soviet history at the American University in Bulgaria, where he is also the chair of the Arts and Humanities Division.

Typeset in 9/13 ITC Stone Serif
with Helvetica Neue Extended display
Designed by Paula Newcomb
Composed by Jim Proefrock
at the University of Illinois Press
Manufactured by Thomson-Shore, Inc.

University of Illinois Press
1325 South Oak Street
Champaign, IL 61820-6903
www.press.uillinois.edu